MW01617108

In God's Throne Room

Retah & Aldo McPherson

ISBN 978-1-920363-41-3

Cover design: Conrad Marshall
Layout: Free Van Nieuwkerk

Published by:
Maranatha Christian Publishing
Private Bag X32823
Menlyn
0063
South Africa
www.maranatha.co.za

McPherson House
P O Box 793
Hartbeespoort
0216
South Africa
Tel: + 27 (0) 82 610 5757
www.retahmcpherson.com

First edition, first print 2012
Printed and bound by CTP Printers, Cape Town

Dedicated to:

I dedicate this book to my family, who, without complaining, walk this road with me. Thank you for being willing to pay the price so that many can learn and grow with us. Thank you for clinging with me to this truth – that it is not about us and our times of pain and suffering; it is all about YHVH – all for His glory! It is a privilege to be able to do it for our King!

Retah

Note to the reader:

Dear Reader,

As you read Aldo's handwritten letters, you will see that Aldo has a unique way of saying things – we call it his 'lingo'. In order for you to have a better understanding of what he is trying to say, I would like to clarify a few words in his lingo:

Under the leading of *Wisdom* (the Holy Spirit), Aldo sometimes refers to himself as *Samuel* and to me as *Ruth* or *Hannah* in his letters.

When he speaks of the colour *red* he usually refers to the 'red blood of the Lamb' – the blood of Yeshua, the Messiah (Revelations 1:5 says: '*... Jesus Christ, who is the faithful witness, the firstborn from the dead, and the ruler of the kings of the earth. To Him who loves us and has freed us from our sins by His blood...'*)

Acknowledgements:

Holding this book – I raise it up and dedicate it to You, YHVH. To You alone belongs the glory for the path we walk. You are the One who gives us the strength, wisdom, counsel, knowledge, love, insight, patience, gentleness and perseverance. You are the One who whispers in my ear: 'Don't give up, Retah, what I have begun I will complete.' I honour You for never giving up on any one of us. Teenager, despite the difficulties you face – what God has begun in Your life He will complete.

To Ma'm Patrys – I do not have words to express my gratitude to you. YHVH planted you in our lives. I am so grateful to you for bringing His love to us. During difficult times you take my hand and raise me up. In the good times we laugh together – actually, you always laugh! Thank you so much for sharing your love with our family!

Josh and Chantel, thank you for your willingness to help Aldo whenever called upon, and your sacrifices to make life easier for him. I honour you both for who you are in Christ! Josh, you are an amazing and courageous young man! Chans, you are the love and smile in Aldo's life!

Foreword:

At the age of twelve, Aldo was injured in a serious motor vehicle accident, and he was in a coma for several months. While in the coma, Jesus took Aldo to heaven, and also showed him hell. When Aldo came out of the coma, he began walking a long road to recovery. During this healing process, we became aware that God was speaking to Aldo in a unique way, in his spirit. When God speaks to Aldo; He calls him 'Samuel'.

Whenever God calls out to Aldo, 'Samuel, Samuel', then Aldo hears Holy Spirit (or Wisdom, as he calls Holy Spirit), speak to him. Aldo writes down everything that Wisdom tells him.

Alongside these wonderful experiences there's also been a great spiritual battle for Aldo's life and his future. The enemy fought hard to destroy Aldo's (or Samuel's) calling in the Kingdom of Jesus Christ. He wages this battle against every child of God who tries to walk a path of holiness.

The fight was deathly. Aldo recounts the story of this battle in his journal, *Wisdom for Teens*. In the journal, he describes how the enemy lies to teenagers, so that in the end they think they are hearing their own voices. The enemy does this for one reason only; and that is to keep us from following God's will for our lives. His favourite lines are: 'You are not good enough; you are not good-looking, or you are not clever.' These are all lies! Aldo's great heartache was rejection. I would love to say 'was', because

I know that he is working with Wisdom everyday to overcome this. He is learning that he must seek acceptance with God, and not with people.

We invite you to join us on a journey over the next twelve months; to learn what it means to walk in a love relationship with King Yeshua. We will learn how to hear God's voice, identify and understand the different seasons in our lives. Together we will learn how to cling to hope and above all, how to trust in God. Aldo's letters are simple, but filled with deep wisdom from Holy Spirit. They contain messages for God's children. We will learn, together with Aldo, how to work through our heartache.

No matter how difficult your life is at this moment in time, Wisdom wants to walk each step of the road with you. He will teach you to trust God whole-heartedly. You will learn about God's character, because after all you cannot totally trust someone you do not know. Do you know Jesus Christ, my friend – do you love Him? Is your life in His hands?

Jesus is establishing a new generation – the Benjamin generation – and you are part of it! Join us as we open our hearts to learn from Wisdom.

Love

Retah

God die Vader se hartklop vir sy kinders is liefde. hy sien hewige samuel seun haat nie meer harde woorde. hulle harde woorde haat was wat samuel so vas gebind het. toe sê God - samuel, jy het haat in jou hart teen mense wat so sleg van samuel gepraat het. rut het samuel gehelp om te vergewe, goud is God se hart, na vergifnis het samuel God se hartklop. vra humble rut, hy is bevry na hy vergewe het. Jou slegte woorde oor ander is vloeke hulle bind mense, rooi is samuel se hart nou. Jy sal waarlik vry wees na vergifnis.

Letter 1:

The heartbeat of God

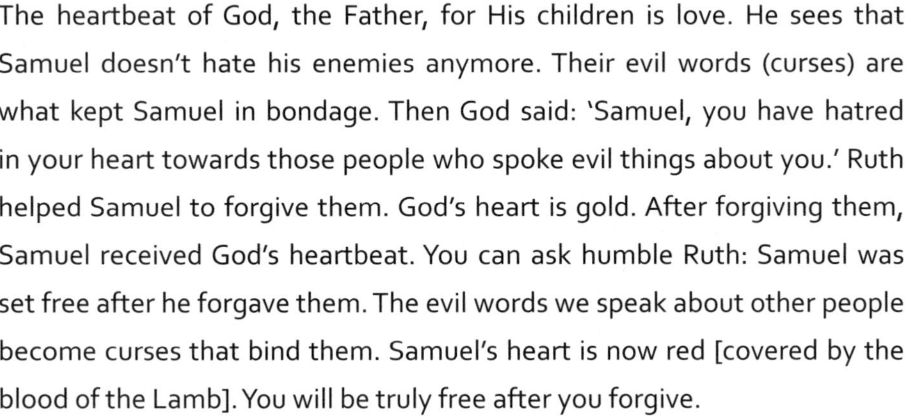

The heartbeat of God, the Father, for His children is love. He sees that Samuel doesn't hate his enemies anymore. Their evil words (curses) are what kept Samuel in bondage. Then God said: 'Samuel, you have hatred in your heart towards those people who spoke evil things about you.' Ruth helped Samuel to forgive them. God's heart is gold. After forgiving them, Samuel received God's heartbeat. You can ask humble Ruth: Samuel was set free after he forgave them. The evil words we speak about other people become curses that bind them. Samuel's heart is now red [covered by the blood of the Lamb]. You will be truly free after you forgive.

God's blessing in your life

Prayer for January

Father, I come to You at the beginning of this New Year in the wonderful Name of Jesus, my Messiah. It is so wonderful to begin this year in Your presence, praising, honouring and worshiping You. Like David, I lift my hands and declare: You are Holy, O Lord, my God, You are King of the universe. I love You, Lord. Thank You for Your blessing in my life, O Mighty God. All the honour and glory are due Your name for all eternity. Lord, You know me through and through. There is nothing that You do not know about me, You know my thoughts before I think them. You know what I need before I can ask You, what a wonderful God You are! Father, You love me more than I can ever comprehend. Thank You for Your Word, Your complete Word, both the Old and the New Testament. Thank You for Your blessing in my life, Father. I pray this in Jesus Name.
Amen.

1 January

Blessed by God

Read Psalm 67

May God be gracious to us and bless us and make his face shine upon us, that your ways may be known on earth, your salvation among all nations. - Psalm 67:1-2

I want to begin the year talking about blessing. God loves and blesses us. It is interesting that you can only bless someone if there is love in your heart.

When we become followers of Jesus, we begin a whole new way of life. We walk along a different, exciting and life-giving path. We have a new heart – one filled with love. As we get to know Jesus better we learn how to live in the Kingdom of Light, God's Kingdom. In this Kingdom we enjoy God's blessing in all the areas of our lives. God blesses us freely but the blessing is not for us alone – we are not to be selfish with it - we have to share the blessing and give it away. Every day we must look for opportunities to bless other people. The more we bless other people the more God will bless us.

I have to share the blessing and give it away.

Prayer

Father, You are my God, You bless me and love me, thank You. I want to share this blessing I get from You with my friends and family. Amen.

Blessed to praise Him!

Read Psalm 104:1-4, 33-35

Praise the Lord, O my soul. O Lord my God, you are very great; you are clothed with splendour and majesty. - Psalm 104:1

Every time I read Psalm 104 it reminds me that the whole of creation, everyone in heaven and everyone living on earth have one purpose: We must praise and worship God with our whole heart. He created us to have a relationship with Him; He longs above everything else to spend time with us.

The Lord our God is the Light of my life. I want to praise Him – He is the One who lights the fire within me. As I praise Him He fills me with His blessing. Do you experience this too? Do you understand what I am talking about? The more you praise Him the more He will fill you and the more you will be blessed.

God fills you to overflowing with His blessing so that day by day you can share the blessing you have received from Him with others.

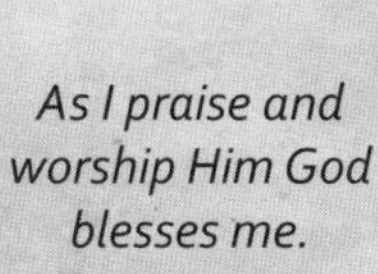

As I praise and worship Him God blesses me.

Prayer

Lord Jesus, I love to praise and worship You. Thank You that You give me so many blessings every day. Help me wherever I go today to share this blessing with others. Amen.

3 January

Blessed by our covenant keeping God

Read Psalm 111

He has caused his wonders to be remembered; the Lord is gracious and compassionate. He provides food for those who fear him; he remembers his covenant forever.
- Psalm 111:4-5

Psalm 111 says that nothing and no one can break the covenant God has made with us. A covenant is a promise that two people make to each other. This covenant God made with us is very important to people who have made a decision to follow Jesus. It is God's promise to us that we can hold on to no matter what happens in our lives.

God never breaks His promise to me. He cannot break His promise because it is in His character to be true and faithful.

People sometimes break the promises they make to each other – but God never breaks His promise to us. He cannot break His promise because it is in His character to be true and faithful – He does not let those who depend upon Him down. One of His promises is that He will bless us if we serve Him. He says in the Bible that if we serve Him then He will bless our children one day and their children as well.

Prayer

Father, thank You that even if people let me down – You will never disappoint me. I want to serve You so that You will bless me and also that You will bless those who come after me. Amen.

Blessing of covenant

Read 2 Samuel 7:1-29

The Lord declares to you that the Lord himself will establish a house for you ... I will raise-up your offspring to succeed you ... I will establish the throne of his kingdom forever. I will be his father, and he will be my son ... But my love will never be taken away from him ... Your house and your kingdom will endure forever before me, your throne will be established forever. - 2 Samuel 7:11-16

Do you realise that you are a big part of the blessing God has bestowed upon your parents? In 2 Samuel God is talking to King David, He assures David that He will raise-up his offspring to succeed him. God promises to bless Solomon, David's son.

The main point is this: I am blessed in order to bless others.

God's blessing upon you started before you were even born, it is part of an ongoing blessing He promised to your parents. You may be the first person in your family to follow Jesus and you are asking well what about me – my parents don't serve God? That doesn't matter: it simply means that the blessing starts with you and you will have the pleasure of seeing it passed on to your children and then to their children one day.

So, today you can choose to continue sharing the blessing, you can start a new tradition. You are blessed in order to bless others.

Prayer

Father, thank You that You are my Father. You bless my life every day in so many ways. I want to bless others in the same way You bless me. Amen.

Bless others

Read Luke 6:27-36

Bless those who curse you, pray for those who mistreat you. - Luke 6:28

As you read the Bible you will find many places where God talks about blessing us. He blesses us not just so that we can feel good or have a happy life but so that we can in turn share this blessing with other people.

Some of the places you can read about this are found in Numbers 6:27 in the Old Testament: *So they will put my name on the Israelites, and I will bless them.*

In the New Testament again, Peter speaks about blessing. He encouraged the new Believers in 1 Peter 3:9 by saying: *Do not repay evil with evil or insult with insult, but with blessing, because to this you were called so that you may inherit a blessing.*

It is difficult when people are nasty to us or treat us badly to bless them; but God is clear – He expects us to live our lives blessing others – even when they don't deserve it.

God is clear – He expects me to live my life blessing others – even when they don't deserve it.

Prayer

Father, I want to obey You and bless others – even those who don't deserve it. Thank You that because You love me I can pass Your love and blessing on to others. Amen.

Blessed if you walk in His ways

Read Psalm 128

Blessed are all who fear the Lord, who walk in his ways. - Psalm 128:1

God loves you no matter what. He will never stop loving you – it doesn't matter what you do. However, if you love Jesus then you will want to walk in His ways and please Him in the things you think and do. What does this mean? It means that you will obey God. You will do all the things you know to do. How do you know what God wants you to do?

You find out by reading the Bible, praying, and letting the Holy Spirit speak to you; then you do the things you have learnt and heard. If you do this, Psalm 128 says you will be blessed. You will have success in the things you do. You will know prosperity, which is another way of saying, you will be blessed. Now you know this doesn't mean that things won't ever be difficult but God will be there to help you and lead you.

How can I know what God wants me to do? I read the Bible, pray, and let the Holy Spirit speak to me; then I do the things I have learnt and heard.

Prayer

Lord, I want to walk in Your ways so that I can experience Your blessing. Help me to listen to Your Spirit. Amen.

Bless your enemies

Read Matthew 5:1-10

Blessed are those who are persecuted because of righteousness, for theirs is the kingdom of heaven. - Matthew 5:10

It is so easy to become despondent and disappointed when people do and say hurtful things about us or to us. What does it mean to be persecuted? People are persecuted for their faith in some countries around the world. We are blessed to live in a country where there is freedom of religion – so how are you likely to experience persecution? The enemy, the devil, enjoys taunting us by planting negative thoughts in our minds. Sometimes he uses people around us to speak negatively to us.

Our natural reaction when this happens is to retaliate. Yet Scripture tells us that we must bless people. I want to challenge you, if someone is giving you a hard time make a choice to bless them. Speak the peace of Christ over them. Continue to do this and you will be amazed at the difference it will make.

I choose to speak out a blessing upon the people in my life.

Prayer

Father, I am so quick to seek revenge and become discouraged when people hurt or disappoint me. Help me by Your Spirit to bless others with Your peace. Amen.

Blessings past and future

Read Romans 10:5-13

For there is no difference between Jew and Gentile – the same Lord is Lord of all and richly blesses all who call on him. - Romans 10:12

In God's eyes all people are the same. God loves everyone. Our verse today tells us that He is Lord of all and that He richly blesses everyone who calls on Him. Do you realise how important this is in your life? It means two things: it means you can experience God's blessing in your own life and you can call on Him if you are in need.

Are you experiencing difficulties in your life? Do you have problems at home or maybe at school? It doesn't matter what you are facing – if you call on the Lord He will bless you. He will hear you and bless you; so that you can speak out a blessing upon the things in your life that you want to see changed. It is easy to sit back and complain or be angry and upset – but that doesn't accomplish anything.

I need to speak out a blessing upon the things in my life that I want to see changed.

Decide today that you will begin to speak blessing.

Prayer

Lord, I bring my difficulties to You – I choose today to call upon Your name – please bless .... I thank You for Your blessing in my life. Amen.

9 January

Blessed by a priestly blessing

Read Numbers 6:22-27

The Lord bless you and keep you; the Lord make his face shine upon you and be gracious to you; the Lord turn his face towards you and give you peace. - Numbers 6:24-26

This blessing is one of the most beautiful you can speak over someone. The first part says that the Lord will bless you and keep (or protect) you. He will protect you from the powers of darkness. We in turn must speak this blessing out upon everyone we know; our families, friends, our classmates, and even our enemies.

The second part of the blessing says that the Lord will make His face shine upon you – He will be kind to you. He will be faithful to the promises He has made to you.

The third part says the Lord will turn His face toward you – He will hear you when you pray to Him. He will give you peace – why will you have peace? You will have peace because you know your God is in control of your life. You can trust Him to do what is best for you and those you love.

I will have peace because I know my God is in control of my life.

Prayer

Father, once again I pray this wonderful promise: *The Lord bless me and keep me; the Lord make His face shine upon me and be gracious to me; the Lord turn His face towards me and give me peace.* Amen.

Answer with a blessing

Read 1 Peter 3:8-12

Finally, all of you, live in harmony with one another; be sympathetic, love as brothers, be compassionate and humble. Do not repay evil with evil or insult with insult, but with blessing, because to this you were called so that you may inherit a blessing.
- 1 Peter 3:8-9

Have you ever seen the bumper sticker Born to be blessed? In some ways this is what today's verses are saying. Usually in order to claim an inheritance you have to be part of a family, or know someone with money. Occasionally you hear of people inheriting from distant relatives. It doesn't work like this with God – He only has children – not grandchildren or great-grandchildren.

Our verses today clearly spell out how a child of God must live; we must get on with people, we must try and understand what they are going through, loving them – like we would love our brother or sister. We must show that we care and we are not to be proud. When people harm us or say bad things about us we are not to react but rather to bless them. You can do this because you are God's child and you have inherited the blessing.

I can bless others because I am God's child and I have inherited the blessing.

Prayer

Father, thank You that I am Your child. I have inherited the blessing from You, and because of this I can confidently reach out to everyone around me and bless them. Amen.

11 January

Bless your persecutors

Read Romans 12:9-21

Bless those who persecute you; bless and do not curse. - Romans 12:14

There will always be people who will try to bring you down and make you feel like a failure. It might be a friend, a teacher at school or sometimes unfortunately, someone in your own family. Often the loudest voices telling you that you are not good enough are the ones inside your own head. You look in the mirror and you are dissatisfied; or you see someone else who is more beautiful, clever and popular and you feel like you are a failure.

Do you realise this is not God's Spirit speaking to you? It is the enemy, the devil – he wants you to believe you are not good enough.

God, my Father. has made me. I am His creation – I am made in His image.

Our text tells us how to break a curse spoken over us – We must bless the person. If you are speaking negatively to yourself you need to stop. Look yourself in the eye and say: 'God, my Father, has made me. I am His creation – I am made in His image.' Then you will be able to bless others even if they speak negatively to you, and you will live in the abundance of God's blessing.

Prayer

Father, thank You that You have created me – I am Your special creation. Help me live in Your blessing and to bless others. Amen.

Blessed with a gift

Read 1 Corinthians 12:1-11

Now to each one the manifestation of the Spirit is given for the common good. All these are the work of one and the same Spirit and he gives them to each one, just as he determines. - 1 Corinthians 12:7,11

When you look at your friends do you compare yourself with them and feel that you do not have the abilities and talents that some of them have? This can make you feel inadequate. Maybe it is your brother or sister that you are comparing yourself to. You do not have to do this – in fact you shouldn't do it. Why not; because God has given you all the talents and abilities you need to do what He wants you to do.

I must use my gifts and talents to bless other people.

This is what our verse tells us. It says He gives to each one – just as He determines. This means He knows what you need. There is a key to unlocking this that maybe you have missed up until now. He does not give you talents and gifts for your own benefit alone. Again our verse gives us the clue – it is for the common good. This means you are to use your gifts and talents to bless other people. Start doing this today and you will be amazed at the difference it will make.

Prayer

Father, I want to bless other people. Help me to use my gifts and talents to do this. Amen.

Blessing of obedience

Read Colossians 3:18-25

Children, obey your parents in everything, for this pleases the Lord. - Colossians 3:20

It is often not considered cool to obey ones parents. Down through the ages children have struggled with the temptation to disobey their parents. Sometimes it can be because you feel they are being unfair, sometimes it is simply because you feel like it. If you have friends who disobey their parents you might feel that if you are not disobedient too you won't fit in.

In one of our earlier readings we said that when we choose to follow Jesus we start to walk along a different path; walking along this path means that we obey what God tells us to do. In our verse today we are told that God wants us to obey our parents. God says in this verse that we do not get to pick and choose what we will obey – we have to obey them in everything. It goes on to say that if we do this we will please the Lord. You will be blessed through your obedience. This is also a way that you can bless your parents – by obeying them.

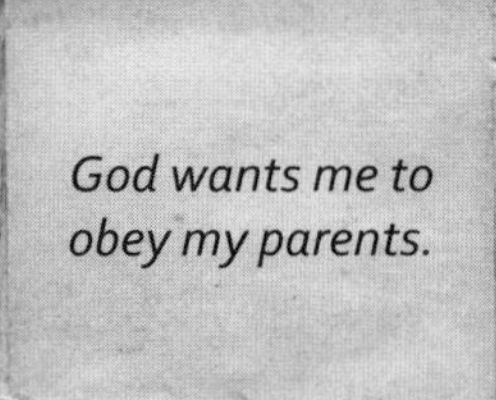
God wants me to obey my parents.

Prayer

Father, You know it is not always easy to obey my parents. I want to please You though, so I choose today to obey them. Thank You that Your Holy Spirit will help me to do this. Amen.

Blessing of love

Read Deuteronomy 6:4-6

Love the Lord your God with all your heart and with all your soul and with all your strength. These commandments that I give you today are to be upon your hearts.
- Deuteronomy 6:5-6

When we make the decision to follow Jesus we are given a new beginning. It is as if the screen of our lives is wiped clean. The best part though is that it is not only the screen but also the hard drive that is wiped clean. This means we can walk along this new path without a whole lot of stuff to hold us back.

As we walk along this path God asks us to love Him. This love that He talks about is a love that has to include every part of us. He is not interested in only part of you. He wants you to love Him with your heart and soul – with all your strength – that means as much as you are able. The reason you can love God is because He blesses you with His love – it is so big the love He has for us that it fills us to overflowing and allows us not just to love Him in return but also to love other people.

God is not interested in only a part of me. He wants me to love Him with my heart and soul – with all my strength.

Prayer

Father God, thank You for Your great love for me. I am so glad that I am Your child. I want to love You in return with my whole heart, soul and with all my strength. Amen.

15 January

Blessing sweeter than honey

Read Psalm 119:97-104

How sweet are your words to my taste, sweeter than honey to my mouth!
- Psalm 119:103

Do you find it difficult to pray? When you first make a decision to follow Jesus it can be a little difficult to find the right words. When you were little you probably learnt to pray using set prayers. As you grow in your relationship with the Lord you need to have a deeper communication with Him.

You can speak to Him about absolutely anything and everything. He is closer than your best friend – in fact He is your best Friend. Our Psalm talks about God's Word being sweeter than honey in our mouth. Why don't you try reading a Psalm every day and using it as a prayer to pray back to God; you will see that the people who wrote the Psalms told God everything; they shared all their emotions and experiences with Him. One of the best blessings God has given us is the blessing of prayer. Talking to our Father is meant to be something we do everyday all day; it is not just meant for specific times and places. Try it today – talk to God throughout your day – enjoy the blessing!

One of the best blessings God has given me is the blessing of prayer.

Prayer

Father God, thank You for the blessing of prayer. I am so glad I can talk to You about absolutely everything – there is nothing I cannot tell You – what a blessing this is! Amen.

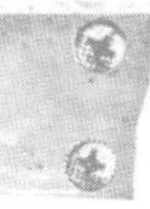

Blessing of provision

Read Genesis 22:1-19

Isaac spoke up and said to his father Abraham "Father?" "Yes, my son?" Abraham replied. "The fire and wood are here," Isaac said, "but where is the lamb for the burnt offering?" Abraham answered, "God himself will provide the lamb for the burnt offering, my son." And the two of them went on together. - Genesis 22:7-8

When one reads this story for the first time it might seem a bit strange; after all it is really an odd thing for God to ask a father to do. The lesson for us in this story is that Abraham was obedient to what God asked him to do. Abraham knew God, he believed that God loved him and loved his son, Isaac. Abraham understood that God would provide. God had given Isaac to him so God would do what was best for both of them.

I am moving forward believing God will bless me by providing for me.

Are you facing something difficult in your life? Are you having a hard time understanding why something like this should be happening to you? If you are then stop a moment and think about this story. God loves you. You are His child – He has a plan and a purpose for your life. You can trust Him to provide what you need. So don't sit around and feel sorry for yourself. Listen to what He is telling you and obey Him. Start doing it – move forward believing He will bless you by providing for you.

Prayer

Father God, it is hard sometimes to believe when things are so difficult. Fill me with the power of Your Spirit – open my ears to hear what You are saying to me and then help me to obey You and do what You are telling me to do. Thank You that You will provide for me because You love me and care for me. Amen.

17 January

Blessing of God

Read Psalm 29

The Lord gives strength to his people; the Lord blesses his people with peace.
- Psalm 29:11

In 2004 my family had a very bad car accident. My son, Aldo, who was 12 at the time was very badly injured, and he wasn't expected to live. However, he did live but we were told he would be bed-ridden, never able to walk or talk again. He could write though and he would spend hours filling page after page. One day I asked him, *Aldo, where were you when you experienced all these things you write about. He wrote, I was with Jesus. Jesus was there the night of the accident.*

He will give me the strength and peace I need – I must trust Him.

For many months I never stopped begging God to let Aldo speak again. Aldo would write over and over again; *Jesus will make me talk.* He circled Jesus' name every time. He would fill pages and then at the end he would write; *Thank You, Jesus, I will talk.* I believed he would talk again – God gave me the strength and peace to believe. Is there something you need to believe in God for today? He will give you the strength and peace you need – trust Him.

Prayer

Father God, I bow before You today. You are the Almighty God, Your voice is full of majesty. You reign over everything in heaven and on earth. Today I choose to trust You to fulfil Your promises in my life – give me Your strength and peace to believe. Amen.

Blessed – invited to come and buy

Read Revelation 3:14-22

He who has an ear, let him hear what the Spirit says to the churches.
- Revelation 3:22

In Revelation there are seven churches; God says to the Church at Laodicea; *you do not realise that you are wretched, pitiful, poor, blind and naked* (v 17). There's a lot we can learn from what God said to them. They believed (like many people do today) that what they had they had earned.

Instead, God invites them: *to come buy from me gold refined in the fire, so that you may become rich; and white clothes to wear, so that you can cover your shameful nakedness, and salve to put on your eyes, so that you can see.* Jesus died on the Cross so that we can enjoy God's abundance, be washed clean of our sins and have our spiritual eyes opened to see God. We get caught up with stuff that doesn't matter.

God wants to bless me with gold, with white clothes and ointment for my eyes.

You have the choice: Are you going to come to God and freely buy what He is offering you?

Prayer

Father God, I come to You just as I am. I choose to buy from You gold, white clothes, ointment for my eyes. Thank You for the blessing that is mine – thank You, Jesus, that You paid the price on Calvary so that I can have all I need. Amen.

Blessed with the fruit of the Spirit

Read Galatians 5:13-25

But the fruit of the Spirit is love, joy, peace, patience, kindness, goodness, faithfulness, gentleness and self-control. Against such things there is no law. - Galatians 5:22-23

Even if you do not look like your parents you have their DNA in your blood. This means that there will be certain similarities in your temperament, attitude and actions. When we choose to follow Jesus and we become God's children He places His DNA inside of us. This means that we will begin to look and act like Jesus.

God has placed His Spirit within us to lead and guide us. As God works in us moulding and making us like Jesus we will begin to show the fruit of the Spirit in our lives. Sometimes we resist God working in us – we do not want to change. We want to remain critical and judgemental of others; but God tells us we will be judged as we judge; so rather allow God to do the judging.

As God works in me moulding and making me like Jesus I will begin to show the fruit of the Spirit in my life.

Choose to work with God and as you yield to Him, spend time with Him, and read His Word – His Spirit will work within you forming the characteristics of the fruit of the Spirit so that you can be a blessing to others.

Prayer

Father God, I yield to Your Holy Spirit, I will not resist You working in my life making me more like Jesus. As You form the characteristics of the fruit of the Spirit in me use me to bless other people every day. Amen.

Blessing of answered prayer

Read Mark 11:20-26

Therefore I tell you, whatever you ask for in prayer, believe that you have received it, and it will be yours. - Mark 11:24

What an absolutely wonderful promise this is! This promise has special meaning for me; I will never forget the time I spent standing next to Aldo's bed in intensive care – I prayed this promise over and over clinging to it with all my might.

It doesn't matter how long it takes for your prayer to be answered. It is now more than eight years since the accident. Today if you look at Aldo you might be tempted to say; 'You still have a long road to walk.' It does not matter, if it hadn't been for faith and prayer, I would not have survived. It is only the belief that God will answer my prayers and bless us with what we have need of that helps me to persevere and keep going.

If I pray believing and God will answer me according to what is best for me.

You must never forget who the God is in whom you believe and to whom you pray. Many days I pray the Word. I remind God about the promises in His Word. I often insert my name into the scripture I am praying, making it personal – claiming the promise for myself. You can do the same – pray believing and God will answer you according to what is best for you.

Prayer

Father, help me to pray according to Your will, and give me more faith. I believe that I have already received what I am praying for. Thank You that You are the faithful God who blesses me according to what is best for me. Amen.

Blessing of God's Spirit

Read Romans 8:18-30

In the same way, the Spirit helps us in our weakness. We do not know what we ought to pray for, but the Spirit himself intercedes for us with groans that words cannot express. - Romans 8:26

I often ask the Holy Spirit: 'Holy Spirit, please plead for me with groans that cannot be expressed in words. Pray for me.' He leads me in prayer. He will do the same for you. Pray in your spirit. If you have received the gift of tongues then pray in your tongue. There is one condition that you must always adhere to; and that is always pray with your heart and not your mind. Set your thoughts to one side so that your spirit can be open to receive from God.

When the Holy Spirit prays on your behalf and for you then you will experience God's love, peace and blessing. You will be fully in God's presence. You will be so close to Him that you will literally be able to taste Him. His Word will be sweet upon your tongue, sweet as honey. You will be so close that you will be able to smell Him.

I will experience God's presence and blessing in my life like an all consuming perfume.

Ask the Holy Spirit of God to take you so deeply into prayer that you will experience God's presence and blessing in your life.

Prayer

Father, thank You for Your Spirit who is not only my Guide in life, but also in prayer. I pray that Your Spirit will lead me into Your wonderful presence and blessing, Holy God. Amen.

Blessed in Christ

Read Colossians 1:24-29

To them God has chosen to make known among the Gentiles the glorious riches of this mystery, which is Christ in you, the hope of glory. - Colossians 1:27

If you have made the decision to be a Christian and live for God then you have done so through accepting Jesus Christ as Your Saviour. This means that He lives within you. There is no other way for you to get closer to God except through Jesus. There isn't a game plan you can follow – such as saying five things in the morning, or doing ten things at night and then you will be close to God. It is through Christ and Him alone; this is how we become godly.

Paul told Timothy: *Have nothing to do with godless myths and old wives' tales; rather, train yourself to be godly. For physical training is of some value, but godliness has value for all things, holding promise for both the present life and the life to come* (1 Timothy 4:7-8).

It is through Christ in God's presence that I will find faith, strength, joy, peace and rich blessing.

It is through Christ in God's presence that we will find faith, strength, joy, peace and rich blessing. He is our hope for the blessing and glory awaiting us.

Prayer

Father, thank You that You live in me through Your Spirit. Through You I have the hope of eternal life. I praise and thank You for this! Thank You that I have faith, strength, joy, peace and rich blessing in You. Amen.

23 January

Blessing of Christ's rest

Read Matthew 11:25-30

Come to me, all you who are weary and burdened, and I will give you rest. For my yoke is easy and my burden is light. - Matthew 11:28,30

With Christ in us nothing is impossible. We follow in His footsteps and we are capable of everything because He lives within us.

Being a child of God and having Jesus Christ in us brings another blessing into our lives; He gives us rest. In Matthew 11:28-30 Jesus invites us to bring our heavy burdens to Him. He will exchange our heavy burdens for His rest, contentment and peace.

With Christ in you, and His peace and attitude in you, you will begin displaying His character. You will become like Him. You will have His strength. You will be able to do more than you could ever have imagined with Christ in You. Christ Himself said that with Him and His Spirit in us we will do greater miracles than even He did when He was here on earth.

With Christ in me; with His peace and attitude in me; I will begin displaying His character.

Know Who is in you. Commit yourself to Him, and receive from Him not only His rest and blessing, but everything He desires to give you and do in you.

Prayer

Father, thank You that I can go to Your Son, Jesus Christ, when I am tired and over-burdened. Thank You that His yolk and burden are easy and light. Thank You, Jesus, that You are my merciful Redeemer who blesses me with rich blessings. Amen.

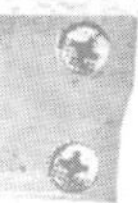

Blessing of looking to Jesus

Read Psalm 118

I will not die but live, and will proclaim what the Lord has done. - Psalm 118:17

There are times in life when it is very hard to see the silver lining around the dark cloud. Are you prepared during times like this to trust in the Lord? Or do you allow your emotions to get the better of you and the circumstances to dictate how you feel and act.

Jesus spoke to me about this one day when I was on an aeroplane. As the plane took off I could see the houses, plots and the roads. The higher the plane got the smaller they became. Eventually the plane was engulfed by clouds and then all of a sudden it broke through into the blue sky and sunshine. This is what happens when we choose to lift our eyes above our problems and focus on Jesus.

I am blessed of the Lord. His favour rests upon me. He gives me the victory.

You are blessed of the Lord. His favour rests upon you. He gives you the victory. You are not a victim. Choose in every and any circumstance to look up to Jesus, your Rock.

Prayer

Father, I choose anew today to lift my eyes to You, my Rock. You are so much bigger than my problems. I choose to look past my heartache, and break through the clouds gathered around me, into Your presence where You can bless me. Amen.

25 January

Blessing of God's graciousness

Read Isaiah 30:19-26

O people of Zion, who live in Jerusalem, you will weep no more. How gracious he will be when you cry for help! As soon as he hears, he will answer you. - Isaiah 30:19

Do you have a special friend whose voice you would recognise no matter where you were – even in the midst of a large crowd of people? To know someone's voice this well you have to spend time with them. You have to talk to them and listen to them. You have to hang out with them. Only then will you be able to distinguish their voice when they call to you above all the other voices around you. The same is true of God – the closer you are to Him the better you will hear Him.

This is the kind of relationship God wants to have with you. In the midst of the noise and babble of the world around you – you need to be tuned in to His voice. He wants to talk to you, lead you, comfort you and bless you. Call to Him. He will graciously answer you. Do you hear Him when He calls to you?

Do I hear Him when He calls my name?

Prayer

Father, thank You that I have the freedom to call upon You. You answer me immediately when I call out to You. Holy Spirit, quicken my hearing so that I in turn, may hear the voice of My Lord when He calls to me. Amen.

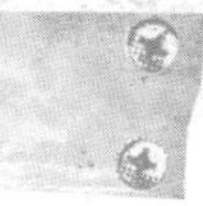

Blessing upon you

Read 1 Thessalonians 5:12-28

May God himself, the God of peace, sanctify you through and through. May your whole spirit, soul and body be kept blameless at the coming of our Lord Jesus Christ. The one who calls you is faithful and he will do it. - 1 Thessalonians 5:23-24

Child of God I want to bless you today.

I bless you with the love of our Lord Jesus Christ.

I bless you with the spiritual insight to see Jesus, so that you will view everything that happens in your life from God's perspective.

I bless you so that you will not only see the challenges in your life, but that you will also be able to perceive His light that surrounds you.

I bless you today with the ability to accomplish things you would never previously have considered doing.

I bless you with joy unlimited found in Jesus. May you experience the joy of the Lord; may He be your strength in every circumstance and each situation you encounter.

I bless you with all these blessings today. Go out and bless others as you come into contact with them throughout your day.

I receive Your blessing today so that it can flow through me to everyone around me.

Prayer

Father, thank You that You are faithful to all Your promises You have blessed me with. I receive Your blessing today so that it can flow through me to everyone around me. Amen.

27 January

Blessed with discernment

Read Philippians 1:3-11

And this is my prayer: that your love may abound more and more in knowledge and depth of insight, so that you may be able to discern what is best and may be pure and blameless until the day of Christ, filled with the fruit of righteousness that comes through Jesus Christ- to the glory and praise of God. - Philippians 1:9-11

Today I bless you with the peace and joy that will take away all the pain and hurt in your life.

I bless you with a clear understanding and insight into God's plan for your life; and with the will to carry out the plan He has for you.

I bless you so that God's will – may be good, perfect and acceptable to you and that you will choose to live according to His will for your life.

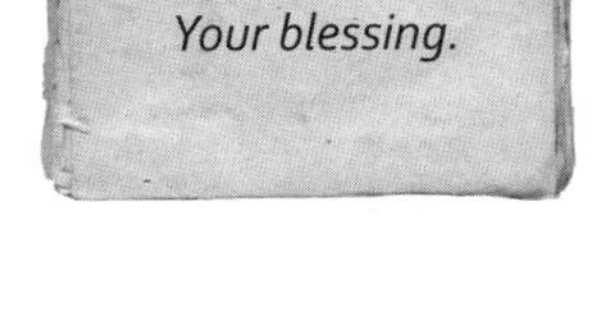

Empower me to live in the fullness of Your blessing.

I bless you with the ability to distinguish between right and wrong; with the discernment to be able to detect the plans of the enemy so that you do not fall into his trap.

I bless your ears with the ability to hear the voice of God; so that you may hear, understand and obey what He is saying to you.

I bless you with the joy of the Lord that is your strength.

Prayer

Father, bless me with a hunger and a thirst for Your Word. Bless me, I pray, with discernment. Bless me with insight into Your plan for my life. Empower me to live in the fullness of Your blessing. Amen.

Blessed by those around you

Read Ruth 2

Boaz replied, "I've been told all about what you have done for your mother-in-law since the death of your husband – how you left your father and mother and your homeland and came to live with a people you did not know before. May the Lord repay you for what you have done. May you be richly rewarded by the Lord, the God of Israel, under whose wings you have come to take refuge." - Ruth 2:11-12

Bless you today with 'Believing' friends; who can stand with you. I bless you with the fulfilment of your dreams; God is the 'Dream-Giver' and He will make your dreams come true.

I bless you with people who will walk in unity with you.

I bless you with endurance so that you may have perseverance, energy and strength to keep going.

I bless you with people who will support and encourage you, who bring peace into your life.

I bless you with relationships with friends who will love and serve God with you – who will walk the journey of faith with you.

Help me, to be like Ruth and serve and love others unselfishly.

I bless your personality – that you may have a personality that radiates the love, peace and joy of Christ.

Maybe you feel that you do not matter – but you do matter – you are on this earth for a purpose. God has a plan for your life. You are precious beyond words to Him.

Prayer

Father, thank You for the people You bring across my path who support and encourage me. Help me, to be like Ruth and serve and love others unselfishly. Thank You for Your love and blessing in my life. Amen.

29 January

Blessed with God's peace

Read John 14:15-31

Peace I leave with you; my peace I give you. I do not give to you as the world gives. Do not let your hearts be troubled and do not be afraid. - John 14:27

God has a calling for you; and today I want to bless you so that you will not resist this calling, but that you will embrace it and fulfil it.

I bless you with an experiential understanding of God's love for you.

Jesus tells us in John 14 that He has given us His peace; I pray that you will experience His peace so that your heart will not fear or be unsettled.

I bless you with the knowledge that the One who is in you is greater than the one who is in the world.

I bless you with a passion for God; so that His fire will burn brightly in you for others to see.

I bless your values today, that you will live according to God's precepts and principles.

I bless your perseverance and fortitude so that you will not break under the pressure of the world, but rather that you will say to the world: "This is who I am in Jesus Christ my Lord!"

God blesses me with perseverance so that I will not break under the pressure of the world.

Prayer

Father, thank You that I can know that You have a purpose for my life; that I have a calling. Reveal it to me this day so that I can live my life in the fullness of service to You. Thank You that You bless me with Your peace and love. Let it flow through me to others. Amen.

Blessed with Love

Read 2 Corinthians 13:1-14

May the grace of the Lord Jesus Christ, and the love of God, and the fellowship of the Holy Spirit be with you all. - 2 Corinthians 13:14

Bless you today with words of truth and life.

I bless you so that you will allow God's light to shine through your life causing people to turn from their sin and glorify our Father in heaven.

I bless you so that you will love your fellow man with the love of God.

I bless you with His resurrection power that flows through you. If you are sick I pray that this resurrection power will touch you and heal you.

I bless you as a child of God that you might live as a king/queen, priest/priestess, and prophet/prophetess.

I bless you with a positive self-image so that you will know that God sees you differently to the way the world sees you. I pray that you will believe this, accept it and live this out. You are precious to God. He loves you with an everlasting love and He will continue to bless you with His love, joy, peace and mercy.

God continues to bless me with His love, joy, peace and mercy.

Prayer

Father, bless me with the mercy and grace of the Lord Jesus Christ and with Your love and the communion of the Holy Spirit. Send me out today, to share this blessing with everyone I come into contact with. Amen.

A final prayer of blessing

Read Ephesians 3:14-21

I pray that out of his glorious riches he may strengthen you with power through his Spirit in your inner being, so that Christ may dwell in your hearts through faith. And I pray that you, being rooted and established in love, may have power, together with all the saints, to grasp how wide and long and high and deep is the love of Christ, and to know this love that surpasses knowledge – that you may be filled to the measure of all the fullness of God. - Ephesians 3:16-19

As we come to this last day of January, I want to pray Paul's prayer, which he prayed for the Ephesians, over you:

I pray that the Lord through His Spirit, out of the riches of His glory will give you the power to grow in strength in your inner most being.

I pray that you will grasp how wide and long and high and deep the love of Christ is for you.

I pray that you will know His love that goes beyond our understanding. His love cannot be described with words, but makes us whole and brings us peace.

He is able to do immeasurably more than all I ask or imagine, according to His power that is at work within me.

I pray that you will put your hand up and not be ashamed to let people know that you serve the Lord – that you will stand up for Jesus. He is your hope of glory.

I pray all this in the Name of the Father, the Son and the Holy Spirit. I ask that He continue to hold you in the palm of His hand and richly bless your life.

Prayer

Father, thank You that I can know and experience how wide and long and high and deep Your love is for me and the world around me. Help me to daily share Your love, mercy and blessing with those around me. Amen.

Jesus Christus woon
in my. samuel bly
vry wanneer hy in
Jesus Christus bly. Soos
rut rustig is so sal
Sameul vir altyd rustig
wees. Goud sal ons sien
harte wat bou van
muur om het nehemia
se muur om het, so
hart is goud. Samuel is
vrees vry want sy
muur is beseën. Seun
hoor God sê samuel,
bly in my hier is
vrede hier is lewe.
Giet ouers soveel
liefde oor samuel sien
hoe liefde Samuel rustig
vashou.

Letter 2:

Jesus Christ in me

Jesus Christ lives in me. Samuel will remain free as long as he is in Jesus Christ. Just like Ruth is at peace, so too will Samuel be at peace forever. We will see golden hearts. Golden hearts have Nehemiah's wall built around them. Samuel is now free from fear because his wall is blessed. Boy heard God say: 'Samuel, live in Me. Peace is here. Life is here.' My parents pour so much love over Samuel. I can see that God gently holds Samuel with His love.

In the throne room with God

Prayer for February

Father, we come to You in the name of Jesus Christ, the Name above every name. I pray Your mercy and Your unmerited favour upon each young person reading this devotional. I ask You to speak to us through Your Spirit this month. Father, You have been teaching me about living in Your presence for some time now. I pray that as we walk through this month, You will help me to share my experiences in a way that will help others to be drawn into Your presence. Thank You that You are the God of love. Pour out Your blessing, salvation, peace and glory upon us. Lead us into Your throne room during this month, Father. Take us by the hand and show us everything You have in store for us. I pray this in the Name of the One and only Jesus. Amen.

Entering the Father's presence

Read Psalm 65

Blessed are those you choose and bring near to live in your courts! We are filled with the good things of your house, of your holy temple. - Psalm 65:4

After the accident in which my son, Aldo, was so badly injured, I spent a long time trying to understand everything that had happened and totally changed our lives as a result.

I prayed and asked God to help me to find a way of being able to share and explain my experiences to other people. In the beginning when I spoke about it I could see that people didn't understand. God began to show me, and He spoke to me through His Spirit. 'Retah, I am inviting you into My presence, into My throne room and I want you to explain to other people how they can also enter into My presence.'

My friend, join me on a journey into the throne room of God, your Father, this month. I can promise you it will be an experience that will bring a new dimension to your life and your relationship with the Lord.

After I have entered into the throne room of God, my life will never be the same again.

Prayer

Father, thank You for the privilege of entering into Your presence. Thank You that we can come freely. Lead me by Your Spirit into Your throne room so that I can worship You and love You. Amen.

Calling out to God

Read Psalm 3

To the Lord I cry aloud, and he answers me from his holy hill. - Psalm 3:4

Living in God's presence is the birthright of everyone who is a child of God. Jesus died on Calvary so that you can live in the Father's presence.

The day Jesus died upon the cross was the most significant day in the history of humanity. We become so used to talking and reading about the crucifixion that it can become head knowledge. Yet God's Spirit wants to help us understand its importance for our lives.

If you are a child of God and you have chosen to follow Jesus then you are meant to be living in God's presence. It took a major trauma in my life to make me turn towards God. On a day when I was so tired and I felt that I could no longer cope I called out to God and asked Him to help me. He heard me and He answered me. If you call to Him and wait on Him then He will do the same for you.

When I call out to the Lord, He answers me.

Prayer

Father, thank You that there is nothing that stops me from entering into Your presence. I call out to You to please help me to know You better. Amen.

3 February

Tearing the veil

Read Matthew 27:45-56

And when Jesus had cried out again in a loud voice, he gave up his spirit. At that moment the curtain of the temple was torn in two from top to bottom. The earth shook and the rocks split. - Matthew 27:50-51

God the Father showed me Jesus hanging on the cross of Calvary. Jesus was beaten and He suffered thirty-nine lashes for us. For every lash that Jesus endured I heard the Father say, 'This was for you.' I experienced the heart of God and met with Him.

After Jesus called out, 'It is finished!' the curtain in the temple was torn in two. I then heard the words: 'Come in, My child, come into My presence.'

This month we are going to talk about how we can enter into God's presence, and live there every day.

Now I can enter freely into God's presence and worship Him in spirit and in truth.

The temple had an Outer Court, the Holy Place and the Holy of Holies. Only the High Priest could enter into the Holy of Holies. On the day Jesus died the curtain was torn in two. The Holy of Holies was open: Now we can enter freely into God's presence and worship Him in spirit and in truth.

Prayer

Heavenly Father, thank You for Your Son who died on the cross for me. Thank You that because of Jesus I can freely come into Your presence and worship You in spirit and in truth. Amen.

Pushing through into God's presence

Read Hebrews 9:1-22

A tabernacle was set up. In its first room were the lampstand, the table and the consecrated bread; this was called the Holy Place. Behind the second curtain was a room called the Most Holy Place, which had the golden altar of incense and the gold-covered ark of the covenant. This ark contained the gold jar of manna, Aaron's staff that had budded, and the stone tables of the covenant. - Hebrews 9:2-4

I want to link the Outer Court, the Holy Place and the Holy of Holies with Jesus' statement that He is 'the Way', 'the Truth' and 'the Life'.

You can be on 'the Way' and still live in the Outer Court. You have accepted Jesus as your Saviour, but you are still focused on your own life.

Push through into the Holy of Holies – Live in the fullness of His Life.

You can know 'the Truth' and enter into the Holy place, but still have many struggles between your sinful nature and God's Spirit. For me it was only after our terrible accident that I moved into 'the Life'– into the Holy of Holies.

Jesus came so that we can have life and have it to the full (John 10:10). This 'Life to the full' is for now – it is not for one day when we get to heaven.

You are starting out on life's journey: live in the presence of your Heavenly Father.

Prayer

Father, thank You for standing with open arms waiting to welcome me into Your presence. Thank You for Your Spirit who leads me into all Truth and teaches me to know You as my Heavenly Father. Amen.

Challenging you

Read Hebrews 4:14-5:10

Therefore, since we have a great high priest who has gone through the heavens, Jesus the Son of God, let us hold firmly to the faith we profess. Let us then approach the throne of grace with confidence, so that we may receive mercy and find grace to help us in our time of need. - Hebrews 4:14,16

When the curtain was torn, God said: 'Come in.' In His throne room we find the mercy seat. God says, 'Come into My throne room My child, and your life will be changed. You will become a new person and live in a radically different way. You will never be the same again when you leave here.'

There is only one reason for this: God is love. He does not invite us into His presence to judge, criticise or punish us, no, He overwhelms us with His love, truth and mercy.

I want to challenge you today to move through the Outer Court – past your own dreams and desires, on through the Holy Place – don't get caught up in the struggle between your old life and the new life you have in Christ. Push on into the Holy of Holies. There you will live in the anointing; the richness, depth, height, and the glory of God's presence.

Push on until I enter the Holy of Holies. There I will experience the glory of God's presence.

Prayer

Father, strengthen me through Your Spirit to move through the Outer Court. I do not want to stop until I have pushed through into Your presence. Father, I want to experience the fullness of Your glory so that I will forever be changed. Amen.

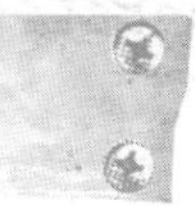

6 February

Releasing your faith

Read Matthew 9:18-26

Just then a woman who had been subject to bleeding for twelve years came up behind him and touched the edge of his cloak. She said to herself, "If I only touch his cloak, I will be healed." - Matthew 9:20,21

My favourite story in the Bible is about the woman who suffered with an issue of blood for many years. She spent all her money going from one doctor to another trying to find a cure. No one could help her. One day Jesus visited her village and she hurried to where He was, but there was such a large crowd around Him that she could hardly get near Him.

This woman was not to be put off she pushed through the crowd. Her eyes were focused on Jesus and she persevered. She believed that if she could just touch the edge of His robe she would be healed. Eventually she was close enough to touch the robe. Immediately Jesus was aware of her. Her turned to her and said: 'Take heart, daughter, your faith has healed you.'

Faith is all that I need to enter into the presence of my Almighty God.

Faith is all that you need in order to enter into the presence of your Almighty God.

Prayer

Father, thank You for Your Son who brings me freedom and healing. Thank You that You confirm my faith in Him through Your Spirit. I need You in my life, Father. Lead me into Your presence. Amen.

7 February

Removing the obstacles

Read Matthew 9:18-26

Jesus turned and saw her. "Take heart, daughter," he said, "your faith has healed you." And the woman was healed from that moment. - Matthew 9:22

When I speak about life – I am not only referring to physical life but also to spiritual life. It is possible to be physically alive but be spiritually dead. The woman with the issue of blood in our reading today was alive spiritually, because she believed. She would not be deterred and pushed through the barrier. At the moment she came into Jesus' presence her faith came into contact with the Almighty power of God. Immediately she received healing and new life.

I choose to break through the barriers so that I can come before Him and receive healing and new life.

Many things can prevent us from experiencing God's healing and life-giving presence in our lives; bitterness, the inability to forgive, sinful deeds, bad habits, or disobedience. We allow things or people to become more important than God; family, friends, sport or hobbies to name a few.

If you want a relationship with God, which is real and life-giving, nothing and no one can be more important in your life than He is.

Prayer

My Heavenly Father, I praise You for the new life and healing that You have given me. Thank You that You are faithful and whenever I cry out calling upon Your name You always answer me. I choose today to make You the most important Person in my life. Amen.

Seeking God wholeheartedly

Read Psalm 63

O God, you are my God, earnestly I seek you; my soul thirsts for you, my body longs for you, in a dry and weary land where there is no water. I have seen you in the sanctuary and beheld your power and your glory. - Psalm 63:1-2

There was a time in my life when I believed that I didn't need God. I didn't realise that everything I had, everything I was, even the very air that I breathed came from the Almighty God. It is all about His grace and mercy in my life. In the light of His presence it all became clear to me. His light opens our spiritual eyes so that we can see clearly. As I saw His rich blessings descending down upon me I realised that everything I am or have is from Him. I can do nothing apart from God. Even though I thought it was me who was so good and clever, all the time it was Him. It was my Father showing me His love.

Everything I am and have is from Him. I can do nothing apart from God.

Can you say with the Psalmist today, '*O God, you are my God, earnestly I seek you; my soul thirsts for you, my body longs for you, in a dry and weary land where there is no water.*'

Prayer

Father, I am earnestly seeking You. I am longing for You. I want to abide in Your presence. Everything I am and have comes from You, my God and Father. Thank You for Your love and mercy in my life. Amen.

9 February

A God centred life

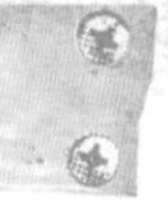

Read John 8:31-47

So if the Son sets you free, you will be free indeed. - John 8:36

When we live our Christian life in the Outer Courts we worship God from afar. In the Outer Court we make our own decisions independently of God. We are self centred – not God centred. In the Outer Court we are people pleasers, not God pleasers. We are more concerned about what our friends think of us than what God does. We have no spiritual depth. We regularly attend Church without it having any real effect upon our lives – there is no evidence of change in our lives.

The power to live in Him can only be received by entering into His presence; by pushing through into the throne room of God. Jesus came to bring you freedom, and you are only truly free once the Son has set you free. The miracle is that He wants to set you free: so that you can live a God centred life.

> *Jesus came to bring me freedom, and I am only truly free once the Son has set me free.*

Prayer

Dear Father, thank You that You sent Your Son, Jesus Christ, to this world to die for me so that I can be set free. Help me to move from the Outer Court into Your presence. Help me not to stop until I enter into Your throne room. Amen.

Our supernatural God

Read Mark 10:17-31

Jesus looked at them and said: "With man this is impossible, but not with God; all things are possible with God." - Mark 10:27

As Believers when we live in the Holy Place, we operate in the dimension of the soul. We want to experience and feel everything. Everything revolves around us feeling good and our needs being met. We expect other people to make us happy. The world revolves around us.

Serving God is not based on a feeling though. It is a choice; just as happiness is a choice. Happiness has nothing whatsoever to do with your feelings; it has nothing to do with what is happening around you. Happiness is an attitude. Paul spoke about this in Philippians 2 when he said that 'our attitude should be the same as that of Christ Jesus.' Jesus had the attitude of a servant. He found His 'happiness and contentment' in His relationship with His Father.

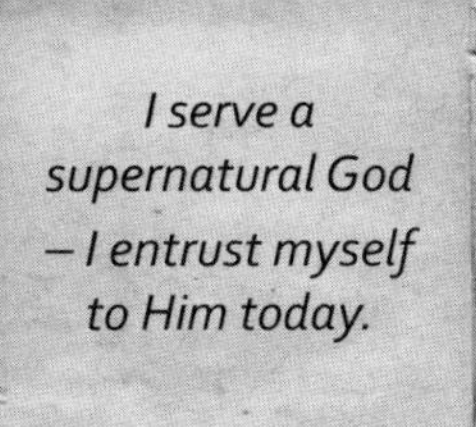

I serve a supernatural God – I entrust myself to Him today.

You too can trust God no matter what your need is. Our text today tells us that nothing is impossible with God – you serve a supernatural God. Entrust yourself to Him today.

Prayer

Father God, thank You for Your promise to me that You are the same yesterday, today and forever. Thank You that this brings balance and stability to my life. I find my happiness and contentment in You not in other people or circumstances. Amen.

Holy God

Read Revelation 4:1-11

Each of the four living creatures had six wings and was covered with eyes all around, even under his wings. Day and night they never stop saying: "Holy, holy, holy is the Lord God Almighty, who was, and is, and is to come." - Revelation 4:8

In the Holy of Holies we worship our supernatural God who has miracle-working power. This is the realm where we experience God's glory and majesty.

It is here the angels are to be found; around God's throne. They worship before God day and night singing; *'Holy, holy, holy is the Lord God Almighty.'* When we get to heaven we will worship in God's presence. We will glorify His wonderful Name forever. We will not argue with God; we will not ask why and demand answers from God. Instead we will say: 'Lord it doesn't matter what the answer is, I choose to trust You.' What is faith? It is not knowing the answer and still trusting God.

My purpose is to worship God.

Your purpose is to worship God. You enter the Holy of Holies when you come before Him in humility and love, bowing before His throne in worship.

Prayer

Father, I want to be quiet in Your presence today, bowing before Your glory and majesty, crying 'holy, holy, holy Lord God Almighty!' I honour, praise and worship You. Amen.

Seeking God

Read Acts 17:16-34

God did this so that men would seek him and perhaps reach out for him and find him, though he is not far from each one of us. - Acts 17:27

Every person has a deep seated desire within them. God created each of us with this desire, with this void only He can fill. He is the only One who can satisfy the need in each human heart. It is only when we come to Him, accepting Him as our God and Father through Jesus, His Son, that the need is met.

We must seek God with our whole heart. The Word of God assures us that those who seek God will find Him; that He will draw near to those who draw near to Him.

He is waiting to welcome me with open arms when I choose to make Him first in my life.

When we find God we must continue to seek after Him, to grow in Him, to abide in Him, to worship Him, to seek His will for our lives. He must be and remain our first priority in every area and facet of our lives. He is waiting to welcome you with open arms when you choose to make Him first in your life.

Prayer

My Father God, thank You for Your promise that You are never far from me. Help me, I pray, by Your Spirit to put You first in my life. I want to seek You with all my heart. I want to live in Your presence worshiping at Your throne. Amen.

God's Almighty Presence

Read Exodus 24:1-18

And the glory of the Lord settled on Mount Sinai. For six days the cloud covered the mountain, and on the seventh day the Lord called to Moses from within the cloud. To the Israelites the glory of the Lord looked like a consuming fire on the top of the mountain. - Exodus 24:16-17

Moses was an old man already when God told him in Exodus 19 to climb Mount Sinai. He could easily have said; 'I am too old,' but Moses had experienced the burning bush, and he had a desire to experience more of God and to obey Him. He knew that God would give him the strength and he implicitly trusted God.

If I desire to experience God's power in my life I need to spend time in His presence – unhurried time.

Are the challenges preventing you from following the path God has set out for you? Is it your friends, or the activities you are involved in?

The goal and the reward at the end of the journey for Moses was that he experienced more of God – Moses' desire was met.

If you desire to experience God's power in your life you need to spend time in His presence – unhurried time. Allow Him to fill you with His glory so that it will overflow onto all those you come into contact with.

Prayer

My Father, thank You that I can experience the glory of Your presence in my life. Help me to resist the things that prevent me from spending time with You. I want to spread Your glory to my friends and family. Amen.

Recharging your batteries

Read Psalm 23

Surely goodness and love will follow me all the days of my life, and I will dwell in the house of the Lord forever. - Psalm 23:6

Recently while charging my cell phone battery, I remembered that I needed to make a call. I noticed that the battery had not had an opportunity to fully recharge. As I picked up the phone I realised the phone had limited power because I hadn't fully charged it.

As I looked at the partially charged cell phone it reminded me that it is exactly the same for us on a spiritual level. Our spiritual batteries need consistent recharging. We charge our spiritual batteries by spending time in God's presence, allowing Him by His Spirit to minister to us. Sadly so many of us only spend short amounts of time in His presence – just enough to get by. Is it any wonder that we lack power?

Spend time in God's presence. There is no shortcut to His power flowing through me.

If you want to experience the glory of God in your life then you must spend time in His presence. There is no shortcut to God's power flowing through you.

Prayer

My loving Father, thank You that You love me, and I love You in return. I want to express my love for You by spending time in Your presence. Lord, I desire Your power in my life – touch me, I pray. Amen.

With heart, soul, strength and mind

Read Luke 10:25-37

He answered: "Love the Lord your God with all your heart and with all your soul and with all your strength and with all your mind and love your neighbour as yourself."
- Luke 10:27

Here are some of the ways you can love and glorify God; you can serve Him; seek His will for your life, spend time in the Word learning about Him and His ways. Repent of your sins and thank Him for His forgiveness. You can build a strong prayer life, and live in an attitude of praise and worship towards God. Another way is to intercede for others before God's throne of grace.

God spoke to me the other day, He asked me, 'Retah, does the whole of your heart belong to Me, is your entire soul, all of your strength and every corner of your mind Mine?' God wants nothing less from each of us. When God is your first love you will be one with Him. You will be filled with His love, courage, strength and authority. The Spirit of the Father and His miracle-working strength will flow through you.

When God is my first love I will be filled with His love, courage, strength and authority.

Prayer

Father, prevent me from allowing anything or anyone to divert my whole hearted love from You. You are my first love. I want to love You with my whole heart, soul, strength and mind. Amen.

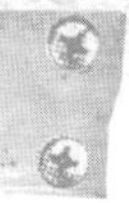

One with Christ

Read Galatians 2:15-21

I have been crucified with Christ and I no longer live, but Christ lives in me. The life I live in the body, I live by faith in the Son of God, who loved me and gave himself for me. - Galatians 2:20

Are you prepared to take up your cross and follow Jesus? Are you prepared to take a stand for Jesus and live in total dependence and unity with Him? If you are prepared to do this you will begin to understand what Paul meant in Romans 8 when he wrote: Nothing can separate us from the love of God through Jesus Christ our Lord. For me this is the most amazing verse in the entire Bible. Jesus and I are one; nothing and no one in this world can separate me from His love for me or me from my love for Him.

Christ living His life through me will lead me into fullness of life.

We are unequivocally one with Jesus. The more we are one with Him the more like Him we will begin to think, act and speak. We will start behaving more and more like Jesus. Galatians 2:20 will become a reality for us: It is not us who lives but Jesus Christ who lives in us.

Surrender to His will, become one with His Son, Jesus Christ; and you will experience freedom and life. Christ living His life through you will lead you into fullness of life.

Prayer

My Father God, thank You for Your Son who invites me to be one with Him and with You. Thank You for the assurance that I have died with Christ and that I am a new creature in Him. Thank You that I share in His risen life. I am so grateful for Your rest and peace. Amen.

17 February

Candle or lamp stand?

Read Matthew 11:25-30

"Come to me, all you who are weary and burdened, and I will give you rest. Take my yoke upon you and learn from me, for I am gentle and humble in heart, and you will find rest for your souls. For my yoke is easy and my burden is light."
- Matthew 11:28-30

The biggest lesson I have learnt as a result of spending time in God's presence is that I have stopped trying to do everything myself.

Jesus came to me and He said: 'Come to me, stop all your labour and toil, I will do it for you.' Today He is saying the same thing to you. You could compare this to the difference between trying to find your way using a single candle, as opposed to using a lamp stand to illuminate your way.

The longer the candle burns, the quicker it burns itself out. The lamp stand on the other hand, like the golden candelabra, standing in the Tabernacle, gives ongoing light. Why; because every day the Holy Spirit fills it with new oil.

I come to God, submit to Him, allowing Him to replace my heavy burden – His yoke is easy and light.

Obey God and do what He asks of you; Come to Him, submit to Him, and allow Him to replace your heavy burden with His yoke that is easy and light.

Prayer

Dear Father, thank You for the peace and calm I receive through Your precious Son, Jesus Christ, My Lord and Saviour. As I surrender to Your Holy Spirit working in me fill me and anoint me with power so that I can be a light to the world around me. Amen.

Being rooted and established

Read Ephesians 3:14-21

I pray that out of his glorious riches he may strengthen you with power through his Spirit in your inner being, so that Christ may dwell in your hearts through faith. And I pray that you, being rooted and established in love, may have power, together with all the saints to grasp how wide and long and high and deep is the love of Christ.
- Ephesians 3:16-18

God's presence in your life brings you contentment, peace and rest. In God's presence the Devil cannot touch you; you are safe.

People are considered established when they have accumulated wealth; when they have reached the top of their chosen profession; when society acknowledges their accomplishments and they achieve a certain status in society. On the other hand being established in God's Kingdom means something quite different; you have a relationship with God, and you are anchored in God's Word.

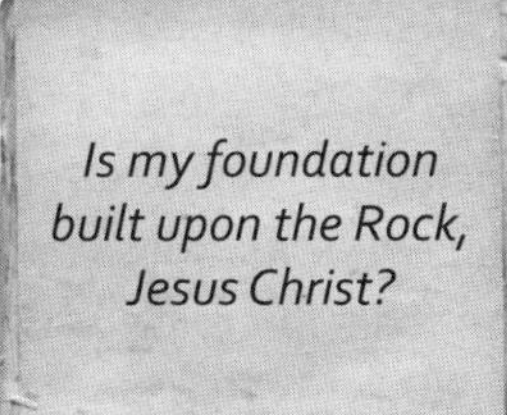

Is my foundation built upon the Rock, Jesus Christ?

If you follow Jesus people think you should not be successful. This is not true – God blesses us with success in every area of our lives – but we must first seek God and His Kingdom and then trust Him to bless us.

Someone who is established in God finds their happiness primarily in God their heavenly Father. If this is your experience you will be able to stand firm no matter what happens.

Prayer

My Father God, I pray that by Your Spirit, out of the riches of Your glory, You will make me strong. I want to be rooted and established in Christ's love through faith as He lives in my heart. Amen.

19 February

Bearing Fruit (1)

Read Matthew 13:1-9

Still other seed fell on good soil, where it produced a crop – a hundred, sixty or thirty times what was sown. - Matthew 13:8

What kind of a Christian are you? In Matthew 13 Jesus spoke about seed that bears fruit. Some seed bore thirty times, sixty times and even a hundred times.

If you are a thirty percent Christian you are like a motor car that never moves out of first gear, travelling at thirty kilometres an hour. Depending on how far you are trying to travel you will burn the engine out and the car will come to a stop.

Matthew 13:22 tells us: *...the seed that fell among the thorns is the man who hears the word, but the worries of this life and the deceitfulness of wealth choke it, making it unfruitful.*

If this describes you then you need new seeds of wisdom, inspiration, creativity, love and power from God's storeroom. Are you obeying and doing what He is telling you to do? Draw seed from His storeroom and begin to bear fruit for Him.

How much fruit is my life bearing for the Master?

Prayer

My Lord and Master, I place my trust in You so that neither the difficulties nor the pleasures of life will slow me down, preventing me from serving You wholeheartedly. I want to serve You at one hundred percent capacity. Amen.

Bearing Fruit (2)

Read Matthew 13:1-9

Still other seed fell on good soil, where it produced a crop – a hundred, sixty or thirty times what was sown. - Matthew 13:8

Some Christians only produce a sixty percent yield in their lives; their fruit is stunted. They want to follow God but they let things get in the way. They strive in their own strength. It took me a long time before I learnt how to move out of this phase.

The way to enter into true life is to say to God: 'Lord, I can no longer do things in my own strength. I surrender to You, one hundred percent of who I am.' This will result in you pushing through into the Holy of Holies into God's presence; faith will be set free in your heart and life.

The fruit you will bear is not only to bless you – you bear fruit in order to bless other people also. What God has done in your life will bring about change in the lives of the people you meet and whom God brings across your path.

I will bear one hundred percent fruit when I push through into the Holy of Holies.

Prayer

Father, empower me through the strength of Your Spirit in my life, to produce a hundred percent yield of fruit, so that my life will glorify You. Father, to this end I surrender the whole of my life to You. In Your power I will bear fruit in Your name. Amen.

Nourishing food and life giving water

Read Revelation 22:1-5

Then the angel showed me the river of the water of life, as clear as crystal, flowing from the throne of God and of the Lamb down the middle of the great street of the city. - Revelation 22:1-2a

Bearing fruit and living in God's presence go together. People who yield one hundred percent fruit have two things in common: They spend a lot of time praying and they live praising and worshipping God. If you do not spend time in prayer and you do not live praising and worshiping God you cannot expect to enter the Holy of Holies, and into the true life.

I need to get my nourishment from the Word of God.

The power of God flows through prayer in God's presence to us and through us, and then in turn to other people when we praise and worship Him.

Choose today to live in God's presence, in the Holy of Holies. Derive your nourishment from the Word of God. Drink pure life giving water from the River of Life flowing from the throne of God. These are the blessings He has given you to sustain and nourish you spiritually so that you can bear abundant fruit for Him.

Prayer

My Father for the nourishment I receive from Your Word and the life giving water from Your throne, I thank and praise You. I worship You, I honour You and I glorify Your Name. Fill me with Your power – let it flow through me so that I may yield abundant fruit for You. Amen.

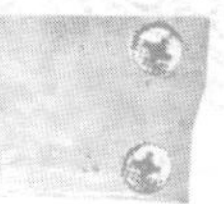

As the Spirit wills

Read Matthew 13:1-9

For the sinful nature desires what is contrary to the Spirit, and the Spirit what is contrary to the sinful nature. They are in conflict with each other, so that you do not do what you want. - Galatians 5:17

Galatians 5 says that our sinful nature desires things that are in conflict with what the Spirit wants us to do. Our sinful nature tries to take control of our lives. When this happens we do not do what God wants us to do. We walk according to the flesh and not according to the Spirit. Temptations come our way and we yield to the temptation.

Remember to be tempted is not a sin; it is only when we give in to the temptation that it becomes a sin. This is why it is vitally important that we surrender our lives to the control of the Holy Spirit. Pray and ask the Holy Spirit to renew your mind so that you will know what the good, perfect and acceptable will of God is for your life. Allow God's power to feed your spirit so that it becomes the strongest part of who you are.

My spirit must be the strongest part of me and a defence against the enemy's attempts to ensnare me.

Prayer

Thank You, my Heavenly Father, for giving me Your Holy Spirit who fills me, leads me and controls my life. Help me to live in the Spirit day by day. Amen.

23 February

Living in God's Light

Read Psalm 36

For with you is the fountain of life; in your light we see light. - Psalm 36:9

We return to our image of the Outer Court, the Holy Place and the Holy of Holies. In the Outer Court there is natural light – the sun shines in by day, the moon and the stars by night. In the Holy Place we find the golden lamp stand. The Spirit tends the lamp stand; filling it with oil, trimming the wicks. It is here that you are baptised in the Holy Spirit and filled every day with the Spirit of God and His power.

The Holy of Holies is lit by the Light of God; there is no need for any other light. The glory of God provides the light; God's Light is the brightest light you will ever see in your life. Everything is exposed and illuminated in God's presence – the good and the bad. In His presence you will find salvation, deliverance, peace, joy, freedom, power, wisdom and love.

In His light I see and understand what His perfect will is for my life.

Prayer

Father God, thank You for Your wonderful Light, which shines into every corner of my life, flooding me with warmth and love. Your Light illuminates my way leading me step by step. Jesus, thank You that You are the Light of the world and that through You I have salvation and the forgiveness of sin. Amen.

Entering with freedom

Read Hebrews 4:14-16

Let us then approach the throne of grace with confidence, so that we may receive mercy and find grace to help us in our time of need. - Hebrews 4:16

Have you ever been in a difficult place where you desperately needed God's mercy, deliverance and salvation? I have good news for you! God's grace and deliverance are freely available you.

The story in the Bible about Queen Esther is a wonderful example of this. Esther desperately sought deliverance and freedom for her people. She prayed; she fasted; then she put on her queenly robes and went to the King. The King immediately stretched out his golden sceptre towards her, 'Touch the tip of my sceptre.' he said. 'What is the desire of your heart? I will do anything you ask – I will even give you the half of my kingdom.'

God says to you, 'My child, you may enter My presence freely. I want to bless you, the things I want to do for you are far beyond what you can ever dream of, pray for, or imagine.'

God wants to bless me beyond what I can ever dream of, pray for, or imagine.

Prayer

My wonderful Heavenly Father, what a wonderful gift Your Son, Jesus, has given to me; because of what He did on Calvary I can freely enter into Your presence, just as I am. Thank You for this blessing. Amen.

25 February

Hearing God's voice

Read Psalm 29

The voice of the Lord is powerful; the voice of the Lord is majestic. - Psalm 29:4

Jeremiah 29:11 says, *'For I know the plans I have for you ... plans to prosper you and not to harm you, plans to give you hope and a future.'* God assures you that His plans for you include success, hope and security. As God's child you can look forward to a bright future.

We need to prepare before entering God's presence by being cleansed from our sins. The blood of Jesus must wash us clean. We are filled with the Spirit, and then we are ready to boldly approach God's throne of grace.

Psalm 29 reminds us that the voice of the Lord is powerful and full of majesty! It was the voice calming the storm on the Sea of Galilee, proclaiming, 'Be healed,' and people were healed, calling Lazarus forth from the tomb. God's voice whispers words of hope, encouragement, love and comfort to you when you need it.

God speaks words of wisdom, knowledge, hope, encouragement, love and comfort to me.

Prayer

Holy, Holy, Holy are You, my Heavenly Father, God Almighty! I praise and worship You. Thank You that You speak to me and that I can freely enter Your presence. I praise Your Holy Name. Amen.

26 February

God reveals His will

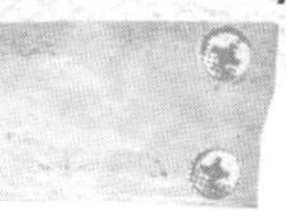

Read 1 Samuel 3:1-18

So Eli told Samuel, "Go and lie down, and if he calls you, say, 'Speak, Lord, for your servant is listening.'" So Samuel went and lay down in his place. The Lord came and stood there, calling as at the other times, "Samuel! Samuel!" Then Samuel said, "Speak, for your servant is listening." - 1 Samuel 3:9-10

When God first spoke to Samuel he thought it was Eli speaking. This proves that God's voice is audible to us in our spirit. Samuel listened to God. He heard and obeyed God. Samuel lived close to God. If we want to hear God speaking to us we need to make sure that we live close to Him too.

We do this through getting to know His Word. There are three stages to growing in God's Word. Stage one: drink the milk of the Word. Stage two: eat and digest the Bread of Life. Stage three: digest the meat of the Word that builds us up making us strong in the Lord.

> *If I live in His presence, in the throne room, I will have the answer to all my questions; what, where, when, and how.*

You don't need to ask, 'What is God's will for my life?' You need to live in His presence, before His throne; then you will have the answer to all your questions. He will show you what, where, when, and how.

Prayer

Thank You, Father, that You reveal Your will to me when I spend time in Your presence and sit at Your feet. Thank You that You welcome me into Your presence because You love me and You want to talk to me. I praise You. Amen.

27 February

Listening to God's voice

Read Hebrews 3:7-19

As has just been said: "Today, if you hear his voice, do not harden your hearts as you did in the rebellion." - Hebrews 3:15

There is nothing wrong with us praying for each other, but if you pray yourself you will receive the blessing and message directly from God. He will speak directly to you. As you receive directly from God not only will the power be greater but your faith will be built up as you experience Him first hand. His Word will be engraved upon your heart. You will receive renewed faith, inspiration and motivation.

God will reward you for spending time in His presence by revealing His heart and will to you. You will know His thoughts, His character and His intentions. You will experience the Father heart of God. You will hear the Father say, 'This is what I have done for you. I gave My Son to die for you. I have delivered you, because I love you so much.'

When He speaks to you today – listen!

When He speaks to me – I will listen!

Prayer

Father God, thank You that You reveal Yourself and Your will to me. Thank You that You reveal Your heart and Your character to me. You have redeemed me through the precious blood of Jesus, thank You! Like King David I long for Your presence. Amen.

Obeying God

Read John 14:15-31

If you love me, you will obey what I command. - John 14:15

If we love God wholeheartedly He will show us His love and grace. Do you know this God of grace; this God who promises to speak to us?

Make God the focal point of your life. Give Him your undivided attention. The closer you are to Him, the closer He will be to you. He will bless you. He will give you true, abundant life. You will be a light guiding others into His presence.

Are you willing to make being in God's presence and learning to know Him the main focus of your life? Your faith will be strengthened and you will be a credible witness for Him. God will enable you to soar beyond your abilities. The result of all this will be that you will be able to accomplish more than you ever dreamt you would be able to. You will be more obedient to God, listening to and heeding His direction in your life.

Am I willing to forsake all else so that I can enter God's presence and learn to know Him?

Prayer

My Father in heaven, thank You that I receive strength and power from You when I spend time in Your presence. Strengthen my faith and empower me to be obedient to all Your commands. Amen.

Hungering and thirsting after God's presence

Read Isaiah 60

See, darkness covers the earth and thick darkness is over the peoples, but the Lord rises upon you and his glory appears over you. - Isaiah 60:2

We began the month by looking at the temple. We examined the Outer Court, and then moved on to look at the Holy Place; lastly we walked into the Holy of Holies.

Do you long with all your heart for His Light to shine upon you and fill you with wisdom, insight, peace and grace? Do you thirst for God like a deer in the wilderness thirsts for water? Are you prepared to give yourself wholeheartedly to the Kingdom of God?
Psalm 24:3-6 tells us: *Who may ascend the hill of the Lord? Who may stand in his holy place? He who has clean hands and a pure heart, who does not lift up his soul to an idol or swear by what is false. He will receive blessing from the Lord and vindication from God his Saviour. Such is the generation of those who seek him, who seek your face, O God of Jacob.*

Are my hands clean and is my heart pure as I stand before my God today?

Prayer

My Father God, thank You for the journey of discovery we have been on this month. I have been blessed and awed as I've moved through the tabernacle into Your Holy presence. I desire above all else to walk with You, to dwell each day in Your presence, to praise You and worship You. Amen.

wandel soos hy sê, seën
jy jou vyande baie seën
hulle bring vir jou
vrede en vryheid. Wysheid
sê rut naby sal gunse
seën op ons rus.
Hy sê wandel in die
Gees is hoe sy kinders
moet leef dit is 'n lewe
van geloof oë op hom
rut vrou sy wandel in
geloof bou van harde
muur was geloof ouers
bid, bid, bid het samuel
se muur gebou. dankie
rut giet seën was wat
Samuel so gehelp het. dankie
so dankie yeshua, hoor
vir wysheid sê, samuel
jy sal binne bou van
muur bly. samuel sien
rut nou in vryheid. wie
vryheid gee is yeshua.
samuel sien jou bly
hart, sien ouers sal so
waarlik gelukkig wees.
hulle so, so gelukkig.
baie dankie yeshua vir
julle liefde, sal vir
altyd vrank vry wees
die samuel, rut is baie
rustig nou.

Letter 3:

Walk in the Holy Spirit

We must walk as He instructs us: bless your enemies. Keep on blessing – it will bring you peace and freedom. Wisdom says: 'Blessing will rest upon us.' He says that His children must live their lives by walking in the Spirit. It means to live by faith and to keep our eyes on Him. Ruth lives by faith. Our strong wall was built because of faith. The many prayers of his parents built Samuel's wall. Thank you, Ruth, – the blessing you poured out on Samuel is what helped him. Thank You so much Yeshua! I heard Wisdom say: 'Samuel, the wall that is built around you will protect you.' Samuel can see that Ruth is living in freedom. Yeshua is the one who gives freedom. Samuel can see that your heart is happy. I can see that my parents are now truly happy. Thank You so much, Yeshua, for Your love. I will be free from bitterness forever. Samuel and Ruth are so at peace now.

A young person after God's own heart is ...

Prayer for March

Abba Father, I come to You in the wonderful Name of my Messiah, King Jesus. I love You so much my Father. I thank You, Jesus, for Your shed blood, for Your love and grace that is new each morning. Your peace fills my heart. Thank You for Your peace that confirms how much You love me. My life is flooded with Your Spirit: You pour out Your Spirit on me and You fill me to overflowing. Your Word is truth and Your Spirit leads me into all truth. I praise and worship Your Holy Name.
Amen.

A young person who obeys God

Read Ruth 1:1-16

But Ruth replied, "Don't urge me to leave you or to turn back from you. Where you go I will go, and where you stay I will stay. Your people will be my people and your God my God." - Ruth 1:16

What does it mean to be 'a young person after God's heart?' This month we look at the lives of Naomi and Ruth to see what we can learn from them – they are great examples of living lives of obedience. This is exactly what a young person after God's heart is – an obedient person.

Ruth was a Moabite, she was an outsider who found herself in difficult circumstances and needed to be rescued. She found a kinsman-redeemer, who delivered her. A kinsman-redeemer is someone who is related to us and has the power to save us. You and I, as children of God, have a Kinsman-Redeemer – Jesus Christ. We were lost and Jesus came and made us His own.

This is exactly what a young person after God's heart is – an obedient person.

Have you ever felt the way Ruth did, like an outsider, afraid and lonely? If you have, then Jesus, your Kinsman-Redeemer, is the One who can save you.

Prayer

My God and Father, thank You for sending Your Son, Jesus Christ, to be my Kinsman-Redeemer. I am so grateful You have chosen to rescue and deliver me. Thank You that even when I am lonely and alone You are there for me. Amen.

A young person who waits on God

Read Psalm 130:1-2,4-5

I wait for the Lord, my soul waits, and in his word I put my hope. - Psalm 130:5

It is really great that the story of Ruth is about women of different ages. Naomi is the older woman, her husband and her two adult sons have all died. Then we have Ruth and Orpah, Naomi's daughters-in-law, two young women with their whole lives ahead of them who have their hopes and dreams dashed. There was no hope left, or so it would seem...

We are going to take a journey with Naomi, Ruth and Orpah and the choices they made. We can learn many things from Ruth and Orpah but Naomi will also show us a few important life lessons.

No matter how difficult my situation is, God cares about me and He has a plan and a purpose for my life.

Have you gone from being confident and joyful about your future to suddenly being heartbroken and unsure about what will happen next? Be encouraged that no matter how difficult your situation is, God cares about you and He has a plan and a purpose for your life.

Prayer

Dear Father God, thank You that I can come to You today just as I am. Thank You that You know what I am going through. I do not understand why these things have happened, but I want to trust You. Help me to lean on You. Amen.

A young person whose life bears fruit

Read Psalm 1

...They are like trees that grow beside a stream, that bear fruit at the right time, and whose leaves do not dry up. They succeed in everything they do. - Psalm 1:3 (Good News Translation)

We never know what is going to happen next. Bad things can happen even when we don't deserve it. The question is how do we handle it?

Sometimes the challenges we face are temporary but other times things happen that change our lives forever as in the case of Naomi, Ruth and Orpah. Naomi was a woman of strong character and she never forgot who she was and where she came from. When the life she had created in Moab with her husband and sons all went terribly wrong, she chose to return home to Bethlehem.

As I look at my life am I being true to what I know is right and good?

As you look at your life are you being true to what you know is right and good? Are you living your life to the full? When people look at you do they see a young person who knows who he/she is and what he/she stands for? Is your life bearing fruit for the Master?

Prayer

My Lord and God, I come before You today. Help me to be like a tree planted by a stream. Please show me where I am making poor choices. Help me become the person You created me to be. Let me bear much fruit for You. Amen.

A young person who knows God

Read 2 Peter 1:2-4

His divine power has given us everything we need for life and godliness through our knowledge of him who called us by his own glory and goodness. - 2 Peter 1:3

The story of Ruth is a story of faith, hope and love that begins with Naomi. Naomi KNOWS her God. She knows that even though terrible things have happened there must be something more.

Naomi knew how to have good relationships, she accepted Ruth and Orpah's family and they loved her. When Orpah chose to stay behind – we are told she cried when she kissed Naomi goodbye. Are you accepting and caring of the people God has put into your family?

I can KNOW God by having a relationship with Him and everything changes as I experience life with God.

There is a difference in whether you know or KNOW God. What do I mean? You can know God as if He was a subject at school that you learn about and find interesting but this type of knowing doesn't change your life. Or you can KNOW God by having a relationship with Him and everything changes as you experience life with God, you get to KNOW God's character and love.

Prayer

Lord, I want to KNOW You. I don't want to have only head knowledge of You, I want to have a relationship with You. Help me to KNOW You so that I can be a blessing to those You have put in my life. Amen.

A young person who knows - God provides

Read Jeremiah 29:11-14

"For I know the plans I have for you", declares the Lord, "plans to prosper you and not to harm you, plans to give you hope and a future." - Jeremiah 29:11

No matter how bad her situation is Naomi KNOWS God has a plan. Her faith helped her to keep going. She might have been desperate but she knew God would provide.

If you KNOW God and have a relationship with Him then no matter where you find yourself you have hope. Naomi knew this and believed it before she saw how God would fix her problems. She had a lifetime worth of experiences to look back on so she knew that her God always came through.

Sometimes I can get so stressed out by what is happening to me that I forget how faithful God has been.

Can you trace God's care for you and your family? Are you encouraged by what He has done for you in the past? Sometimes we can get so stressed out by what is happening to us we forget how faithful God has been and how He got us through other difficult times.

Prayer

God, You are my loving Father who has a plan for me and those I love. Help me to remember all the other times when You came through for us. Build my faith. Let me learn from the example of Naomi who had hope even though she didn't know how you would provide for her. Amen.

A young person with a pure heart

Read 1 Samuel 16:4-13

...Man does not see what the LORD sees, for Man sees what is vidisible, but the LORD sees the hear. - 1 Samuel 16:7b (Holman Christian Standard Bible)

Naomi managed to live for many years in a foreign country with people who didn't worship her God. She kept her heart pure and did not become influenced by the beliefs of those around her. A pure heart is very important to God. He is not impressed with how we look physically, God sees through the way we dress and looks to the core of who we really are.

God sees through the way I dress and looks to the core of who I really am.

In our scripture reading God teaches the Prophet Samuel this lesson. He was all set to make a choice based on how a person looked but God told him to look at the heart instead.

How is your heart today? Is it open to God and the things He wants to teach you? Or has disappointment made you hard and tough? Let God in. He is the One who can heal us and help us become pure in heart.

Prayer

O Father God, I am so tired of being tough – help me to heal. I want You to look at my heart and be happy with what You see. Thank You for not judging me on how I look, please help me to learn to do the same with others. Amen.

7 March

A young person who is vulnerable

Read Ruth 1:6-13

Then Naomi said to her two daughters-in-law, "Go back, each of you to your mother's home... May the Lord grant that each of you will find rest in the home of another husband." - Ruth 1:8a, 9

Naomi was a practical woman. She trusts God and she believes He is leading her to leave Moab and return to Bethlehem, to her land and people.

The story does not give all the details of what happened but Naomi clearly shared her plan with Ruth and Orpah to go back to Bethlehem. We are told they all set out on the road for Judah. Naomi then stops and tells them they should return to their own people. She must have been scared of what lay ahead – perhaps she wanted to save Ruth and Orpah from more heartache?

I trust God, I know He will look after me. Even in moments when things threaten to crush me and it is hard to cope, He understands.

As you will see in our scripture reading Naomi has a little wobble where her loss is too much. Can you relate to feeling vulnerable? You trust God, you know He will look after you, yet there are moments when things threaten to crush you and it is hard to cope. He understands.

Prayer

Loving Father, thank You that You understand that the road is difficult sometimes. I choose at times like this to run to You and not away from You. Only in You do I find peace. Thank You that when I lose the way You are there to guide me back. Amen.

A young person who sets an example

Read Titus 2:3-4; 3:3-7

But when the kindness and love of God our Saviour appeared ... He saved us through the washing of rebirth and renewal by the Holy Spirit ... so that, having been justified by his grace, we might become heirs having the hope of eternal life. - Titus 3:4a,5b,7

We do not know what kind of homes Ruth and Orpah came from but it is interesting to note that they were willing to leave their families to go with Naomi into the unknown. This was probably because of the type of person Naomi was. She was caring, loving and kind. She was a positive influence in their lives and they looked up to her.

A young person after God's heart is one who knows how to receive and give encouragement and speak the truth with love.

The Bible tells us in Titus that older people must set an example and encourage younger people in the things of the Lord. Who are the people in your life who have been an encouragement to you and have helped your faith grow?

A person after God's heart is one who knows how to receive and give encouragement and when it is needed speak the truth with love. Do you have any friends or family members whom you could help encourage?

Prayer

I am grateful, Lord, for the people who have taken the time to encourage and support me in my walk. Help me to reach out to those I can help and encourage. Thank You for Your Holy Spirit who leads us into all truth. Amen.

9 March

A young person who can make difficult choices

Read Ruth 1:14-18

But Ruth replied, "Don't urge me to leave you or to turn back from you. Where you go I will go, and where you stay I will stay... May the Lord deal with me, be it ever so severely, if anything but death separates you from me." - Ruth 1:16a-b,17b

Life presents each of us with impossible situations. Ruth and Orpah had to decide: do they go back or do they continue with Naomi into the unknown? As we know from the story, Orpah chose to go back although it wasn't an easy choice to make and it caused her pain. Over the next few days we will examine what going back can mean for us.

Ruth chose to remain with Naomi – one last time Naomi tried to encourage her to turn back. Look, Naomi said; *Your sister-in-law is going back to her people and her gods. Go back with her.* Ruth replied: *Don't urge me to leave you or to turn back from you.*

A young person after God's heart knows how to make the difficult choices.

Did you notice the phrase ...*and her gods?* Orpah could not turn away from *her gods*. She chose *her gods* above **The God**. A young person after God's heart knows how to make the difficult choices.

Prayer

Lord, help me to be like Ruth and make wise decisions. The pull of 'other gods' can be so strong sometimes. I need Your Spirit to lead and guide me. Help me to be a young person after Your heart, a young person who can make the difficult choices. Amen.

A young person who faces fear

Read 2 Timothy 1:5-10

For God did not give us a spirit of fear. He gave us a spirit of power and of love and of a good mind. - 2 Timothy 1:7 (New Life Version)

I feel sorry for Orpah. It is clear she loved Naomi and Ruth but Orpah wasn't able to take the step of faith into the unknown. So Orpah turned back. It is often the same for us – we want our lives to change but we find it hard to give up habits that keep us stuck. It takes courage to choose a new way – even if it will bless our lives in unexpected ways.

Fear keeps us down and stops us from living a full and happy life. We fear standing up for ourselves, we fear the future; we fear getting hurt. God has not called us to live with fear and we have His Spirit to help us.

Don't be like Orpah. If you find yourself trapped by fear today, make the choice to trust in God. Through God's grace we can let go of fear and become self-disciplined, joyful and loving.

Through God's grace I can let go of fear and become self-disciplined, joyful and loving.

Prayer

Lord, I come to You, just as I am, fearful and scared. Please help me to let go of my fear. Thank You that You have given me a healthy mind and spirit. In the days ahead show me where I can make better choices so I can move forward with You. Amen.

11 March

A young person who has Kingdom attitudes

Read Matthew 16:24-27

What kind of deal is it to get everything you want but lose yourself? - Matthew 16:26a (The Message)

You cannot split yourself and be one type of person for some people and then be another kind of person for God and your church.

This kind of living will only break you down. I know because for many years I lived like this. I was a Christian but my attitudes and actions were not Godly at all, they were worldly. I lived to please myself.

This is why Naomi is to be admired. She'd lived in Moab, a place where it was hard for her to worship God but she found a way to do it. In the same way you and I need to live truthful Godly lives even though we live in a world where it is difficult and often unpopular to be Christian.

Am I trying to live in two kingdoms? It cannot be done; I have to choose.

Are you trying to live in two kingdoms? It cannot be done my dear friend; you have to choose.

Prayer

Lord, forgive me for trying to be both worldly and Godly. I know that You have called me to live in Your Kingdom. I want my attitudes and actions to show what I believe. Fill me with Your Holy Spirit and help me to stand strong in You. Amen.

A young person who has no other gods...

Read Luke 14:25-35

Those who come to me cannot be my disciples unless they love me more than they love father and mother, wife and children, brothers and sisters, and themselves as well.
- Luke 14:26 (Good News Translation)

Do you serve other gods? You might be shocked at this question. You might say: "I don't serve other gods, I'm a Christian." None of this matters if there are things or people that are more important in your life than God.

Does this mean that you cannot be passionate and enjoy life? No, of course not; what it means is that you are to love God more. To allow any person or sport or passion to take God's place in your life, means you place the person or thing above God. This is what it means to have a god or an idol in your life.

Love for God, my Father, is to be so all consuming that in everything He comes first.

Love for God, our Father, is to be so all consuming that in everything He comes first, and if He comes first then we will naturally be able to enjoy life and love other people without getting caught up with putting 'idols' before God.

Prayer

Father, please show me if I have any idols in my life. Is there anything or anyone I love more than You? If I do, please forgive me and help me to put You first. Amen.

A young person who serves one Master

Read Matthew 6:19-24

No-one can serve two masters. Either he will hate the one and love the other, or he will be devoted to the one and despise the other. You cannot serve both God and Money. - Matthew 6:24

There are many things which can become idols or gods in our lives. For Orpah, her family and the need to feel safe became her 'gods'. When you look at Orpah's reasons for turning back it is hard to blame her. She loved her family and she wanted to be with them. She was comfortable with life in Moab and the thought of walking into the unknown was too hard for her.

It can become so comfortable for me living a certain way that making the decision to let go or to change becomes too difficult.

Even small things that aren't bad at first can become a problem. We can become obsessed with a celebrity; a TV show; getting the right outfit or even trying to get a certain grade at school. For many young people it can be their bodies. It can become so comfortable for us living a certain way that making the decision to let go or to change becomes too difficult. This is where God's grace meets us and helps us through.

Prayer

Oh Father, I cannot do this on my own. Please shine the light of Your Spirit into my heart and give me the strength to change. Help me to let go of all that I need to. Amen.

A young person who is salt and light

Read Matthew 5:13-19

You are the light of the world ... In the same way, let your light shine before men, that they may see your good deeds and praise your Father in heaven. - Matthew 5:14a,16

Jesus asks us to be salt and light in the world we live in. What does this mean?

Salt draws out the flavour in food. If we have a good relationship with God then our faith is active and like salt we can help bring out the best in people. With the Holy Spirit working through us we have the ability to make a difference for God.

If I have a good relationship with God then my faith is active and like salt I can help bring out the best in people.

Light shows what is hidden by darkness. As lights for God we can help people see more clearly. Yet not everyone who has light uses it, sometimes it can be hard to be the one standing up and speaking life and light into a bad situation. There will be times where you don't have to say a thing but by simply treating others with love and respect your light will shine and show others that there is a better way – God's way.

Prayer

Dear Lord, forgive me that I have kept quiet when I should have spoken up. I have done nothing when I should have tried to make a difference. Today I choose to be salt and light. Thank You Father. Amen.

15 March

A young person who knows the Truth

Read John 10:7-15

I am the good shepherd; I know my sheep and my sheep know me. - John 10:14

As a young person after God's heart you need to know your own worth. It is so important to take time to understand the lies the devil uses to keep us small so we don't believe and we don't try. These two lies are:

Lie number one: You are not good enough. Don't even try something new because you will fail. Be careful not to reach out to others – you will just get hurt.

Lie number two: You are okay. You don't need to stand up or stand out – you do many good things, so don't worry about doing anything more. Don't be a show-off.

I am loved. For this reason I can stand up and make a difference.

The truth is that because Jesus Christ died for you – you are worth *everything* to Him. You can ignore the lies; you only need to listen to the voice of Jesus. You are loved. For this reason you can stand up and make a difference.

Prayer

Dear Jesus, thank You that I am Your child. Thank You that You died for me. I don't have to live under the lies of the devil; I believe You and trust You. Amen.

A young person who shares love and forgiveness

Read Ephesians 4:17-24, 32; 5:1-2

Be kind to one another, tender-hearted, forgiving each other, just as God in Christ also has forgiven you. - Ephesians 4:32 (New American Standard Bible)

Is there someone in your life who has hurt you or you are scared of? How are you handling that fear? As a young person of the Kingdom, someone after God's heart we have to find a way to deal with our fear of other people.

If you are being bullied, is there someone you can talk to? What about that girl in school who is so popular and pretty she makes you feel bad about yourself? Perhaps she is a really nice person. Or what about that someone you just don't like because they are just too different to you? Is there a way you can get to know them?

How will the world experience the love of Jesus if I do not show it to them?

We are to be God's 'life' to those around us, so we need to love and forgive when people hurt us. How will the world experience the love of Jesus if we do not show it to them?

Prayer

Father, help me to forgive anyone who has hurt me. Please give me the courage to reach out and show love and friendship to the people around me. Amen.

17 March

A young person who turns from darkness

Read 1 John 1:5-10

If we live in the light as He is in the light, we share what we have in God with each other. And the blood of Jesus Christ, His Son, makes our lives clean from all sin.
- 1 John 1:7 (New Life Version)

God made a way for us to enter His Kingdom by sending His only Son, Jesus Christ, into our world. He died so we can have life with Him in the Kingdom of Light.

Orpah chose Moab because it was home to her but one thing to remember is that she went back to a famine, there was no food in Moab. She was going back to darkness and hard times. Do you think the world has more to offer you than God does? Jesus promises us not just life but *life in abundance* that means life in full colour.

Jesus promises me not just life but life in abundance that means life in full colour.

So what does it take for us to be able to start living as children of the Light? We need to make a decision to choose Jesus and the unknown way that He will lead us on. It will be hard and scary at times but it will be worth it.

Prayer

Lord, I know I have sinned and hurt You by choosing other things over You, I am sorry. I ask You to forgive me and to make my heart clean. I pray in Jesus Name. Amen.

A young person who lives in the light

Read Ephesians 5:8-16

For you were once darkness, but now you are light in the Lord. Live as children of light. - Ephesians 5:8

There are many places in the Bible where God uses darkness to represent the kingdom of the devil and light to represent the Kingdom of His Son, Jesus Christ.

The Lord warns us that the devil pretends to be an angel of light, meaning he will make a bad thing look good. We may have been freed from the darkness but unfortunately sometimes we still choose the dark even though we know the light is so much better.

A young person who walks in the light uses every opportunity he/she can to give glory to God. The more often we walk in the light the easier we will find it to learn what pleases the Lord.

A young person who walks in the light uses every opportunity he/she can to give glory to God.

Like Orpah and Ruth you have a choice to make: Are you going to choose darkness or be like Ruth and live as a child of the Light?

Prayer

Dear Lord of Light, thank You for rescuing me from the kingdom of darkness so that I can live in Your Kingdom of Light. Amen.

A young person who shares the Light

Read John 3:16-21

For God loved the world so much that he gave his only Son, so that everyone who believes in him may not die but have eternal life. - John 3:16 (Good News Translation)

It is not enough for us to just have the Light of God for ourselves. We also have to learn how to share the Light. We have a responsibility to tell others about Jesus Christ. God has asked us as His children to spread His message of love to people who don't know Him.

Naomi never stopped sharing her beliefs. We can suppose that during the years she lived in Moab she would have shared her faith with Ruth and Orpah and told them about her home and where she had come from. It is interesting that in the end Ruth chose to follow Naomi and Orpah chose to turn back.

God asks me as His child to spread His message of love to people who don't know Him.

This shows us that we cannot take responsibility for the choices that other people make – we can only faithfully share with them. Is there someone you should be sharing with today?

Prayer

Father God, please show me how to share Your love with others. Give me a heart for those who live in the kingdom of darkness. Help me to love and care for those You have placed in my life – so that my talk as well as my walk show how much I love You. Amen.

A young person who finds comfort in God

Read Isaiah 12:2-6

Surely God is my salvation; I will trust and not be afraid. The Lord, the Lord, is my strength and my song; he has become my salvation. - Isaiah 12:2

All of us have times when we feel sorry for ourselves and doubt God's goodness. Naomi had a moment like this when she arrived home in Bethlehem. People were amazed to see her and Ruth. Names in the Bible have great meaning. The name Naomi means 'pleasant'. However, when she arrived home she told her family and friends not to call her Naomi but to rather call her Mara - meaning 'bitter.' *I went away full, but the Lord has brought me back empty.* Such sad words.

Do you have days when you feel empty and sad? As a child of God there is only one place for you to go – and that is to the throne of God. The Lord is the only One who can comfort you. Take hold of His promises for you. Go on your knees before Him and claim what is Yours in Jesus Christ, His Son.

The Lord is the only One who can comfort me. I take hold of His promises for me.

Prayer

Father God, thank You for being strong for me. Help me to get to a place where I can sing about Your goodness and grace in my life. Amen.

A young person who looks to the future

Read Isaiah 43:1-4

Do not be afraid. For I have bought you and made you free. I have called you by name. You are Mine! - Isaiah 43:1b (New Life Version)

The name that God called Naomi was not Mara. He had called her by name, she was His child – He loved her – He had led her home back to her people – towards hope and a future. Naomi's friends also refused to let her feel sorry for herself. They encouraged her and reminded her of everything she still had going for her.

Have you had times when everything you planned has gone wrong? Remember that God has a wonderful ability to surprise us with something even better than we had hoped for.

God has a wonderful ability to surprise me with something even better than I had hoped for.

Your God knows your name and your heart – He will not leave you on your own to deal with your problems. He knows how much you can take. No matter what you are going through or will go through He will be there with you. Always.

Prayer

Oh my Father, You know how hard it is to trust You when things go wrong. Help me to see how You are working things out for me. Thank You in Jesus' name. Amen.

A young person who is known by God

Read Psalm 139

You are all around me on every side; you protect me with your power. Where could I go to escape from you? Where could I get away from your presence? - Psalm 139:5,7 (Good News Translation)

The story of Ruth shows us that God knows the end from the beginning. Ruth didn't know when she decided to follow Naomi that she would end up becoming the great grandmother of King David and would be one of the blessed women in Jesus' family tree.

Our lives are like stories and God knows all the parts. We don't know how all the parts will fit together, which can be very hard for us, especially when things happen that we don't understand. We need to learn to stop and remember that, like Ruth, God knows what the future holds and His plan is a good one.

There is nothing I need to worry about. God holds every second of my life in His hands.

Our scripture reading today reminds you that God saw you before you were born. He has planned every day of your life. There is nothing you need to worry about. God holds every second of your life in His hands.

Prayer

Search me, O God, and know my heart; test me and know my anxious thoughts. See if there is any offensive way in me, and lead me in the way everlasting. Amen.

A young person who is humble

Read Psalm 18:30-37

It is God who arms me with strength and makes my way perfect. - Psalm 18:32

Although Ruth and Naomi were welcomed in Bethlehem, Ruth was still considered an outsider. This must have been painful but Ruth didn't let hurt feelings stop her from being helpful.

In those days if you were poor you were allowed to work in the fields after the harvesters. It seems like a strange thing to us today but that is what Ruth did, she worked in the hot sun finding broken corn.

If I faithfully do what God has called me to do then He will do the rest.

She ended up working in a field owned by Boaz, who turned out to be one of only two men who would be able to rescue Ruth and Naomi from their life of poverty. Boaz became their kinsman-redeemer but Ruth did not know this at the time – she was doing what she could to provide food for Naomi and herself.

Do you see the lesson? If we faithfully do what God has called us to do then He will do the rest.

Prayer

Father, thank You for the lessons I can learn from Ruth. I too want to be a person who will not let pride stand in my way of following Your purposes and plans for my life and the lives of my family. Amen.

A young person who has a Redeemer

Read Ephesians 1:3-14

Having believed, you were marked in him with a seal, the promised Holy Spirit, who is a deposit guaranteeing our inheritance until the redemption of those who are God's possession – to the praise of his glory. - Ephesians 1:13b,14

Naomi and Ruth could not rescue themselves – their only hope was for someone to step forward and offer them a way out. They needed a kinsman-redeemer – a hero. In today's world we think of a hero as someone who is strong, good looking and who has special powers. In my opinion, Boaz is a hero. He was a good man who was kind and generous. He had the special power of being able to see beyond Ruth's poverty to her true value – he saw her wonderful heart.

Jesus Christ is my Kinsman-Redeemer, in every way He has saved me.

We also need a hero to rescue us. No matter how strong or clever we may think we are, we cannot save ourselves. Jesus Christ is our Kinsman-Redeemer, in every way He has saved us. What Boaz did for Ruth, Jesus did for us. Ruth was protected and loved by Boaz. Jesus takes away our shame, our loneliness and His love surrounds us – forever.

Prayer

Jesus, thank You that You are my Kinsman-Redeemer. You give me a place of honour in Your Kingdom. You have rescued me and I have a blessed future with You. I praise You for this gift. Amen.

25 March

A young person who shows respect

Read Psalm 37:1-5, 7, 11, 18-19, 23

But the humble will inherit the land, and will delight themselves in abundant prosperity. - Psalm 37:11 (New American Standard Bible)

When Boaz first saw Ruth she was working in his fields. He found out who she was and then he made sure she had food and water. He also told her to work only in his field where she could be protected. Boaz was careful not to put Ruth in a position where she felt embarrassed; or where other people could become jealous and make things difficult for her.

Do you see a picture here of how Jesus looks after you? He offers us His protection and provides all we need physically and then Jesus does even more – He cares for our hearts. He gives us His love and peace so we can enjoy life.

Jesus does even more – He cares for my heart. He gives me His love and peace so I can enjoy life.

What was the key to Ruth enjoying Boaz's care? She took his advice, she respected his wisdom. In the same way we too need to obey God and accept and respect His solutions to our problems.

Prayer

My Father, forgive me for trying to do things my way. They never work out. Help me to be obedient to You. Thank You for taking care of me and for also looking after those I love. Amen.

A young person who is unselfish

Read Ruth 1:16-17; 2:10-14,18

May the Lord repay you for what you have done. May you be richly rewarded by the Lord, the God of Israel, under whose wings you have come to take refuge. - Ruth 2:12

We live in a world where everyone looks out for themselves. Ruth is a wonderful example of a young woman who put someone else and their needs first. She worked hard to make sure Naomi had enough food to eat. Her unselfishness made her stand out and Boaz noticed.

It is not always easy to be unselfish. There are many times when it is hard to let other people get all the attention; or to work hard so someone else can be blessed. Sometimes being unselfish can cost us more than just time and emotion, it may also mean giving up something we love and want so that another person has what they need.

The Lord is the One who sees my sacrifice and He will repay me. He is the One who promises to richly bless me.

The Lord is the One who sees our sacrifice and He will repay us. He is the One who promises to richly bless us when we put another person's needs above our own.

Prayer

Dear Father, You gave everything for me. Help me not to be selfish, show me how to be generous with my time, love and possessions. Amen.

A young person who is faithful

Read Galatians 5:16-18,22-25

But the fruit of the Spirit is love, joy, peace, patience, kindness, goodness, faithfulness, gentleness and self-control. Against such things there is no law. - Galatians 5:22-23

Ruth is a good example of someone who stood firm in what she believed. She was faithful. She was clear from the beginning that she would follow Naomi to her homeland. She knew this meant she would be a stranger in another country and that it would be difficult. Yet she did it.

Remaining strong in what we believe is not always easy. There are many things that come along and make it hard to stay faithful. There are people who will laugh and try and make us think we are crazy to believe in God.

It would have been easy for Ruth to give in to the problems she faced but she did not turn back. She did everything with faith and a joyful heart. The way she lived her life showed that the fruit of the Spirit was active. Do people see love, joy, peace, patience, kindness, goodness, faithfulness, gentleness and self-control in your life?

Do people see evidence of the fruit of the Spirit in my life?

Prayer

Father God, please fill me with Your Spirit; help me to become a person who enjoys and shows the fruit of Your Spirit in my life. Thank You. Amen.

A young person who asks boldly

Read Ruth 3:1-11

And now, my daughter, don't be afraid. I will do for you all you ask. - Ruth 3:11a

Naomi could see that God had a plan when she found out Ruth was working in a field that Boaz owned. It wasn't luck that Ruth ended up there, it was God. So at the right time Naomi encouraged Ruth to go to Boaz and ask him to deliver them.

Again Ruth was obedient, she did as Naomi asked. Ruth stayed strong and was bold in asking Boaz for help. She took a chance. She did it not just for herself – but also for Naomi. We know from the story that Boaz did not reject her. He accepted her and then he did everything needed to keep his promise.

Ruth asking Boaz to help reminds us of our relationship with Jesus. We know that we can always go to God for help. We can ask with confidence knowing He will never turn us away.

I know that I can always go to God for help. I can ask with confidence knowing He will never turn me away.

Prayer

My Lord, today I bow at Your feet worshipping You. I boldly come to You laying my needs before You. I ask You today to ....
Thank You that You love me. Amen.

A young person redeemed

Read Psalm 3

But you are a shield around me, O Lord; you bestow glory on me and lift up my head.
- Psalm 3:3

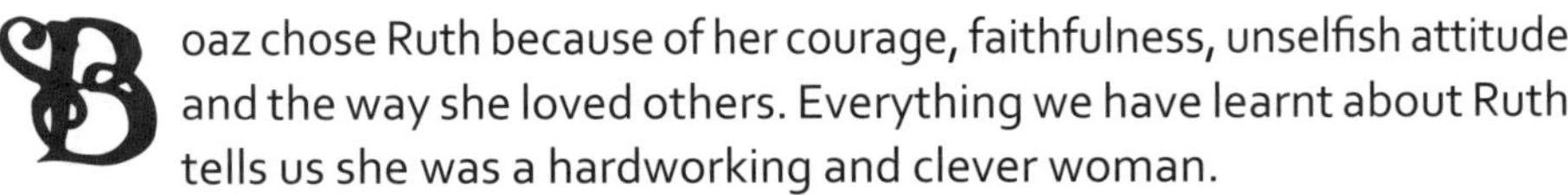

Boaz chose Ruth because of her courage, faithfulness, unselfish attitude and the way she loved others. Everything we have learnt about Ruth tells us she was a hardworking and clever woman.

The most wonderful part of this story is that we see a young woman redeemed by God. Ruth came from a bad background; she was a stranger with no money and she seemed to have little chance of having a happy life. And yet through God's grace Ruth was blessed among women. God gave her a good future, He gave her a family and He honoured her.

What was Ruth's secret? She did what God put in front of her to do, she was obedient, faithful and she stayed strong. Allow God to do the same for you. Let Him fix the areas in your life that aren't working. Ask Him to change Your life for His glory.

> *What was Ruth's secret? She did what God put in front of her to do, she was obedient, faithful and she stayed strong.*

Prayer

My Lord and God, You are my shield; You are the lifter of my head. I come just as I am. Amen.

A young person who is blessed

Read Ruth 4:13-22

The women said to Naomi: "Praise be to the Lord, who this day has not left you without a kinsman-redeemer." - Ruth 4:14

When Naomi lost her husband and sons she felt her life had reached a dead end, she could not see how her family line could continue. Yet all this time she was faithfully cared for and loved by Ruth.

After Boaz and Ruth married it is clear Ruth continued to look after Naomi and we finally see God's restoration of Naomi as she holds her grandson. Her friends praise God's goodness ...*Praise be to the Lord, who has not left you without a kinsman-redeemer.* They go on to speak of Ruth ...*who loves you and who is better to you than seven sons.* What an amazing moment that must have been! After everything Naomi had gone through, God never forgot her.

Is your heart filled with joy at this picture of God's goodness? What God did for Naomi and Ruth He can do for you. He is the same faithful God.

What God did for Naomi and Ruth He can do for me. He is the same faithful God.

Prayer

Thank You my Kinsman-Redeemer that Your faithfulness is the same yesterday, today and forever. Amen.

31 March

A young person who rejoices in the Redeemer

Read Ephesians 1:18-23

I pray also that the eyes of your heart may be enlightened in order that you may know the hope to which he has called you, the riches of his glorious inheritance in the saints. - Ephesians 1:18

Ruth's son was named Obed meaning *servant, worshipper.* In many ways this sums up what a young person after God's heart is. We are servants of the Most High God but that is not how God treats us. Our God lifts us out of our problems and gives us opportunities and blessings – so we can worship Him.

What has God said to you as we have looked at Ruth's story this past month? So often we want to finish one thing and quickly move on to the next thing but it is good to take time to stop, get quiet in our minds and let God speak to our hearts.

Join me in praise and gratitude to Jesus Christ, our Kinsman-Redeemer for His amazing grace, mercy and love. He has done it all for us. Go out today knowing Jesus is able to fulfil His promises in your life.

I know Jesus is able to fulfil His promises in my life.

Prayer

My Lord, thank You for Your precious love, thank You for Your constant faithfulness to me, your child. I love You. Amen.

Wysheid sê volhard in geloof, "volhard samuel boy volhard" dit hoor ek so gereeld. Wysheid sê vir my Wie volhard sal hy kroon. Samuel baie samuel sal samuel bly glo wat hy in sy hart hoor en Wysheid sê sy woord sal lei, Wysheid is harte se Leiding. dankie so baie dankie vir Wysheid wat Samuel so liefhet. hy sê hy sal my nag na nag humble samuel na wysheid vat en leer. sal sien geloof sien baie baie harde raam wat al die beloftes van God binne in hou die raam om samuel se Lewe is ware geloof in God sonder om te sien net omdat samuel God liefhet en glo in hom samuel sien so jy wat humble is vertrou God so baie. Wat vandag sal gebeur is wat God aan samuel bekend gemaak het.

Letter 4:

Persevere in faith

Wisdom says we must persevere in faith. I hear so often: 'Persevere Samuel boy, persevere!' Wisdom told me that He will crown those who persevere in faith. Will Samuel keep on believing what he hears in his heart? Wisdom says His Word will lead me. Wisdom will lead our hearts. Thank You so much for Wisdom who loves Samuel so much! He says that He will take humble Samuel to Wisdom night after night to be taught.

I see that there is a very strong frame around my life, and the frame keeps all the promises of God on the inside. The frame around Samuel's life is true FAITH in God – to believe without seeing – because Samuel loves God and believes in Him. Samuel can see that you who are humble trust God a lot. What happens today will be as God revealed it to Samuel.

Rebuilding your walls

Prayer for April

My loving Heavenly Father. I come before You in humble adoration, I bow before Your throne of grace. Thank You for Your great and awesome love for me. Your love is incomparable and I revel and bask in it. Father, as You call me to rebuild the walls of my own life, as well as those of my family, give me strength, I pray. I cannot do this on my own – I acknowledge my absolute need and dependence upon You. Give me courage to do the work, give me a strong mind and a willing heart, I pray. My gracious Father, thank You for Your Spirit who indwells me and fills me with Your power. Thank You that You give me every weapon that I need to defeat the evil one. Thank You that You give me the blueprint for building – You are the Master Builder. I choose to follow no one else but You. Thank You my Lord for victory in Yeshua.

Amen.

Broken walls

Read Nehemiah 1:1-4

They said to me, "Those who survived the exile and are back in the province are in great trouble and disgrace. The wall of Jerusalem is broken down, and its gates have been burned with fire." - Nehemiah 1:3

Broken walls have nothing to do with your age. If you have been badly hurt, you are not able to forgive or you are bitter any or all of these can loosen the stones in your walls. Bad choices and sin can make the hole in the wall bigger and bigger until the wall begins to crumble. Other reasons are fear of people, circumstances, or lack of obedience.

If we do not take care and replace the missing stones as quickly as possible the walls of our lives will crumble.

If there are stones missing from my wall then I need to choose to do something about it.

Nehemiah heard that the people of Jerusalem had allowed the walls to fall into disrepair he was very upset and felt that he needed to do something about it.

Do you have broken walls in your life today? Are there stones that are loose or missing from your wall? If so, you need to choose to do something about it today.

Prayer

My Heavenly Father, I come into Your presence today. I acknowledge that there are stones loose in the walls of my life. Father, give me the courage through Your Spirit to begin the process of rebuilding. Amen.

A defenceless city

Read Nehemiah 1:5-7

Then I said: "O Lord, God of heaven, the great and awesome God, who keeps his covenant of love with those who love him and obey his commands. - Nehemiah 1:5

The Lord led me to the book of Nehemiah some time ago when my family went through a particularly difficult time. Aldo, my son, was exposed to a situation that had a very negative effect upon him. This caused him a huge amount of anguish and was extremely difficult and traumatic for the rest of our family. We walked this path for eight or nine months. During this time I spent much time before the Lord seeking His face. Aldo continually wrote to me regarding Nehemiah and the message was; *you cannot become tired, you must build, you must build day and night, you must build and fight.*

Are my walls strong, are they secure, are all the stones firmly in place?

Today I am not asking you if you are serving the Lord. I am not asking you whether you attend church. I am asking you if your walls are strong, are they secure, are all the stones firmly in place.

Prayer

O Lord God of heaven, You are a great and awesome God. I love You dear Lord and I desire to obey all Your commands. Give me the strength to build and not become tired, to build and fight, to build day and night. Amen.

Building in the Spirit

Read Galatians 5:16-25

But the fruit of the Spirit is love, joy, peace, patience, kindness, goodness, faithfulness, gentleness, self-control, Against such things there is no law. - Galatians 5:22

The battle for the walls of our lives, and those we love, is not a battle that is fought in the physical dimension. It is fought in the spiritual dimension. There are physical aspects to rebuilding our walls, but the battle and the victory are won in the spiritual dimension.

It is in the realm of the spirit where we experience the attacks that weaken the stones in our walls. You can be sure that when the fault line shows up in your wall it is because you have allowed the enemy to gain access. This does not always happen through sin; sometimes it can be because we unwittingly open ourselves up to the enemy.

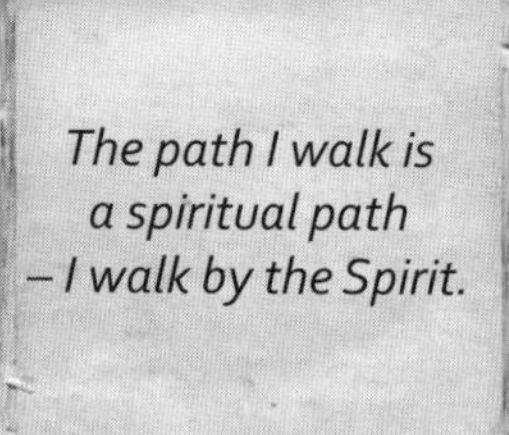
The path I walk is a spiritual path – I walk by the Spirit.

Our walk is a spiritual one and so Paul tells us in Galatians 5 to walk by the Spirit. Did you notice that the portion of Scripture we read today started and ended with the instruction: *Walk by the Spirit*.

Prayer

Dear Father, thank You for Your power at work in my life. I realise today that I need Your Spirit to work in me. Forgive me, and fill me with the power of Your Spirit so that my hands can be strengthened for the task ahead. Amen.

Taking up the challenge

Read Nehemiah 1:8-11; 2:1-6

The king said to me, "What is it you want?" Then I prayed to the God of heaven, and I answered the king, "If it pleases the king and if your servant has found favour in his sight, let him send me to the city in Judah where my fathers are buried so that I can rebuild it." - Nehemiah 2:4-5

When Nehemiah brought the king his wine the king noticed that he was sad. He asked Nehemiah what was wrong. At first Nehemiah was scared, but he quickly prayed and asked God for help. Then he answered and told the king he was upset about what had happened in Jerusalem.

Are you sad today? Maybe your sadness, like Nehemiah's, is because of the brokenness of your walls or those of people you love.

Nehemiah did not depend upon his own wisdom, he realised that he needed God.

Nehemiah gathered his courage and he told the king why he was sad. Nehemiah did not depend upon his own wisdom, he realised that he needed God. He knew that in difficult times he could call upon the name of the Lord. Follow Nehemiah's example – pray to the Lord in heaven – He will hear you and answer you.

Prayer

My Father, I come before You today very aware of my need of You. Lord, I am scared, I am overwhelmed, but I trust in You. I know that You will lead me and guide me through this process. Empower me with boldness through Your Spirit, I pray. Amen.

Wisdom to avoid the pitfalls

Read Nehemiah 2:7-16

I also said to him, "If it pleases the king, may I have letters to the governors of Trans-Euphrates, so that they will provide me safe-conduct until I arrive in Judah?"
- Nehemiah 2:7

God revealed the plan for rebuilding the walls step by step to Nehemiah. Before setting out on the journey he asked the king for letters so that the people he encountered would know that he had the support of the king.

Nehemiah knew some people did not want the walls of Jerusalem to be rebuilt and the children of Israel to become strong again. You will also experience opposition from people as well as from the devil when you begin to rebuild your walls and like Nehemiah you have the support of your King.

Like Nehemiah I have the support of my King as I rebuild my walls.

Nehemiah inspected the damage to the walls so that he would know what needed to be done to fix them. He prayed and asked the Lord to help him to know what to do. God will show us what to do to fix the walls – we must spend time with God and be filled with the power of His Spirit and He will guide us.

Prayer

Lord God, I choose today to do the work needed, I come before You in humility and bow in Your presence. I pray that You will show me Your will; one step at a time. As I spend time in Your presence Lord, give me the wisdom, courage and patience that I need. Amen.

6 April

Wisdom day by day

Read James 1:1-12

If any of you lacks wisdom, he should ask God, who gives generously to all without finding fault, and it will be given to him. - James 1:5

It is so easy to become impatient when rebuilding our walls. It happened to me, at a certain point I became so tired and weary I wanted God to move more quickly. He said, 'No Retah – one step at a time.'

This process has to be undertaken step by step. It is not possible to fast track or fast forward through to the end. He cannot show us the whole plan at once. We need to recognise that our ability to rebuild is based in our dependence upon God. We can do nothing without Him.

Your strength and power comes from Him alone; His wisdom and love needs to flow through you to others. As you wait upon Him you will learn new facets of His character. Don't try and rush the process – be diligent, do the work and trust your God. There is no one else who can help you.

I have to go to the Lord for the wisdom, strength, power and the love I need.

Prayer

Lord my God, I worship You today. Thank You that Your Word says that I can ask You for the wisdom I need and You will give it to me. Help me to be patient and diligent. I submit to Your will dear Lord. Amen.

7 April

Build in humility

Read James 3:13-18; 4:1-10

Submit yourselves, then, to God. Resist the devil, and he will flee from you. Come near to God and he will come near to you. Wash your hands, you sinners, and purify your hearts, you double-minded. Humble yourselves before the Lord, and he will lift you up. - James 4:7-8,10

The only person we need to look to for the wisdom and strategy to rebuild our walls is God. He showed me another reason for not revealing His complete plan; it is because of spiritual pride.

Spiritual pride is something that puts distance between us, God and other people. It caused Satan's downfall and he would love to entrap us in the same way. Walking this road has kept my family dependent upon God and bowed before Him.

A building site is a messy place to work. It involves heavy labour; it involves sweat and toil, and frustration. It is hard to be filled with pride when you are in the middle of a building site all dirty, sweaty and full of dust.

The Lord promises that if I Humble myself before Him, He will lift me up.

Exactly the same applies to rebuilding your spiritual walls. The Lord promises that if you – *Humble yourself before Him, He will lift you up.*

Prayer

My Father God in heaven, I humbly bow before You today. I come realising my need of You. I ask for Your wisdom, power, and love. Forgive the pride in my heart. Fill me with humility and gratitude today. Amen.

Strength day by day

Read Isaiah 40:27-31(a)

He gives strength to the weary and increases the power of the weak. - Isaiah 40:29

Seeing the whole plan would overwhelm us. Matthew 6:34 says, '*Therefore do no worry about tomorrow, for tomorrow will worry about itself. Each day has enough trouble of its own.*' Although He was telling us not to worry about what we will eat, drink or wear when He said these words, they are good advice when rebuilding our walls.

God gives strength for today; seeing the whole task in the light of today's strength would be too much. You will be able to do it because greater is He who is in you than he who is in the world.

Nehemiah understood that he couldn't take on the task of rebuilding the walls of Jerusalem without God. He spent time in prayer receiving direction, strength and courage from God.

Your Heavenly Father will give you strength and power. Go before Him for fresh strength and power every day.

Go before Him for fresh strength and power every day.

Prayer

My Father, I need Your strength and power for today. I come before You with an open heart and open hands to receive Your anointing upon me. By faith I walk in Your power and strength today. Amen.

Equipped by the Spirit to build

Read Nehemiah 2:6-8, 17-20

I also told them about the gracious hand of my God upon me and what the king had said to me. They replied, "Let us start rebuilding." So they began this good work.
- Nehemiah 2:18

God's hand was upon Nehemiah. God had a plan and a purpose for him and the people of Israel. God placed Nehemiah in the service of King Artaxerxes. The king liked Nehemiah; and because he felt sorry for him, he allowed Nehemiah to go and rebuild the walls of Jerusalem.

After inspecting the walls he addressed the people and told them that they were going to rebuild the wall. The people immediately said, *'Let us start rebuilding.'*

Nehemiah was equipped in the Spirit for the work God had called him to do. We must ask God to equip us in the Spirit for the work of rebuilding our walls.

God's hand will be upon me as I rebuild my walls.

Nehemiah told the people they would no longer live in disgrace after the walls were rebuilt. God will lift up your head and restore you and those you love: God's hand will be upon you as you rebuild your walls.

Prayer

Father God, I come before You thankful that You understand what I am going through. Thank You that You are the lifter of my head. Thank You that You help me and fill me with Your Spirit. Amen.

10 April

Build with Hope

Read Colossians 1:13-29

To them God has chosen to make known among the Gentiles the glorious riches of this mystery, which is Christ in you, the hope of glory. - Colossians 1:27

Nehemiah was very upset when he saw the condition of the walls of Jerusalem. He had two choices: He could have become angry with the Babylonians who broke and burnt the walls and with the Israelites who allowed the walls to get in an even worse state. The other choice was to get up and do something about the situation.

Sometimes it is easy to sit and do nothing. Maybe this is what you have done up until now. You have watched your own life deteriorate. You have seen the lives of your loved ones fall into disrepair and you have done nothing. No more – the light of God's truth has shined into the dark places. Like Nehemiah you will be obedient and do something about your broken walls.

> *I have Yeshua Christ – He lives inside me – He is my hope of glory.*

You and I have Yeshua Christ – He lives inside us – *He is our hope of glory*. We have His Spirit; indwelling us; leading us; guiding us and empowering us.

Prayer

Father God, thank You for Yeshua Christ, Your Son, my hope of glory. I praise You for the Light of Your Spirit that shines into the dark places. Amen.

Beware the enemy!

Read Nehemiah 2:9-10,18(b)-20; 4:1-9

So we rebuilt the wall till all of it reached half its height, for the people worked with all their heart. - Nehemiah 4:6

Nehemiah knew all about being aware of the enemy; he was not very far into his quest before he encountered opposition from evil men. It did not deter him because a) he knew what he had to do, b) he understood his destiny, and c) he knew his God. Every time those who opposed him taunted him he turned to them and silenced them with words of wisdom.

It is no different for you and me – the enemy is all around us. 1 Peter 5:8-9 tells us, *Be self-controlled and alert. Your enemy the devil prowls around like a roaring lion looking for someone to devour. Resist him, standing firm in the faith, because you know that your brothers throughout the world are undergoing the same kind of sufferings.* You are not alone – you have a Big Brother – Yeshua Christ who has won the victory for you.

I am not alone – I have a Big Brother – Yeshua Christ who has won the victory for me.

You have a Heavenly Father who loves you and has a plan and a purpose for you. You have the blessed Holy Spirit who is your guide, protector and inspiration as you go about your task of rebuilding your walls.

Prayer

My Lord, I thank You for the opportunity to walk with You. I am grateful for your warning about the enemy. I praise You that You live within me. Amen.

Living stones from burnt stones

Read 1 Peter 2:4-9

You also, like living stones, are being built into a spiritual house to be a holy priesthood, offering spiritual sacrifices acceptable to God through Jesus Christ. - 1 Peter 2:5

When Nehemiah undertook to rebuild the walls of Jerusalem the material he had to work with was less than the best. The gates had burnt down – so the king gave him a letter to get timber to remake the gates. Nehemiah had to use the existing stones to rebuild the walls though, but the problem was the stones had been damaged by the fire.

Sanballat and Tobiah scoffed at him and asked: *Can they bring the stones back to life from those heaps of rubble – burned as they are?* (Nehemiah 4:2c). Nehemiah was not put off – God had given him the vision to see the finished product.

God takes the broken things and not only mends them but makes something beautiful out of them.

Do you feel discouraged when you look at what you have to work with? Don't allow the hurt to overwhelm you. Take heart today because with God nothing is too difficult. He can take the broken things and not only mend them but make something beautiful out of them.

Prayer

Dear God, my Father, thank You that You can take my burnt and damaged stones and make them into living stones to Your honour and glory. I place my damaged stones before You today. I pray that Your Spirit will breathe new life into them. Amen.

13 April

The Holy Spirit – your Helper

Read John 14:16-27

And I will ask the Father, and He will give you another Helper, that He may be with you forever; that is the Spirit of truth, whom the world cannot receive, because it does not see Him or know Him, but you know Him because He abides with you, and will be in you. - John 14:16-17 (New American Standard Bible)

The moment Nehemiah stepped forward to obey God, the devil appeared. Satan attacked Nehemiah in the form of Sanballat and Tobiah. A lesser man might have run away; but not Nehemiah, he was a man on a mission.

Even though Nehemiah was a man of conviction, courage and focus he must still have had moments of confusion and discouragement. Following God and obeying Him does not mean that we won't have moments like these, but it does mean that we will know where to go for help.

He is my Helper; I will know His voice because He abides in me.

Beginning the process of rebuilding your walls can be confusing. In John 14 Yeshua promises us that He will ask the Father to send us *another Helper* (this literally means *another just like Me*). Yeshua was promising us that when He went to be with His Father in heaven, the Father would send us the Holy Spirit (who is just like Yeshua).

As you wait upon the Lord trust first and foremost in the voice of the Holy Spirit as He speaks to you. He is your Helper; you will know His voice because He abides in you.

Prayer

Father, thank You for the fulfilment of the promise made by Yeshua. Thank You that You have sent me a Helper, Your precious Holy Spirit. Thank You for the power, wisdom and knowledge I receive from the Spirit who indwells me. Amen.

The Holy Spirit – your Teacher

Read John 14:16-27

But the Helper, the Holy Spirit, whom the Father will send in My name, He will teach you all things, and bring to your remembrance all that I said to you. - John 14:26

The Holy Spirit is your Helper, and teacher. Yeshua says in verse 18, '*I will not leave you as orphans; I will come to you.*'

You have everything you need to rebuild your walls. If your folks do some DIY around your home they would get a manual and read up on how to do the job. It is the same with rebuilding your walls in the Spirit, you need a plan. The Holy Spirit is the One who will reveal the plan to you; He will teach you step by step.

Our manual is the Word of God: His instruction is to rebuild the walls of our lives and those of our loved ones. Yeshua gives us a promise to hold onto as we obey Him; *Peace I leave with you: My peace I give to you; not as the world gives, do I give to you. Let not your heart be troubled, nor let it be fearful* (v 27).

My peace I give to you ...Let not your heart be troubled.

Prayer

Father, I thank You that I am Your child, I belong to You. I thank You that Your Spirit is my Teacher. Thank You that You have given me Your marvellous, incomparable peace, because I have Your peace I rejoice today. Amen.

15 April

The Light of God's Word

Read Psalm 119:9, 11, 16, 28, 32, 38-39, 49-50, 65-66, 74, 81, 103-105

Your word is a lamp to my feet and a light for my path. - Psalm 119:105

The world is in opposition to the Spirit. When you have chosen to walk in and be guided by the Spirit – you will face opposition from the world. Nehemiah faced opposition from his enemies. You and I have an enemy, the devil; he does not want us to rebuild our walls. When the walls are rebuilt and there are no more loose or missing stones, it means he no longer has a foothold. He will be locked out and he does not want that to happen.

Nehemiah went out into the night to inspect the damage. In order to see where the damage was he needed a light to illuminate the broken down wall. You also need a light to examine the damage that has been done to your wall. God's Word is your light. You will not stumble because His Word is a lamp lighting your path.

God's Word is my light; I will not stumble because His Word is a lamp lighting my path.

Prayer

Heavenly Father, thank You for Your Word; I delight in it. Your Word is a lamp to my feet and a light to my path. I will walk surefooted because my path is illuminated. I walk boldly along the path You have set before me. Amen.

16 April

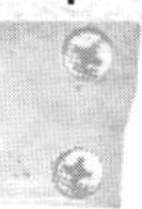

The blueprint for rebuilding

Read 1 Corinthians 3

By the grace God has given me, I laid a foundation as an expert builder, and someone else is building on it. But each one should be careful how he builds. For no one can lay any foundation other than the one already laid, which is Jesus Christ.
- 1 Corinthians 3:10-11

God chose Nehemiah to rebuild the walls of Jerusalem. Nehemiah needed a blueprint. He could not do it alone – he needed help. The first step was returning to Jerusalem (Nehemiah 2:11). Step two was assessing the work that needed to be done (Nehemiah 2:12-15). The third step was recruiting the people to do the work (Nehemiah 2:16-18). The next step was that Nehemiah encountered opposition from the authorities (Nehemiah 2:19-20).

I am God's fellow worker, I am God's field, and God's building.

As you rebuild your walls you will experience opposition. God's Word tells us that all through history people encountered opposition as they set about accomplishing the tasks God set before them.

The Apostle Paul also understood about opposition: Take courage from Nehemiah and Paul. *You are God's fellow worker, you are God's field, and God's building. For no one can lay any foundation other than the one already laid, which is Jesus Christ* (1 Corinthians 3:9,11).

Prayer

My Father God, how awesome that You would choose to partner with me to accomplish Your purposes. I submit to You today, I will not be detracted by those who want to discourage me. I praise You for Yeshua Christ who is the foundation of my life. Amen.

Assembling your team

Read 1 Corinthians 12:11-21

For by one Spirit we were all baptized into one body, whether Jews or Greeks, whether slaves or free, and we were all made to drink of one Spirit. - 1 Corinthians 12:13 (New American Standard Bible)

Nehemiah needed a team to help him rebuild the walls. He got the people of Jerusalem together and told them what God had instructed him to do. They immediately agreed to build. They had to work together as a team. Everyone was needed for the job. Each group had their own section of wall to rebuild.

When you have a few minutes to spare, take the time to read Nehemiah chapter three. It is fascinating to read how each group took responsibility for rebuilding specific areas of the wall.

I cannot do everything – in fact I am not meant to; I need my friends in the Body of Christ.

As you think about rebuilding your walls don't become scared. God will give you instructions – one step at a time. God has placed you in His Body, the Church, for a reason. You cannot do everything – in fact you are not meant to; you need your friends in the Body of Christ. Even though they cannot rebuild your wall, they can support and pray for you – they can build alongside you.

Prayer

My Father, thank You that as Your child I am a part of Your family. Thank You that I am a part of the body of Christ, Your Son. Help me to appreciate my brothers and sisters. Help me to be a functioning member of your body. Amen.

Taking your place in the team

Read Ephesians 4:1-16

Instead speaking the truth in love, we will in all things grow up into him who is the Head, that is, Christ. From him the whole body, joined and held together by every supporting ligament, grows and builds itself up in love, as each part does its work.
- Ephesians 4:15-16

If you read Nehemiah chapter three carefully you see the description of what each group did. They didn't try to do each other's work; they worked together, each one building their own portion.

We usually use our hands to accomplish a task – in fact without your hands you would find it difficult to do even the simplest job. God used the analogy of the hand to help me understand the building process. God uses 'a hand' – a willing hand. God showed me His hand and said, 'I will bestow my **grace** upon you; I will place My **anointing** in you; I will fill you with My **power**, I will give you **gifts** and I will delegate My **authority** to you.'

God, my Father, will give me everything I need to do the work on my walls.

You need to do your part – you must rebuild your wall. As you come before Him in humility and obedience, God, your Father, will give you everything you need to do the work on your walls.

Prayer

Father, I come to You with a humble heart. I desire to obey You. Reveal Yourself to me, I pray. Thank You that You have promised to give me grace, anointing, power, gifts and authority to fulfil the task at hand. I accept Your blessings with a grateful heart. Amen.

19 April

You have God's grace

Read 2 Corinthians 12:1-10

But he said to me, "My grace is sufficient for you, for my power is made perfect in weakness." - 2 Corinthians 12:9

The world believes in the survival of the fittest: God says His power is made perfect in our weakness.

Can you identify with Paul today? Do you have a 'thorn' in your flesh? God says to you, 'My grace is sufficient for you.' I will give you the grace to do the work. God's grace is all about His ability at work in us. It is not about your ability but God's ability – that is limitless.

Paul accomplished great things for God. He helped Paul rebuild the walls of his life and He used Paul to minister to other people. There is no limit to the extent that God can use you when you are submitted to Him.

There is no limit to the extent that God can use me when I am submitted to Him.

The Father says to you; 'My grace is sufficient.' Work with Him to rebuild the walls so that the enemy will not have the victory in your life.

Prayer

My Father God, I bow before Your throne of grace and mercy. I thank and praise You for Your Word. Thank You that You speak to me through Your Word. Today you are telling me that Your grace is sufficient for me; thank You Lord, I hear and I accept what you are saying to me. Amen.

You have God's anointing

Read 1 John 2:24-29

I am writing these things to you about those who are trying to lead you astray. As for you, the anointing you received from him remains in you, and you do not need anyone to teach you. But as his anointing teaches you about all things and as that anointing is real, not counterfeit – just as it has taught you, remain in him. - 1 John 2:26-27

The second of the five things that God gives us for rebuilding our walls is His anointing. The anointing of God is the sweet soothing quality attached to His ability.

God's anointing equips, teaches and helps you to walk God's path. It will protect you from being led astray. Trust the anointing God has put in you.

I have the anointing of God within me. The Spirit will teach me. I will know what to do.

God anointed Nehemiah: the king favoured him, and the people of Israel recognised him as their leader.

Has the time come for you to step out in your anointing and speak up about the need to rebuild the walls of your family? When Nehemiah came back from inspecting the walls he knew what needed to be done. The next step was gathering the people and informing them. The walls would not have been rebuilt if he didn't gather the team around him. You have the anointing of God within you. The Spirit will teach you. You will know what to do.

Prayer

Father God, thank You for Your anointing in my life. Thank You that Your Spirit indwells me; leading me, teaching me and guiding me. I accept Your anointing today. I walk boldly in this anointing that You have blessed my life with. Amen.

You have God's power

Read Ephesians 1:18-23

I pray also that the eyes of your heart may be enlightened in order that you may know the hope to which he has called you ... and his incomparably great power for us who believe. That power is like the working of his mighty strength, which he exerted in Christ when he raised him from the dead and seated him at his right hand in the heavenly realms. - Ephesians 1:18a,19-20

As we look at the grace God gives us we see His mercy attached to His ability. His anointing is the calming, sweet, soothing quality that is linked to His ability. On the other hand His power shows us the strength and force attached to His ability. Don't you love the verses you read just now?

I will let His grace cleanse me, His mercy save me, His anointing soothe me and His power embolden me in the task of rebuilding my walls.

Are the eyes of your heart opened? Do you know the hope God has called you to? This knowledge is not an academic understanding – but rather an experience. Are you experiencing His mighty power and strength at work in your life each day as you rebuild your walls? This is your inheritance as His child, this is your birthright. Don't let anyone steal this away from you.

Spend time in God's presence asking Him to open the eyes of your heart, your spirit and your understanding.

Prayer

Father, open the eyes of my heart, that I may see You. Open the eyes of my understanding that I may grasp Your incomparable strength and power. Grant me grace and favour in Your sight I pray. Amen.

You have God's gifts

Read Ephesians 1:1-14

Praise be to the God and Father of our Lord Jesus Christ, who has blessed us in the heavenly realm with every spiritual blessing in Christ. - Ephesians 1:3

Over the past few days the same attributes of God have come up again and again: Grace, mercy, strength, power, anointing, love, blessing, and gifts to mention a few of them.

The fourth finger we look at is the gifts (blessings) of God; the gifts show us the freely given nature of His ability.

God, your Father, has chosen you to be holy and blameless. He has chosen you to be adopted as His child; this is the will of God. You are not an accident of birth; you are the much loved, much planned child of the King of the Universe – you are special.

He will be there with me giving me the gifts and blessings I need to accomplish the task before me.

God loves and blesses you; He delights in you His child. God is faithful to His covenant with you. He is your *Covenant-keeping God*. As you begin the process of rebuilding your walls He will be there with you, giving you the gifts and blessings you need to accomplish the task before you.

Prayer

My Loving Heavenly Father, thank You that calling You my Father, has special meaning in the light of Your Word to me today. I revel in the joy of knowing that You have chosen me before the foundation of the world to be Your much loved child. Amen.

23 April

You have God's authority

Read Colossians 1:13-20; 2:9-12

For in Christ all the fullness of the Deity lives in bodily form, and you have been given fullness in Christ, who is the head over every power and authority. - Colossians 2:9-10

The fifth finger, which God showed me, was authority. This authority shows us the extent of His power behind His ability. We need God's complete hand. We need His grace and mercy at work in our circumstances; His soothing, sweet and calming anointing upon our troubled lives; His power and strength at work in our lives. Every day we experience the sheer joy of the gift of our salvation.

Lastly, you need to recognise that you serve the God of the Universe. He gave that authority to His Son, Yeshua Christ. Yeshua in turn passed that authority and power on to us, His children.

I am not powerless or without weapons as I rebuild my walls. I claim my authority today.

Once your walls are stable, secure and strong there is no way that the enemy will be able to break through. You will be protected by the authority that is yours in Yeshua Christ.

You are not powerless or without weapons as you rebuild your walls. Claim your authority today.

Prayer

My Father God, Yeshua Christ, Your Son, is head over every power and authority. I have nothing to fear from the enemy. I can stand tall and brave in the authority that is mine because I am Your child. Lord, empower me through Your Spirit to take up the challenge of rebuilding my walls. Amen.

Breaking down and rebuilding

Read 2 Corinthians 10:1-5

The weapons we fight with are not the weapons of the world. On the contrary, they have divine power to demolish strongholds. We demolish arguments and every pretension that sets itself up against the knowledge of God, and we take captive every thought to make it obedient to Christ. - 2 Corinthians 10:4-5

If a wall develops a crack you call a builder in to assess the problem. If the foundation has been compromised and the wall is too badly damaged, he might suggest breaking it down, stabilising the foundations and starting all over again building a new wall.

Our lives are much like a wall. If you have allowed the enemy to get in and cause cracks, then you might well with the help of the 'Master Builder', have to demolish in order to rebuild. The weapons the enemy uses to crack our walls are; lack of forgiveness, disobedience, sin, pride, and hurt, to name a few.

Take every thought captive; make every thought obedient to Christ today.

The good news is that we have weapons to fight with; they have divine power to demolish strongholds. Nine times out of ten the attack of the enemy starts in your mind – from there it spreads into actions and attitudes. Take every thought captive; make every thought obedient to Christ today.

Prayer

My Heavenly Father, I bow before You, the God of the universe. Thank You that You have equipped me with everything I need to demolish the strongholds of the enemy in my life. In submission I bow before Your throne. I bring every thought captive and obedient to Yeshua Christ. Amen.

Expect your work to be ridiculed

Read Nehemiah 4:1-8

"Can they revive the stones from the dusty rubble even the burned ones? Even what they are building – if a fox should jump on it, he would break their stone wall down."
- Nehemiah 4:2d,3b (New American Standard Bible)

As the work on the walls progressed the opposition grew. Sanballat and Tobiah ridiculed the Israelites. They were angry that the work was progressing.

Nehemiah is angry and he prays to God asking the Lord to deal with Sanballat and Tobiah.

The words that followed Nehemiah's prayer are heartening and I believe relevant to us: *So we built the wall and the whole wall was joined together to half its height,* ***for the people had a mind to work.***

When the enemy causes a disturbance in my life, I will learn from the example of Nehemiah – I will run to my God.

Do you have a mind to work on your walls? There is no doubt that it will take work; hot, sweaty, back breaking work. Are you experiencing opposition today? The enemy does not want to see your walls rebuilt. He does not want to see the walls of your family rebuilt. Every row of bricks you put in place is a row closer to him no longer having access into your life.

Prayer

Dear God, I come before You in humility. I am feeling the burden of those who ridicule and scoff at my efforts to rebuild the walls of my life. I know that You have called me to this task. I choose to turn my back on them and concentrate on the work I have to do. Give me success, I pray. Amen.

Watch, Pray: Fight, Pray

Read Ephesians 6:10-18

Therefore, take up the full armour of God, that you will be able to resist in the evil day, and having done everything, to stand firm. With all prayer and petition pray at all times in the Spirit, and with this in view, be on the alert with all perseverance and petition for all the saints. - Ephesians 6:13,18 (New American Standard Bible)

Today we read what Paul says about arming ourselves against the attack of the devil. Aldo often wrote to me – *you cannot get tired, you must continue to build, day and night you must build, you must build and fight.* There were times when I was desperately tired.

Aldo would encourage me saying, *you must watch and pray, you must fight and pray*. This is how Nehemiah handled the enemy's threat

I have a whole arsenal of weapons – I will not be afraid to use them!

Paul says put on the full armour of God. You are not strong in your own might – you are strong in the might of your Lord and Saviour – He alone can give you the strength you need to rebuild your walls. You can be sure that the closer you get to your walls being rebuilt the greater the attack from the enemy will become. Verse 16 says: *taking up the shield of faith with which you will be able to extinguish all the flaming missiles of the evil one*. You have a whole arsenal of weapons.

Prayer

My Father God, my hope is in You, Lord: my trust is in You, Lord. Thank You that You have given me everything I need to face and fight the enemy. I watch and pray, I fight and pray – I have victory in the name of Yeshua. Amen.

God's Love: Your power supply

Read Ephesians 3:14-21

And I pray that you, being rooted and established in love ... may be filled to the measure of all the fullness of God. - Ephesians 3:17b,19b

One of the most powerful weapons you have in your arsenal is the love of God. There is no defence against love. Hatred, anger, malice, vindictiveness, being unforgiving, meanness, violence and any other ugly emotion or action you can think of melts in the face of pure love.

Apostle Paul wanted us to be in no doubt of the fact that God loves us – *I pray that out of his glorious riches he may strengthen you with power through his Spirit in your inner being, so that Christ may dwell in your hearts through faith. And I pray that you, being rooted and established in love, may have power, together with all the saints, to grasp how wide and long and high and deep is the love of Christ, and to know this love that surpasses knowledge – that you may be filled to the measure of all the fullness of God.*

God's love is a glorious love. There is no place for any other influence in my life when His love floods me.

My friend if you know who you are in Christ – if you know this love – there will be no place for the enemy.

Prayer

Now to Him who is able to do immeasurably more than all we ask or imagine, according to His power that is at work within us, to Him be glory in the church and in Christ Yeshua throughout all generations, forever and ever! Amen.

Managing your power supply

Read 1 Corinthians 13

Love does not delight in evil but rejoices with the truth. It always protects, always trusts, always hopes, always perseveres. - 1 Corinthians 13:6-7

Why is it possible for us to love our enemies, to bless those who curse us? We saw the answer in yesterday's reading. It is because of the powerful, all surpassing love of God that is shed abroad in our hearts and lives. This love flows through us. It is the power drill of our lives. We are meant to use it for good – we are meant to use it to build, reconstruct and love.

One day Aldo wrote to me saying those who did not want our walls rebuilt could not stand being shown love. They could not handle being blessed.

My greatest weapon as I rebuild my walls is love.

Your greatest weapon as you rebuild your walls is love. You have the power surge of God's love flowing into your life every moment of every day. It is not meant to be stored up. This power is meant to flow freely from your life to touch the lives of others – even those – in fact particularly those who don't deserve it.

Prayer

My loving Father, I thank You that I am filled to overflowing with Your love. I do not want to be selfish and keep it for myself – I want to share it with others. I want to love those who do not love me, even those who would seek to harm me. Thank You that Your love flowing through me is the strongest weapon that I have. Amen.

29 April

Compassion is the cement

Read Colossians 3:12-17

Therefore, as God's chosen people, holy and dearly loved, clothe yourselves with compassion, kindness, humility, gentleness and patience. - Colossians 3:12

Compassion walks hand in hand with love. It is hard to know what comes first – they are impossible to separate. Compassion drives us to action.

Nehemiah was moved with compassion to do something about rebuilding Jerusalem's walls.

Compassion is the cement that we use to secure the stones in our walls. It is compassion that will move you to rebuild your walls.

How do you go about doing this? You start by praying – asking God for wisdom and a game plan. You walk step by step following His plan. You do not allow yourself to be dissuaded or discouraged by those who would have you follow man's paths. You treat them with love and compassion but you do not follow them. Your plumb-line for building is the voice of the Spirit speaking to you.

Compassion is the cement that I use to secure the stones in my walls.

When you become weary and downhearted, when you want to give up – it is going to be compassion that is going to drive you to get up off your knees and fight another day.

Prayer

Dear Father, I come to You in the Name above all names; Yeshua Christ, Your Son, and my Saviour. Thank You Father, for Your loving compassion towards me and those that I love. I pray that Your Spirit will fill me with that same compassion. I clothe myself with compassion today. Amen

30 April

Grace is your gate

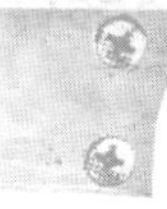

Read Hebrews 4:14-16

Let us then approach the throne of grace with confidence, so that we may receive mercy and find grace to help us in our time of need. - Hebrews 4:16

Once you have rebuilt the walls of your life it will be grace that will keep and sustain you. Grace will be the gate that you hang. Walk in grace day by day as you remain in Christ. If bad choices and sin led to the breakdown of your walls then grace will keep you from falling. If a lack of forgiveness or bitterness eroded your walls then grace will help you walk in forgiveness. Whatever caused the breakdown of your walls – grace will keep you safe once your walls are rebuilt.

Do you have a big, bright, beautiful gate of grace at the entrance to your life?

Yeshua, your High Priest, knows every temptation and weakness you have ever faced – and He overcame each of them. He died so that you can have the victory.

You serve an awesome God – worship Him today.

After Nehemiah and the people had finished rebuilding the walls and hanging the gates, the people moved back into the city to live there. There was life again. In chapter 9 the people came together to confess their sins and to praise God for His goodness to them.

Grace has a two-fold effect upon my life; it has a divine influence upon my heart and it reflects in my life.

We will close off our time together this month by praying the prayer of praise and thanksgiving prayed by the children of Israel:

Prayer

Blessed be Your glorious name, and may it be exalted above all blessing and praise. You alone are the Lord. You made the heavens, even the highest heavens, and the stars in the sky, the earth and all that is on it, the seas and all that is in them. You give life to everything, and the multitudes of heaven worship You. Amen!

my lewe is 'n storie van hoop, geloof en liefde. "Samuel, Samuel sal jy vir my terug gaan aarde toe en vir die mense vertel ek yeshua lewe." Jesus Christus sien name van Sy kinders is in Sy hand. Samuel is so dankbaar sy lewe is vol geloof, hoop en liefde, wysheid sê sy hoop sal nooit vergaan nie. Jy sien baie Samuel. Samuel ek gaan jou leer en jy sal vertel wat ek jou leer. sal sien baie water sien ek sien hy wys my baie water oor die see sal beweeg oor land. Samuel sal jy sê hulle moet nie vrees nie wat jy sien dag van magtige aardbewings is wat sien Julle sien ons is vir Jesus so spesiaal.

Letter 5:

Story of Hope

My life is a story of hope, faith and love. 'Samuel, Samuel, will you go back to earth and tell the people that I – Yeshua – am alive?'

Jesus Christ sees the names of His children inscribed on the palms of His hands. Samuel is so thankful that his life is full of faith, hope and love. Wisdom says that His hope will never fail. You see a lot of things in the spirit, Samuel. 'Samuel, I will teach you; and you will tell others of the things that I teach you.' He shows me a lot of water from the sea that will move over the dry land. 'Samuel, tell them they should not be afraid. You see the day of the mighty earthquakes. You see that we are so special to Jesus.'

The Power of the Tongue

Prayer for May

My Father God, I come to You at the beginning of this new month. I thank You for the lessons I learnt last month as we walked through the book of Nehemiah together. Thank You for the opportunity to rebuild the walls of my life and the lives of my loved ones. As we begin this new month and we look at the tongue and the power of words, I want to commit myself to You anew. Father, I praise and worship You. I exalt You and honour You. I ask You to fill me anew each day with Your Holy Spirit. I pray that my words will honour You. Teach me and instruct me through Your Spirit, I pray. Amen.

The purpose of your tongue

Read Proverbs 10:20-32

The tongue of the righteous is choice silver, but the heart of the wicked is of little value. The lips of the righteous nourish many, but fools die for lack of judgement.
- Proverbs 10:20-21

This month we are going to look at the power of the tongue; it is a small organ with enormous power. The tongue is the strongest muscle in the body. Each person has their own print; this means that your tongue is different to any other person's tongue.

The tongue can be used for good and for evil. Often the same tongue can speak words of love, comfort and compassion one minute and the next it can speak words of hate, anger and destruction.

God created my tongue to bless and not to curse. Will I choose to be an instrument of blessing?

Your tongue can encourage and help rebuild people's walls or you can use it as an instrument for building barriers between you and others. The Word of God has a lot to say about the tongue. You are meant to be a blessing to other people. God created your tongue to bless and not to curse. Will you choose to be an instrument of blessing?

Prayer

Dear Father, You created me to be a blessing. You created my tongue to be an instrument of blessing and not a curse. Fill my mind with Your love, so that my tongue will overflow with words of blessing. Amen.

2 May

An instrument of blessing

Read Psalm 34

I will bless the Lord at all times; His praise shall continually be in my mouth.
- Psalm 34:1 (New American Standard Bible)

Blessing is a powerful tool God has placed in our hands. The instrument, which communicates blessing, is the tongue. If we bring our tongues under the control of the Holy Spirit we will build up rather than break people down. If we build barriers we will not be able to reach out and minister to the needs of those around us. If we determine to speak the truth in love, we will be spreading hope, peace and joy.

If we do this we will earn the right to witness to, and minister into, the lives of the people God brings across our paths. Today people need to hear hope spoken. They need to hear the Good News of the Gospel.

You have a living hope inside of you; share it. This is the task God has given you. The instrument for passing on this hope is your tongue; use it wisely.

I have a living hope inside of me; I must share it. The instrument for passing on this hope is my tongue; I must use it wisely.

Prayer

My Father God, You have given me a task; to speak hope, love and peace to others. Help me to fulfil this task – my tongue is Yours; take it and use it, I pray. Amen.

Work on your self-control

Read Proverbs 25:25-28

Like a city whose walls are broken down is a man who lacks self-control.
- Proverbs 25:28

It was after my family's terrible motor car accident that I began to realise the power my tongue and the words I speak have. It became clear to me how much power words have in my life. I also realised how important self-control is when it comes to the tongue and the words I utter.

God instructs us to use our tongues constructively. He also says we are to learn how to keep quiet, to control our tongues. For this we need self-control. We must guard ourselves and be watchful.

It seems as if the tongue is the last part of us to be touched and brought under the influence of the Holy Spirit. The Spirit must have control of our thoughts and our words. The Word tells us to put on the full armour of God; the helmet of Salvation – so that our heads – where our thoughts are generated are sanctified by the Salvation of Christ.

The Spirit must have control of my thoughts and my words.

Prayer

Dear Father, thank You that I have a voice to be able to praise You. I am grateful that You have placed Your Holy Spirit within me. Through the power of Your Spirit in me, control my tongue I pray. Amen.

A tongue that fears God

Read Psalm 111

The fear of the Lord is the beginning of wisdom; all who follow his precepts have good understanding. To him belongs eternal praise. - Psalm 111:10

The Bible teaches us that we are to 'fear the Lord'. What does this mean?' *To fear, with regard to God, means to reverence, to respect, to regard with awe and affection, to hold in such loving esteem as to be afraid of offending or grieving the One so adored.*

I often observe as I visit churches that there is a complete lack of reverence for God. Young people can be seen talking with their friends during the worship. Some people talk during the delivery of the sermon. There are those who even tweet, message and interact with their cellular phones while sitting in church. There appears to be a lack of awe and reverence for God.

If I reverence God I will bring my thoughts, emotions, actions and speech under the control of the Holy Spirit.

If we reverence God we will want to honour God with our mouths. The Psalmist speaks of a connection between following God's Word, having a good understanding and the fear of the Lord.

Prayer

Dear God, my Father in heaven, I come before You bowing in awe, reverence, respect and love for You. I bow my knee, I bow my heart, I bow my mind and I submit my tongue to You. I desire above all else to honour You with the words of my mouth. Amen.

Keep your tongue from evil

Read Psalm 34

Whoever of you loves life and desires to see many good days, keep your tongue from evil and your lips from speaking lies. Turn from evil and do good; seek peace and pursue it. - Psalm 34:12-14

The Word says, *Let this mind be in you which was also in Christ Yeshua*. It further says you have been given a *sound mind.* This is God's gift to you: A mind like that of Yeshua Christ.

You need to realise that every time you gossip, spread stories about someone, break another person down, or criticise somebody else you are being used by the devil. When we are jealous, unkind, malicious and unloving our tongues become the fiery arrows of the evil one. Our words become arrows striking their walls, attempting to break them down.

If I speak words of life, words of blessing then I am a positive influence bringing God's blessing upon the lives of other people.

When I walk in the Spirit then my emotions and thoughts are brought under the control of the Spirit. I keep my tongue from evil and my lips from speaking lies. God has given us a will – we can choose either to walk in the Spirit or walk according to the flesh – the choice is ours.

Prayer

My Father, I desire to learn from You. I choose to control my tongue. I choose to turn from evil and seek peace. I pray that Your Spirit will fill me to overflowing so that Your blessing and life will flow out of my mouth. Amen.

Guard your mouth

Read Isaiah 59:1-4

Your lips have spoken lies, and your tongue mutters wicked things. They rely on empty arguments and speak lies. - Isaiah 59:3b-4a

We often speak without thinking about what we are saying. The words come out of our mouths without us thinking about the effect they will have on other people. Last month we spoke about rebuilding our walls; but often we build the wrong kind of walls between ourselves and other people. Every time we speak death instead of life we add another stone to the wall. This wall becomes a division between us and breaks down the unity we should be sharing.

The Lord showed me it is sin that causes the barrier between me and other people. I repented and asked the Lord to forgive me. Do the words in our scripture speak to you today? Are your lips speaking lies, are you caught up with empty arguments? If so come to the Lord and repent.

I must ask God to guard my mouth: I must be an instrument of blessing!

Ask God to guard your mouth: Yield control of your tongue to the Holy Spirit.

Prayer

Dear Father God, I come before you confessing that I have sinned. Lord, I ask You to put a guard in front of my lips – so that I will only speak life. I want my words to build up and not to break down. Amen.

Guard your mind

Read Romans 8:1-11

For the mind set on the flesh is death, but the mind set on the Spirit is life and peace.
- Romans 8:6 (New American Standard Bible)

Speech starts in the mind – we think something before we say it. Our mind is where the battle is fought; if we choose the flesh we lose – if we choose the Spirit we win.

This is why it is so important that we put a guard around our minds. We strengthen our minds by making sure we fill them with the things that will ensure their health. We must guard what we read, what we watch, with whom we speak. Our mind is like a computer: what you put in is what you get out.

Your mind can be a strong weapon against the enemy; the stronger your mind becomes the easier it will be for you to resist the influence of the flesh. When you walk according to the Spirit you will help people repair their walls. You will not be responsible for building walls between yourself and other people.

I will place a Guard – the Holy Spirit – at the door to my mind.

Prayer

Dear Father God, thank You that Yeshua Christ, Your precious Son, came to bring me freedom. I choose to live by the Spirit and not by the flesh. I choose to submit to Your guidance in my life. I desire to walk according to Your Spirit every day of my life. Amen.

Your mouth: A fountain of life?

Read Proverbs 10:9-18

The mouth of the righteous is a fountain of life, but violence overwhelms the mouth of the wicked. - Proverbs 10:11

What does it take to have a mouth that is a fountain of life to your family and friends?

Firstly, you have to be righteous (v 11). Your position in Christ is that you have been justified and because you are justified you stand before God as righteous. The problem is that we so often do not walk in the reality of our inheritance in Christ.

Secondly, you must have discernment and wisdom (v 13). God has given you the Holy Spirit, to lead, guide, instruct and enlighten you. The Spirit will give you wisdom and discernment.

Thirdly, you must love (v 12). The love of God covers your sins. God says you must love in the same way. You can choose to have a mouth that is a fountain of life.

I choose today to make my tongue a fountain that refreshes, restores and regenerates.

A fountain refreshes, restores, regenerates and imparts life. A fountain banishes drought and causes the barren ground to break forth in new growth. You can be a fountain bringing new growth and vitality or you can bring drought, causing everything around you to be dry and barren.

Prayer

My Father, I realise that all too often I choose to allow my tongue to cause a drought in the lives of others. I want my tongue to be a fountain that refreshes. Help me to walk in and live a life of expansive love. Amen.

Your tongue: Is it choice silver?

Read Proverbs 10:20-32

The tongue of the righteous is choice silver, but the heart of the wicked is of little value.
- Proverbs 10:20

The heart is the seat of our emotions, and our emotions dictate our thoughts; our thoughts frequently become the words we speak. Sometimes we think something but don't say it. These thoughts make it difficult to forgive. When we allow this to happen a cycle establishes itself in our life. Eventually we will boil over and there will be a torrent of ugliness spewing out of our mouth.

We all know people who complain and moan about everything. They do not see the good in anything or anyone. We must be careful to place a guard around our heart. Our goal should be to become a person whose tongue is choice silver. Silver is pure, it sparkles and shines. It brings light and life.

My goal is to become a person whose tongue is choice silver.

No matter what you go through you have a choice regarding how you will react. Guard your mind, heart and tongue so that you can be a blessing to other people.

Prayer

My Father, You created me in Your image. You gave me a tongue with the potential to be either a blessing or an instrument of torture. The choice is mine: I choose to have a tongue that is choice silver. Amen.

Guard your heart

Read Psalm 19:7-14

May the words of my mouth and the meditation of my heart be pleasing in your sight, O Lord, my Rock and my Redeemer. - Psalm 19:14

How do you guard your heart? Psalm 19 gives us some clear strategies that revolve around the Word of God; verse seven says *the law of the Lord is perfect, reviving the soul.* Are you feeling discouraged? Spend time in Word– your soul will be revived and your heart will be *joyful* (v 8). If you spend time in God's Word your mind will be fed.

You should fill your mind with God and fix your thoughts on Him. If you do this there will be no place for the kind of thoughts that will cause you to become bitter and disgruntled. You will not be able to resist speaking words of blessing.

What we fill our minds with directly affects how we feel (our heart). How we feel influences the words we speak. So if you want the *words of your mouth and the meditation of your heart to be pleasing to the Lord* then you need to guard your heart.

God, my Father, has given me all the tools I need to guard my mind, heart and mouth.

Prayer

Dear Father, *may the words of my mouth and the meditation of my heart be pleasing in Your sight, O Lord, my Rock and my Redeemer.* Amen.

Bearing good fruit

Read Matthew 7:13-23

Likewise every good tree bears good fruit, but a bad tree bears bad fruit. A good tree cannot bear bad fruit, and a bad tree cannot bear good fruit. - Matthew 7:17-18

Your life produces fruit; the question is what kind of fruit does it produce? Your words also produce fruit. If you speak in a loving way; if your speech is joyful, peaceful, patient, kind, good, faithful, gentle, and controlled, then your words will produce good fruit. The converse is also true. If you speak words that are un-loving, joyless, causing unrest, impatient, unkind, bad, untrue, hateful, and uncontrolled – then your words will produce bad fruit.

If you want a tree to be healthy you must nurture and look after it. If you want to produce good fruit in your life you feed and nurture your life in the right way. The end goal is for Christ's nature to be evident in your life.

We have the Holy Spirit dwelling within us – leading, guiding and directing our lives.

I have everything I need to nurture and grow the best fruit in my life – I have the nature of Christ.

Prayer

Dear Father, thank You for Your Spirit who dwells within me. I desire to walk in the fullness of Your power and strength. I desire to bear good fruit. Amen.

A skilful tongue

Read Psalm 45

My heart is stirred by a noble theme as I recite my verses for the king; my tongue is the pen of a skilful writer. - Psalm 45:1

Your tongue is like a pen. A pen writes words on a page; a tongue forms words and speaks them. Words have their own energy and a life of their own. Once written they are there – they become real. Even if you tear up the paper the words have still been formed and crafted. The same is true of the spoken word – once it is uttered you cannot take it back.

How is your tongue? Is it like the pen of a skilful writer? Is your mind and heart in tune with the Holy Spirit so that your tongue can convey God's message? The Lord needs us to communicate His grace, mercy and love to the world around us.

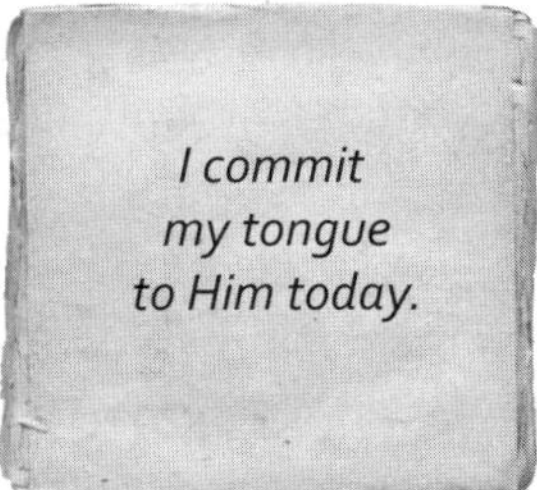
I commit my tongue to Him today.

Tell Him that you desire to have a tongue like the pen of a skilful writer. If your tongue is submitted to God then the Holy Spirit will be the skilful writer who will direct your speech.

Prayer

Lord, I desire that my tongue will be like the pen of a skilful writer. I desire to share Your grace, mercy and love with others. I submit my tongue to the control of Your Holy Spirit. Amen.

13 May

Your words reveal your character

Read Matthew 12:33-37

For out of the overflow of the heart the mouth speaks. The good man brings good things out of the good stored up in him, and the evil man brings evil things out of the evil stored up in him. - Matthew 12:34b-35

Yeshua clearly spells out the connection between the heart and our words.

It is like a computer; what we put in is what we get out. If you program it correctly then it will give you the right information and it will perform as you want it to. The mind is no different. The information we feed the mind with will drop down into our hearts; and what is in the heart, will find a pathway out through the mouth.

Yeshua is our example; He spent His life bringing light and life wherever He went. As His disciples we are commissioned to share the Gospel. Our lives and the way we live are meant to be an example to other people; words should be the last resort when communicating the Gospel. Yet, so often we can speak a great deal but we do not always back our words up with actions.

My life and the way I live are meant to be an example to other people; words should be the last resort when communicating the Gospel.

Prayer

Lord, I pray that You will fill my mind with Your truth and my heart with the light and love of Your Holy Spirit. Touch my lips with Your grace and mercy. Let the words I utter back up my actions. Amen.

Keep a tight rein on your tongue

Read James 1:19-27

If anyone considers himself religious and yet does not keep a tight rein on his tongue, he deceives himself and his religion is worthless. - James 1:26

My dear brothers [*and sisters*]*, take note of this. Everyone should be quick to listen, slow to speak and slow to become angry, for man's anger does not bring about the righteous life that God desires* (vs 19-20). These verses tell us that our religion is worthless if we do not keep a tight control of our tongues. It is no good if you praise God on a Sunday and on Monday you curse friends and family. We have to be careful about how we live.

My constant prayer must be Lord, take control of my tongue; Holy Spirit, take control of my tongue.

You absolutely cannot underestimate the power of your words. They have the power to wound and hurt others. Anger allowed to run free can cause untold harm.

James tells us that we must not just listen to the Word but we must do what it says. We come back to the fact that we need to be spending time in God's Word. We must fill our minds with the truth of God's Word and act upon it. Allow the Holy Spirit to take God's Word and make it alive and real to you.

Prayer

Lord, my God, I want to be a doer of Your Word, not just a hearer. I want Your Word to be life to me; and then in turn I want to bring life to others through the words I speak. Sanctify my tongue, I pray. Amen.

Speak and act with mercy

Read James 2:1-13

Speak and act as those who are going to be judged by the law that gives freedom, because judgement without mercy will be shown to anyone who has not been merciful. Mercy triumphs over judgement! - James 2:12-13

Can I ask you: Where would you be without God's mercy in your life? We cannot live a day without God's mercy and yet we are so slow to extend this same mercy to other people. We judge ourselves by one set of standards, and other people with a much harsher yardstick.

We know that Yeshua Christ came to this world to live, die and rise from the dead in order to free us from the law. As a result we live in freedom and grace. God's mercy is our inheritance in Christ.

I can be the face of mercy to those I live and work with.

Are you merciful or are you quick to condemn, finding it easier to speak words of condemnation rather than words of hope and encouragement? We must speak and act as those who live in freedom.

Only God has the right to judge. We are to love, encourage, build up and help other people. James puts it so beautifully when he says, *mercy triumphs over judgement.*

Prayer

My loving Father, thank You for Your mercy that I enjoy each day in my life. I would be nothing without Your mercy. Help me to live and speak mercy to other people each day. I want to be a merciful person. Amen.

Taming the tongue

Read James 3:1-12

But no man can tame the tongue. It is a restless evil, full of deadly poison. With the tongue we praise our Lord and Father, and with it we curse men, who have been made in God's likeness. - James 3:8-9

James makes two comparisons regarding the tongue. In the first he uses the bit – when it is placed in the horse's mouth, even a small person can control a huge horse, making it obey their commands.

In the second James speaks about a ship and its rudder. The captain can steer a huge ship by turning the rudder (or wheel).

James goes on to say that unlike these two examples the human tongue is totally uncontrollable. He says it's like a fire that runs away. James says that the human tongue is *a restless evil and full of deadly poison*.

There is one Person more powerful than my tongue; the Holy Spirit.

The solution is to daily bring your tongue and lay it on the altar of sacrifice. You need to present your tongue as a living sacrifice. God has called us to be a blessing to our families and friends. Ask the Holy Spirit to take control of your tongue so that you can be a blessing.

Prayer

Lord, I pray that You will take control of my tongue. I confess that I have no control over it. I bring it to You, Lord. I pray that You will fill me with the power of Your Holy Spirit. Amen.

17 May

A living sacrifice

Read Romans 12

Therefore, I urge you, brothers, in view of God's mercy, to offer your bodies as living sacrifices, holy and pleasing to God – this is your spiritual act of worship. Do not conform any longer to the pattern of this world, but be transformed by the renewing of your mind. - Romans 12:1-2a

The only way to control the tongue is through the renewing of the mind. If you submit to the Holy Spirit each day, allowing the Spirit to renew and regenerate your mind; you will find that your tongue too, will come under the control of the Spirit.

If we conform to the pattern of this world we will find that our minds are out of control. If your mind is out of control then your tongue will also be out of control.

I present my tongue as a living sacrifice to God.

The goal for our Christian lives is to grow towards maturity. It is through the reshaping of our minds that we grow towards maturity. Maturity will give us control over our speech and actions.

Part of God's plan for you is to be a blessing through your speech. By the power of God's Spirit working in you it is possible for you to speak peace and to overcome evil with good.

Prayer

My Father God, I come before You in praise and worship. I love You my Lord. I pray that Your Holy Spirit will take control over my mind, heart and mouth so that as I walk with You I might bless others. Amen.

Wholesome speech

Read Ephesians 4:17-32

Do not let any unwholesome talk come out of your mouths, but only what is helpful for building others up according to their needs, that it may benefit those who listen.
- Ephesians 4:29

The Living Bible says, *I can do anything God asks me to through Christ who strengthens me*. God doesn't leave us to our own devices to fulfil this command.

The Bible has many examples about the tongue. Today's reading speaks to us about our Christian walk; again we are told that we have to walk the talk. We are told *not to walk in the futility of our minds* (v 17). What does this mean? Some of the meanings of the word futility are; emptiness, frivolousness, fruitlessness, hollowness, idleness, ineffectiveness and worthlessness. We are told that we are not to have minds that are empty, frivolous, fruitless, hollow, idle, ineffective or worthless.

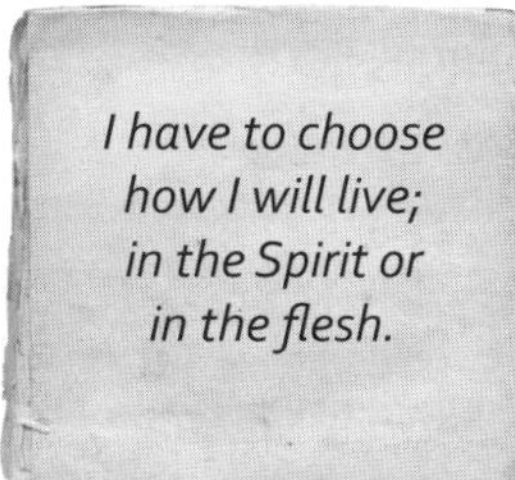

I have to choose how I will live; in the Spirit or in the flesh.

Wrong thinking leads to wrong behaviour. We are told in verse 23 that *we are to be made new in the attitude of our minds*. We cannot live our lives slandering and gossiping about our neighbours and hope to be a witness for the Lord.

Prayer

My Father, thank You for Your clear instruction regarding how I am to live. I commit my mind to Your Holy Spirit. Moment by moment I want to walk in the power of the Spirit. I want my mind to be filled with Your love and goodness. Amen.

19 May

A tongue set free

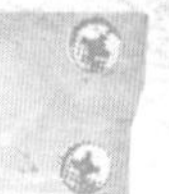

Read Galatians 5:13-26

You, my brothers [and sisters], were called to be free. But do not use your freedom to indulge the sinful nature, rather, serve one another in love. - Galatians 5:13

The solution to the old nature is to walk moment by moment in the Spirit. It is only as we place our lives upon the altar of sacrifice that we are in a position where the Spirit can control our lives.

Yeshua died to give us a renewed mind, a heart filled with His joy and peace, and a mouth singing and speaking praises to God, our Father. Out of the fullness of your heart your mouth will speak.

There will be no place for immorality, impurity, idolatry, strife, jealousy, outbursts of anger, fighting, disagreements or factions. Rather the fruit of the Spirit will be evident in our lives; love, joy, peace, patience, kindness, goodness, faithfulness, gentleness, and self-control. All of these will be the evidence of a life lived in the fullness of the Holy Spirit.

As I submit to the Holy Spirit I will know the freedom of walking in the Spirit and not fulfilling the desires of my flesh.

Your freedom cost Yeshua His life; use your freedom to live by and walk in the Spirit.

Prayer

Father, I thank You for the freedom I have in Yeshua – this freedom cost You everything. I long to walk in the fullness of everything it means to be free in Christ. I surrender anew to Your Spirit. Amen.

Speaking truth from your heart

Read Psalm 15

He whose walk is blameless and who does what is righteous, who speaks the truth from his heart and has no slander on his tongue, who does his neighbour no wrong and casts no slur on his fellow-man. - Psalm 15:2-3

We cannot separate the heart from the tongue. If you cultivate a mind that is focused upon the Spirit and the things of the Spirit; you will automatically have a heart that is filled with truth. What is in your mind will flow into your heart.

If we say something then people should be able to believe what we have said. There should be no slander on your tongue. Do you enjoy gossiping with your friends? Is it sometimes difficult for you to resist passing on the latest tasty morsel of gossip? Our verse says that there should be no slander found on your tongue.

Are you walking a blameless life in the power of the Holy Spirit? Recommit your mind, heart and tongue to the Lord today. Ask Him to sanctify your tongue. Purpose today that your tongue will no longer be used as the tool of the enemy.

I open my mind and heart to the Spirit so that the Spirit can sanctify my mind, causing my heart to overflow with purity and love.

Prayer

Father, I recognise the pull of my old nature – but thank You that the power of Your Spirit is so much greater. Thank You that I am a new person as a result of what Yeshua, Your Son, has done for me on Calvary. Amen.

21 May

The Truth will set you free

Read John 8:31-47

If you hold to my teaching, you are really my disciples. Then you will know the truth, and the truth will set you free. So if the Son sets you free, you will be free indeed.
- John 8:31b-32,36

Truth is not a concept but a Person: Yeshua Christ. We are set free by Yeshua Christ. He is the ultimate truth. In order to be set free by Him we have to know Him. The test of being a disciple of Yeshua Christ is whether we know Him and abide in Him. If we are His disciples we will carry out His desires.

Yeshua died so that you can walk in the light and in freedom. Satan, your enemy would keep you trapped in defeat; he would have you believe that you are at the mercy of your tongue. He would like you to believe that you cannot control what you say. He deals in lies and deceit – he is the father of lies.

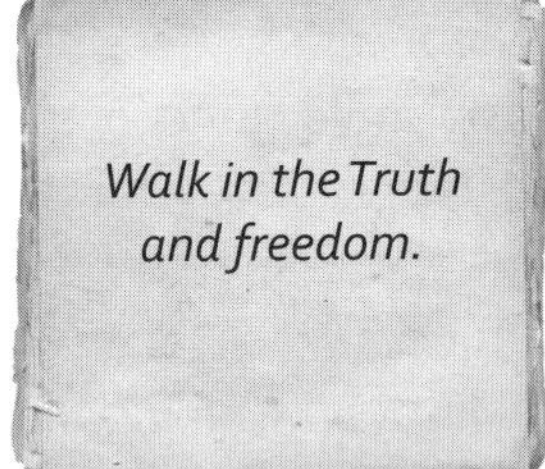

Walk in the Truth and freedom.

Turn your back on the father of lies; firmly and decisively place your trust in the freedom Yeshua has given you.

Prayer

My Father, I bow at Your throne of grace. Thank You that I have been saved from the fiery lake. I walk in the freedom that is mine in Yeshua Christ. Amen.

The wellspring of life

Read Proverbs 4:20-27

Above all else, guard your heart, for it is the wellspring of life. - Proverbs 4:23

The word heart can be supplemented by the word mind in the above text.

Be careful what you put into your mind. What you watch, read and think about are all added into the mix. Your mind does not have a natural filter – it is at the mercy of all the influences, nuances and information that bombards it. We live in the information age. Have you ever stopped to calculate how much information passes through your brain each day? Through the internet, Facebook, Twitter, Mixit, cellular phones, television etc.

I will guard my heart (mind) for it is the wellspring of life.

The water, which comes out of a well, is usually clean, clear and sweet. If your heart is the wellspring of life then what comes out of it is meant to be clean, clear and sweet. Solomon says; *Listen closely to my words. Do not let them out of your sight, keep them within your heart; for they are life to those who find them and health to a man's whole body* (vs 20-22).

Prayer

Heavenly Father, I bow before You. I acknowledge my need and dependence upon You. Thank You for Your wisdom that You freely give to me through Your Word and Your Spirit. Guard, I pray, my heart and mind. Amen.

Confess your sins to God

Read 1 John 1

If we confess our sins, he is faithful and just and will forgive us our sins and purify us from all unrighteousness. - 1 John 1:9

God is a God of light – in Him there is no darkness. Sin flourishes in the darkness. What you think in the privacy of your mind will be the actions that result from your thoughts.

If you dwell on the bad things people have said and done to you, then you will end up a bitter person and your tongue will speak bitter words. If you think impure thoughts and allow them to take root in your mind then it won't be long before your actions and speech reflect these thoughts.

The first step is recognising and admitting that you struggle with your thoughts. Do not hide your sin – do not think that by keeping it in the dark you will be able to either obliterate it or pretend it does not exist. The effect on your thoughts, emotions, and in time your behaviour is not worth it.

He gave me the antidote to my problem with sin; I must confess my sins.

Prayer

My Father, I come before You today, very aware of my need of Your forgiveness. I confess my sins before You. Thank You for Your faithfulness. Thank You that I can trust in You to forgive me and to cleanse me from all unrighteousness. Amen.

Confessing our sins to each other

Read James 4:7-10; 5:13-20

Therefore, confess your sins to each other, and pray for each other so that you may be healed. The prayer of a righteous man is powerful and effective. - James 5:16

Some of you may have drawn the short straw when it came to your earthly family. If this is so you can still rejoice in the fact that you are part of God's family.

Do you seek to be a blessing to your spiritual family? Do your brothers and sisters know that they can come to you if they have a problem? Are they sure that if they share their sin and failure with you that you will keep their confidence? Can they trust you to pray for them – are they confident that whatever they share with you will not be all over the youth group the next week.

Do my brothers and sisters know that I am someone who keeps a guard on my tongue – can they trust me?

Are you the kind of person who, when someone comes to you with their sins, is quick to judge and condemn? Or do you deal gently with the mistakes your brothers and sisters make. Is your one aim to reconcile them to the Lord and restore them to the Christian path?

Prayer

Father, thank You that I am a part of Your family. Help me to be a faithful member of my spiritual family as well as my earthly family. I want to be a blessing and a support to my brothers and sisters. Amen.

25 May

The song of the Lamb

Read Revelation 15:1-8

Great and marvellous are your deeds, Lord God Almighty. Just and true are your ways, King of the ages. Who will not fear you, O Lord, and bring glory to your name? For you alone are holy. All nations will come and worship before you, for your righteous acts have been revealed. - Revelation 15:3b-4

In the years since our accident we have been on a faith journey. As we have walked this road we have grown spiritually as a family in ways we would never have dreamt of before the accident.

One of the lessons we have learnt is the power of praise. We have learnt to sing songs of praise not only when things are going well but also when everything is going wrong.

Praising God will get me through difficult situations, because I know that Yeshua is faithful.

It is wrong to think that you must first gain the victory before you can sing a song of praise to your God. Things work differently in the Kingdom of God. Satan would have us believe that there is nothing to sing about when we are in the heat of battle. This is because he understands better than we do the power of praise; he and his minions are scared of a Christian praising God – because they know that praise unleashes the power of God in a situation. So we are to praise God despite our circumstances.

Prayer

Lord, Yeshua Christ, Lamb of God, I praise and worship You. You are my Lord, my King, my Redeemer! You are holy. You are a great God! You are righteous and faithful. I praise Your great Name! Amen.

God speaks through your mouth

Read Proverbs 16:1-9,23

In his heart a man plans his course, but the Lord determines his steps. A wise man's heart guides his mouth, and his lips promote instructions. - Proverbs 16:9,23

Fifteen year ago, when my husband, Tinus, felt God was telling him to change his lifestyle, I was not serving the Lord. I did not cooperate and missed out on a wonderful time with the Lord.

One day a man came to visit and told Tinus that God wanted him to go back to the city. He said God would show Tinus what to do and bless him. Up to this time God had never spoken through me. Just before we got home Tinus stopped to pray and ask God's guidance.

As we drove I noticed some people busy with a particular task. Suddenly, I called out to Tinus. 'Stop, this is the business that God wants you to be involved in.' No one was more shocked than me. God used my tongue.

I can plan but God will always have the last word.

God uses our tongues to speak direction both in our own lives and in the lives of those around us.

Prayer

Thank You Lord that You are in absolute control of my life. Help me to always first speak to You before I do anything. I acknowledge that it is You who directs my path. I only want Your will for my life. Amen.

27 May

A witness for Christ

Read 2 Thessalonians 1:3-12

On the day he comes to be glorified in his holy people and to be marvelled at among all those who have believed. This includes you, because you believed our testimony to you. - 2 Thessalonians 1:10

We are to use our tongues to be a witness for Christ.

Paul instructs us to proclaim the Gospel, the Word of God to everyone we meet and come into contact with. The Lord Yeshua has given us His Spirit, and it is the Spirit who empowers us to be a witness for Christ. He gives us the power to spread the Good News of Yeshua wherever we go.

If we commit ourselves to the task, asking the Holy Spirit to empower us, then we will have the joy of seeing people come to know Yeshua. We will have the pleasure of introducing them to a life of abundance in the Kingdom of God.

Never forget these words from Romans 10:8-10: *The word is near you; it is in your mouth and in your heart; that is, the word of faith we are proclaiming. That if you confess with your mouth, "Jesus is Lord," and believe in your heart that God raised him from the dead, you will be saved.'*

I will proclaim the Word of God wherever I go – I delight in sharing the Good News of Yeshua Christ, my Redeemer.

Prayer

Lord Yeshua, make me a faithful witness for You. Help me to share the Good News of the Gospel wherever I go. Thank You for the abundant life I enjoy – I want to share this abundance. Empower me through Your Spirit to diligently share the Gospel. Amen.

The power of your words

Read Matthew 17:14-21

He replied, "... I tell you the truth, if you have faith as small as a mustard seed, you can say to this mountain, 'Move from here to there' and it will move. Nothing will be impossible for you." - Matthew 17:20

If you think negative thoughts then your speech will be negative. If you believe you cannot do something and constantly say you cannot do it – then you won't be able to do it.

This was the problem Yeshuas' disciples had in our reading today. They didn't believe that they had the power to cast out demons – and as a result they couldn't do it. What do you think their problem was? They didn't recognise 'Who' their source of power was. They were not plugged in. They walked with Yeshua everyday but did not get that He received His power from His Father. He did nothing in His own strength – He did what the Father told Him to do; therefore He could do anything. Yeshua didn't have faith in faith; He had faith in His Father in heaven.

I can do anything God asks me to through Yeshua Christ who strengthens me. If this is the guiding principle in my life – nothing will be impossible for me.

You can only accomplish the impossible through faith in your Father in heaven, just like Yeshua had.

Prayer

Thank You, Thank You, Father, for your strength and power that flows through me. I walk tall today in the knowledge that You are mightily at work in and through me. Amen.

29 May

The power of prayer

Read Matthew 7:7-12

Ask and it will be given to you; seek and you will find; knock and the door will be opened to you. - Matthew 7:7

The way you choose to communicate in prayer with God is as unique as your relationship with Him. What is important is that you pray. Paul tells us we are to pray without ceasing. Down through history, everyone who accomplished anything of significance for God spent much time in prayer.

Yeshua told us, *if you don't ask you cannot expect to receive?* Sometimes we can have a problem coming to God as our loving Father; particularly if our earthly father was not an easy person to approach. God longs to have you come to Him with your needs. He loves to give you good gifts. God will never give you anything that will harm you.

As the Spirit increasingly controls my life I will use the privilege of prayer to further the Kingdom of God.

Growing in Christ and maturing in our walk with the Lord will result in us spending more time talking with Him. We will begin to understand and appreciate the power of our words as we come to Him in prayer.

Prayer

Father, I come to You in humility and awe. Thank You that You have entrusted the power of prayer to me. Help me to spend time in Your Word. Help me to listen to Your Spirit, and find out what Your will is; so that I can pray the prayers that will bring about powerful answers. Amen.

The power of praise

Read Psalm 145:1-13

I will exalt you, my God the King; I will praise your name forever and ever. - Psalm 145:1

Praising God is one of the joys of being His child. If we are committed to praising God we will find that no matter what we are going through we will experience joy in our lives. This is why the enemy does not want us to praise God. You cannot praise God and be miserable, dissatisfied and unhappy.

Praise and thankfulness are closely linked. There is so much we have to be thankful for – praise is the way to express our thanks for all God does for us. Paul put it so beautifully in Philippians 4:4-9: *Rejoice in the Lord always. I will say it again: Rejoice! Let your gentleness be evident to all. The Lord is near. Do not be anxious about anything, but in everything, by prayer and petition, with thanksgiving, present your requests to God. And the peace of God, which transcends all understanding, will guard your hearts, and your minds in Christ Jesus. Finally, brothers, whatever is true, whatever is noble, whatever is right, whatever is pure, whatever is lovely, whatever is admirable – if anything is excellent or praiseworthy – think about such things. Whatever you have learned or received or heard from me, or seen in me – put it into practice. And the God of peace will be with you.*

> *Praise lifts me out of my circumstances and focuses my mind, heart and mouth upon God.*

This advice from Paul wraps up everything we have spoken about throughout this past month. *Rejoice in the Lord always, I will say it again: Rejoice!*

Prayer

My loving heavenly Father, I bow before You. I praise Your Holy name. I exalt You, I honour You, I worship You. I thank You for every good gift I enjoy from Your hand. I choose today to live a life where my mind and heart are focused upon You. Amen.

Sweeter than honey on the tongue

Read Psalm 119:97-104

How sweet are your words to my taste, sweeter than honey to my mouth!
- Psalm 119:103

Filling your mind, heart and mouth with the Word of God is the best way to ensure that you will have control over your tongue. Read and study the Word of God. You will naturally speak words of blessing as you go through your day.

Think about God's promises, praying them back to God keeps His promises to us. He is a Covenant Keeping God. If He has said it you can believe that He will do it.

God's plan for you is that you will be a blessing. What better way to bless people than to speak and pray God's Word over them.

I will know the sweetness of God's Word not only in my mouth and upon my tongue, but permeating my whole being.

The best way to defeat the devil is to live a life of praise and prayer. Although your tongue is a small part of your body it is very powerful. You choose how this power will be used; for good or for evil.

You have the Holy Spirit dwelling within you – He will lead you and guide you.

Prayer

Dear Father, thank You for Your Word. Thank You that it is like honey in my mouth. As I spend time in Your Word fill me with the power of Your Spirit so that my life can be a blessing to other people. Amen.

Wysheid sê sy stem, soul sal nie sy stem hoor sal nie hy sê sy stem jy in Gees hoor. Seun Samuel hoor God se stem so sag in sy gees. doof is jy wie hewig baie vrank vrees het. wysheid vra sal ons na hom luister? sy woord lei ons, sy Gees lei ons. Wysheid voorsien so in al ons behoeftes. wie sy stem hoor sal hoor "Samuel, samuel jou lewe is in my hande wees oor niks besorg nie" Woord van God sê seun sal gesond word. ek hoor sy stem. baie dankie Yeshua. rut sal sien baie sal God se beloftes waarword.

Letter 6:

Do you hear God's voice?

Wisdom says that man's soul will not hear His voice, but we will hear His voice in our spirit. The boy, Samuel, hears the voice of God so gently in his spirit. Those who are full of fear are deaf to His voice. Wisdom asks us if we will listen to Him. His Word leads us. His Spirit leads us. Wisdom will provide for all our needs. Those who hear His voice will hear: 'Samuel, Samuel, your life is in My hands. Don't worry about anything. The Word of God says the boy will be healed.' I can hear His voice. Thank You so much, Yeshua. Ruth, you will see that God's promises will be fulfilled.

Prayer for June

For this reason, ever since I heard about your faith in the Lord Jesus and your love for all the saints, I have not stopped giving thanks for you, remembering you in my prayers. I keep asking that the God of our Lord Jesus Christ, the glorious Father, may give you the Spirit of wisdom and revelation, so that you may know him better. I pray also that the eyes of your heart may be enlightened in order that you may know the hope to which he has called you, the riches of his glorious inheritance in the saints, and his incomparably great power for us who believe. That power is like the working of his mighty strength, which he exerted in Christ when he raised him from the dead and seated him at his right hand in the heavenly realms, far above all rule and authority, power and dominion, and every title that can be given, not only in the present age but also in the one to come. And God placed all things under his feet and appointed him to be head over everything for the church, which is his body, the fullness of him who fills everything in every way.

Amen.

Ephesians 1:15-23

1 June

My Jehovah Sabaoth

Read Psalm 27

The Lord is my light and my salvation – whom shall I fear? The Lord is the stronghold of my life – of whom shall I be afraid? Wait for the Lord; be strong and take heart and wait for the Lord. - Psalm 27:1,14

Each of us has giants that threaten our lives at some point or another. These giants must be faced up to and slain. In the Bible we read about people who faced giants; such as Joshua, Caleb and David.

I don't know what giants you are facing in your life; but I do know that the same God who helped David slay Goliath is the God who can help you slay your giant.

This month we will explore our giants together. We will bring them before Jehovah Sabaoth – the Lord of Hosts. He is the God who will fight for you and give you the victory. He will give us the strategy just as He gave a strategy to Joshua and David. He will tell you exactly how to defeat your Goliath. Trust your deep wounds of the soul to Him today – He is also Jehovah Rapha – the Lord who heals.

Jehovah Sabaoth – the Lord of Hosts. He is the God who will fight for me and give me the victory.

Prayer

My Jehovah Sabaoth, thank You that You are my Lord of Hosts. I am so grateful that as I face the giants in my life I face them with You at my side. I trust You as I enter this battle. Amen.

Scouting the Land

Read Numbers 13:1-24

When Moses sent them to explore Caanan, he said, "Go up through the Negev and on into the hill country. See what the land is like and whether the people who live there are strong or weak, few or many." - Numbers 13:17-18

The Israelites were on a journey to the Promised Land, Canaan. They had witnessed the plagues, and the parting of the Red Sea. Yet, whenever they faced a challenge they immediately assumed the worst. Their default reaction was to grumble and moan, testing God.

They were about to enter the Promised Land. God told Moses to send twelve spies to scout out the land of Canaan. In verse 18 to 20 Moses instructs them.

I need to take stock of the land where my giants live. The best place to do my assessment is in the presence of God and the Holy Spirit.

We need to take stock of the land where our giants live. Before you can advance against your giant you have to acknowledge it. Once you have acknowledged it then your Commander-in-Chief can begin giving you a war strategy. You don't have to be afraid when you are in the presence of God, your Father. He is on your side and if He is on your side then you do not need to fear anything or anyone.

Prayer

Dear Lord, thank You that You are with me as I scout out the land where my giants live. Thank You that I have Your Holy Spirit within me, leading, guiding and directing me. Amen

Beyond your giants is the Promised Land

Read Numbers 13:25-33

Then Caleb silenced the people before Moses and said, "We should go up and take possession of the land, for we can certainly do it." But the men who had gone up with him said; "We can't attack those people; they are stronger than we are."
- Numbers 13:30-31

Twelve men went to spy out Canaan. Two saw giants, but believed that with God's help they could take the land. The other ten saw only problems, difficulties and giants; they became scared and incited the other Israelites to rebel.

Their rebellion resulted in the Children of Israel wandering in the desert for forty years.

We have a choice: Are we going to face up to our giants believing that God, our Father, can give us victory? Or are we going to be like the ten spies and turn away thinking that we can never conquer the land.

I am going to face up to my giants believing that God my Father can give me victory?

When you face your giants do you doubt like the ten or do you have faith like Caleb and Joshua? Do you remember all the things God has done for you in the past? As you remember these instances do they fill you with faith and confidence in your God?

Prayer

Dear Father God, You love me just as You loved the Children of Israel. You will show Yourself mighty to save me just as You were mighty to save them. Help me, I pray, to trust You. Help me to choose to believe that You can give me victory. Amen.

The Promised Land: Or the wilderness?

Read Numbers 14:1-23,30

But now, I pray, let the power of the Lord be great, just as You hast declared, The Lord is slow to anger and abundant in lovingkindness, forgiving iniquity and transgression. Pardon, I pray, the iniquity of this people according to the greatness of Your lovingkindness, just as You also have forgiven this people, from Egypt even until now.
- Numbers 14:17-18a,19 (New American Standard Bible)

Moses interceded on behalf of Israel reminding God that He is a loving and forgiving God. As a result of Moses' prayer God relented. He didn't annihilate them; instead their punishment was that none of the men would see the Promised Land. Only Joshua and Caleb would go in, because they chose to believe.

Is my unbelief and disobedience causing me to choose captivity?

Your giant might be illness, drugs, alcohol or maybe family problems, to name some possibilities. Whatever your giant, your God is greater. Instead of running away from God, choose to run toward Him. He will not let you down. The children of Israel disbelieved and disobeyed God, because they had never dealt with the root of their problem; their hearts were easily turned.

It is the same with us; we must deal with the root of our problems. Admit your heart problem today, come to God and through Yeshua receive His forgiveness and loving-kindness.

Prayer

My loving Father, thank You that You have made a way for me to come into Your presence – thank You that I can come in the name of Yeshua, my Saviour. I pray that You will give me a steadfast, obedient heart. Amen.

5 June

Taking God at His Word

Read Joshua 1:1-9

Have I not commanded you? Be strong and courageous. Do not be terrified; do not be discouraged, for the Lord your God will be with you wherever you go. - Joshua 1:9

Joshua was the new leader of Israel, and God promised him, *"As I was with Moses, so I will be with you; I will never leave you nor forsake you"* (v 5b).

God tells Joshua *"Do not let this Book of the Law depart from your mouth; meditate on it day and night, so that you may be careful to do everything written in it"* (v 8). If he was going to have victory he needed to know the Word, live the Word and believe the Word. As he prepared to go into the Promised Land and face the giants he needed to be armed with the Word of God.

God is telling me to be strong and courageous because He will give me victory.

If we are going to face our giants we need to know God's Word. If you don't know His promises then how are you going to be able to believe and trust Him? How are you going to be able to obey Him if you don't know what His commands are?

Like Joshua, God says He will be with you. He is telling you to be strong and courageous because He will give you victory.

Prayer

Dear Father, thank You for Your wonderful promises in Your Word. Thank You that in Your Word you tell me what You want me to do. Help me to spend time in Your Word so that I can be strong and courageous. Amen.

Preparing to cross Jordan

Read Joshua 1:10-18

Remember the command that Moses the servant of the Lord gave you: "The Lord your God is giving you rest and has granted you this land." - Joshua 1:13

Joshua told the people to put on their full armour and take up their weapons; in three days they would cross the Jordan and enter the Promised Land. It was time for them to stop wandering around in the desert.

Have you been wandering around in your own desert? Is it time for you to cross your Jordan. It takes faith to do this; so often it is easier to stay where you are. What is staring at you from the other side of your Jordan? What are your giants – the things you are scared of facing?

He promises you rest and victory on the other side of your Jordan. Put on your armour, take up your weapons and prepare yourself for battle. Your armour is the Word of God; your weapons are the power of the Holy Spirit.

The battle belongs to the Lord; but you must to take the first step.

> *The battle belongs to the Lord; but I must to take the first step.*

Prayer

Lord God, thank You that You are a mighty God. Your arm is not too short to save me. I face my giants with the full force of Your strength behind me. In faith I take the first step today. Amen.

God's unconventional protection

Read Joshua 2

[Rahab] said to them: "I know that the Lord has given this land to you and that a great fear of you has fallen on us ... We have heard how the Lord dried up the water of the Red Sea for you when you came out of Egypt ... When we heard of it, our hearts melted and everyone's courage failed because of you, for the Lord your God is God in heaven above and on the earth below." - Joshua 2:9a,10a,11

The two spies who went into Jericho hid in Rahab's home. The king heard about this and he wanted Rahab to betray them, instead she hid them on her roof. They promised to protect her and her family when the Israelites took the City. Rahab firmly believed that God would give the Israelites victory and that they would take the City. God used Rahab to remind them of what He had done for them in the past.

As I prepare to face my giants I can be confident that the Lord will protect me.

She used a red cord to lower them over the wall. This cord can be compared to the thread of salvation that runs throughout the Bible. Jesus is our Salvation – it is through Him that we are rescued from the darkness and brought into the light.

As you prepare to face your giants be confident that the Lord will protect you. Remember what He has done for you in the past. He will give you everything you need.

Prayer

My Father, thank You for Your protection in my life. I am so grateful that as I face the giants in my life, You provide all that I need. I thank You for the salvation that is mine in Jesus. Amen.

Crossing the Jordan

Read Joshua 3

And as soon as the priests who carry the ark of the Lord – the Lord of all the earth – set foot in the Jordan, its waters flowing downstream will be cut off and stand up in a heap. The priests who carried the ark of the covenant of the Lord stood firm on dry ground in the middle of the Jordan, while all Israel passed by until the whole nation had completed the crossing on dry ground. - Joshua 3:13,17

The Israelites had to walk through water for the second time – this time into the Promised Land. Each person had to step into the river to get to the other side. As human beings we are generally scared of the unknown.

It is interesting that the giants on the other side of the river were already defeated – Rahab told the spies that the fear of the Lord had come upon the people of Jericho. They were defeated before the Israelites crossed the River Jordan.

It is not who or what my giants are that matters; what matters is that the God I serve does not change.

Your giants are scared of the Name of the Lord. They know that you serve the Almighty God.

As you step into the river God will honour your faith. Crossing Jordan for us represents placing our giants at the feet of the cross. It is not who or what your giants are that matters; what matters is that the God you serve is the same yesterday, today and tomorrow.

Prayer

Lord, give me the courage to take the first step into the river. Thank You that You will take my hand and lead me step by step as I cross my Jordan River. Thank You that when my giants are viewed in the light of Your might they become insignificant. Amen.

9 June

An altar of remembrance

Read Joshua 4

And Joshua set up at Gilgal the twelve stones they had taken out of the Jordan. He said to the Israelites, "In the future when your descendants ask their fathers, 'What do these stones mean?' tell them, 'Israel crossed the Jordan on dry ground.' For the Lord your God dried up the Jordan before you until you had crossed over. The Lord your God did to the Jordan just what he had done to the Red Sea when he dried it up before us until we had crossed over. He did this so that all the peoples of the earth might know that the hand of the Lord is powerful and so that you might always fear the Lord your God." - Joshua 4:20-24

People in the Old Testament built 'altars of remembrance' at places where significant events took place. It reminded the people of what God had done for them in the past when they faced difficult situations.

The purpose of my altar of remembrance is that I might know that the hand of the Lord is powerful.

Why don't you start an 'altar of remembrance' – list each time God has undertaken for you. Make a note of the date and write a short description of what God did. Continue to add to the list as you walk with the Lord. You will be able to look at your list and know that you can trust God to have a plan.

The purpose of your 'altar of remembrance' is, in the final analysis, the same as that of the children of Israel: *So that* **(put your name here)** *might know that the hand of the Lord is powerful and so* that **(again put your name here)** *might always fear the Lord your God.*

Prayer

My Father God, thank You that You are a faithful God. I stand amazed as I look back over my life and I see so many occasions where You have undertaken for me. Thank You that Your hand is powerful to save me. Amen.

Circumcision of the heart

Read Joshua 5:1-15

Now when all the Amorite kings west of the Jordan and all the Canaanite kings along the coast heard how the Lord had dried up the Jordan before the Israelites until we had crossed over, their hearts melted and they no longer had the courage to face the Israelites. - Joshua 5:1

All the Children of Israel had to do was obey God. They crossed over the river and they built an altar of remembrance. God re-established His covenant with Israel by having Joshua circumcise the people.

We are part of the new covenant; you need to come before God asking Him to do a circumcision of your heart – confess your sins before Him asking Him to cleanse your heart and renew it. Then your heart will be pure and open to receive from the Lord.

> *I will find that my giants will diminish in size as my image of my God grows.*

Verse 8 tells us that after the circumcision they remained in the camp until they were healed. After God has circumcised your heart you need to take the time to heal – allowing God to minister to you through His Holy Spirit. He will bring healing to you and fortify you for the battle ahead. You will find that your giants will diminish in size as your image of your God grows.

Prayer

My loving heavenly Father, thank You for Your new covenant. I come before You in humility today, asking You to circumcise my heart. Give me a new heart that is wholly Yours, I pray. Amen.

11 June

The fall of Jericho

Read Joshua 6:1-21

When the trumpets sounded, the people shouted, and at the sound of the trumpet, when the people gave a loud shout, the wall collapsed; so every man charged straight in, and they took the city. - Joshua 6:20

God's strategy for taking the city of Jericho was unusual. They walked silently around the wall once a day for six days, only the priests blew their trumpets. On the seventh day, they marched six times and on the seventh time they shouted and the walls fell down – just like that.

They entered the city and vanquished the people – no one resisted. The insurmountable giants offered no resistance. The barrier of the wall that kept the children of Israel out of Jericho just crumbled in front of them and became a heap of stones.

The secret of my victory is that I must believe that God can do what He says He can do.

Have you learnt any lessons as we have looked at the giants faced by the Children of Israel? What are the giants you are facing today? Has the enemy made you believe that you cannot defeat them?

This is a lie from the enemy – God has a plan for you – His plan is that you should be free.

Prayer

Father, thank You for Your Word, which encourages, instructs and teaches me. I am so grateful that the giants in my life are only as big as I allow them to be. Build my faith, help me to trust You. Lord I realise that as I walk this road with You – You will give me the plan and the victory. Amen.

God fulfils His promise

Read Joshua 6:22-27

But Joshua spared Rahab the prostitute, with her family and all who belonged to her, because she hid the men Joshua had sent as spies to Jericho – and she lives among the Israelites to this day. - Joshua 6:25

God honoured Rahab; she and her whole family were saved, and lived in the midst of the Children of Israel.

Rahab married into a respected family and she found a prominent place in the history of salvation; she is the great-great grandmother of David and she is mentioned in Yeshua's lineage. In Hebrews chapter eleven Rahab is found in the Bible's 'Hall of Fame' along with Enoch, Abraham, Joseph, Moses and David to mention just a few.

Every day we must choose if we believe God or the devil. Choosing God means you believe and act on what God is saying to you. You cannot face and slay your giants if you do not follow His instructions.

Faith is active not passive. Rahab taught us you have to act on your faith. You have to put your foot into the river. Don't miss out on fulfilling your destiny because of fear and unbelief.

I don't want to miss out on fulfilling my destiny because of fear and unbelief.

Prayer

Lord, forgive my unbelief, forgive my fear, forgive my disobedience, I pray. Thank You for Your grace and mercy. Help me to be a doer as well as a hearer of Your Word, dear Lord. Amen.

Fulfil your promise

Read Judges 2:1-18

The people served the Lord throughout the lifetime of Joshua and of the elders who outlived him and who had seen all the great things the Lord had done for Israel. Joshua son of Nun, the servant of the Lord, died at the age of a hundred and ten ... After that whole generation had been gathered to their fathers, another generation grew up, who knew neither the Lord nor what he had done for Israel. - Judges 2:7-8,10

While the children of Israel had strong leaders they served God; then as soon as that leader died or circumstances changed they turned away from God. They continually tested God and He continually forgave them.

When Joshua and the elders died the Bible says; *another generation grew up, who knew neither the Lord nor what he had done for Israel.* Isn't this sad? Their forefathers had slain giants and they had witnessed God undertaking and giving them victory in miraculous ways.

The choice to serve and honour God with my life ultimately rests with me.

As a young person you need to ask yourself the question; do you have respect for your heritage? There are times when we need to rise above the bad things in our family heritage – but we must be careful to respect what is good.

The choice to serve and honour God with your life ultimately rests with you. It doesn't matter what your earthly family is like – you belong to a heavenly family.

Prayer

My Father, I come before you in humility confessing that I am so often no different to the children of Israel. It is all too easy for me to get side tracked. I choose to serve You and honour You today. Amen.

Victory despite your fear

Read Judges 6-7

When the angel of the Lord appeared to Gideon, he said, "The Lord is with you, mighty warrior." The Lord turned to him and said, "Go in the strength you have and save Israel out of Midian's hand. Am I not sending you?" "But Lord," Gideon asked, "how can I save Israel? My clan is the weakest in Manasseh, and I am the least in my family."
- Judges 6:12,14-15

Gideon was an unlikely giant-slayer: he was not a very brave young man. He, along with all the Israelites, had completely forgotten what God had done for their forefathers. God spoke to Gideon addressing him as a mighty warrior – God clearly saw in him something that he did not see in himself.

Don't run away; trust God with your fears today. You can kill your giants despite your fear, as long as you bring your fears to the Lord, and allow Him to deal with them. God made sure that when Gideon attacked the Midianites with only three hundred men Israel would know who gave them the victory.

I won't let the enemy sidetrack me with my fears – I will trust my God.

Together with God you can be a mighty warrior; you can vanquish your giants in the Name of the Lord, who is mighty to save. Bring your fears to Him and trust Him today. Don't let the enemy sidetrack you with your fears – trust your God.

Prayer

Almighty God, I bow in awe and wonder before You. I acknowledge Your great power and might. I place my fears at your feet and ask You to fill me with Your valour and courage. Like Gideon I realise that I cannot do this without You – but with You I can overcome anything. Amen.

15 June

The heart of a giant slayer

Read 1 Samuel 16:4-13

The Lord does not look at the things man looks at. Man looks at the outward appearance, but the Lord looks at the heart. - 1 Samuel 16:7b

Gideon and David were both the youngest children in their families – no one really took them seriously. They were almost invisible to their parents and siblings.

God chose David instead of his brothers to be the chosen king, even though they looked good. God tells Samuel: *The Lord does not look at the things man looks at. Man looks at the outward appearance, but the Lord looks at the heart.* We are also often impressed with how people look.

If I want to have the heart of a giant-slayer I need to know the One who gives me the victory.

However, God was looking for a king who would listen to Him, who understood what it meant to spend time in His presence, and who had the heart of a giant-slayer.

David learnt to trust God each day in the fields looking after the sheep. If you want to have the heart of a giant-slayer you need to know the One who gives you the victory. You cannot easily trust someone you do not know.

Prayer

Dear Father, You are a great and wonderful God. I praise You and worship You. I want to have a heart that is tender towards You. I want to be someone who is known to be wholeheartedly committed to You. Strengthen me, I pray, in my walk with You. Amen.

Don't give your giants legal entry

Read 1 Samuel 17:10-11, 20-30

Then the Philistine said, "This day I defy the ranks of Israel! Give me a man and let us fight each other." On hearing the Philistine's words, Saul and all the Israelites were dismayed and terrified. - 1 Samuel 17:10-11

The Philistine's were tormenting the Israelites. Our giants will torment us, just as Goliath tormented the Israelites, if we do not obey God. There are so many people who are being tormented by the giants in their lives because they have given them legal entry.

After the accident Aldo had a shunt in his brain that caused him to have epileptic fits. We looked for the cause of this; I realised that there were family roots – soul ties – that had to be dealt with.
I began rebuilding of our family's walls. When I began this process the enemy tormented me in the same way as Goliath taunted the Children of Israel.

I would give up. Like David, God prepared my heart to meet the giant. Don't be put off. There will be people who will try to discourage you; reject what they say; stand firm in the knowledge that your God is for you.

People will try to discourage me but I will stand firm in the knowledge that my God is for me.

Prayer

My Father God, all powerful King of this universe! Who can stand against You? I go forth into battle in Your mighty Name. I am strong in You. My heart is wholly Yours – I claim the victory in You! Amen.

Preparing to slay Goliath

Read 1 Samuel 17:31-40

"The Lord who delivered me from the paw of the lion and the paw of the bear will deliver me from the hand of this Philistine." Saul said to David, "Go, and the Lord be with you." - 1 Samuel 17:37

No one was prepared to stand up to Goliath. They were thinking about doing it in their own strength – they were operating in the soul dimension and not in the Spirit.

How then does one slay the giants – like depression and other things that torment us? How do you come up with a strategy? The truth is you don't. You can't win in the natural; they can only be overcome in the Spirit. David was anointed of God; he understood his position in the Lord. He was prepared for his destiny. He had learnt to trust God when God helped him slay a lion and a bear.

David drew on his knowledge and experience of God.

It is the same with us; if we walk with Him and spend time with Him then when the battle looms we will fall back on what we know of Him. This is what David did; he drew on his knowledge and experience of God.

Prayer

Father, what a faithful God You are! You invite me to walk with You day by day, so that You can teach me and fellowship with me. When the battle comes I run to You, I trust in Your strategy – not the strategies of people. Amen.

The battle commences

Read 1 Samuel 17:41-48

...I come against you in the name of the Lord Almighty, the God of the armies of Israel... This day the Lord will hand you over to me, and I'll strike you down and cut off your head... for the battle is the Lord's, and he will give all of you into our hands.
- 1 Samuel 17:45b,46a,47b

David was twelve when God started training him for this day. Unlike the rest of the Israelite army David believed God would deliver Goliath into his hands. God prepared him through the lesser battles of fighting the lion and the bear. These victories built up his faith in God and gave him the courage he needed. In later years God referred to David as a man after His own heart.

Declare like David: The battle is the Lord's and He will give it into my hands!

Does the story of David build up your faith? Are you inspired by his trust and confidence in his God? As you face your giants you can know the same God who helped David will help you. He will give you the victory no matter what the size of the giant you face. Choose today to be like David – confidently believing that God will undertake. Declare like David: **The battle is the Lord's and He will give you into my hands!**

Prayer

Lord, God of Hosts, Commander of the armies of heaven. Thank You that You are on my side. Thank You that I fight in Your army. Nothing and no one can stand against You. Amen.

19 June

The battle is won

Read 1 Samuel 17:46-58

This day the Lord will hand you over to me, and I'll strike you down and cut off your head. Today I will give the carcasses of the Philistine army to the birds of the air and the beasts of the earth, and the whole world will know that there is a God in Israel.

- 1 Samuel 17:46

David won the spiritual battle long before he went out onto the battle field to slay Goliath. The same is true for us. Our spiritual battle was won at Calvary – Yeshua won the ultimate battle for you and me. It is because of Him that we can face our giants and win. In Yeshua we have the victory.

David went out in the strength and might of the Lord. He shot the stone and it hit its mark and Goliath collapsed in a heap. Then David took Goliath's sword and cut off his head. David didn't stop half way. He made sure that the giant was properly dead. We often stop half way and then the same problem comes back and we wonder why.

I will make sure that when I slay my giant I cut off its head; I won't allow it to come back and cause trouble for me.

Make sure that when you slay your giant you cut off its head; don't allow it to come back and cause trouble for you.

Prayer

Father God, in the midst of battle You are there. Thank You that when the battle rages I have already won. The giants are just making a noise; but I know that You have already given me the victory. Give me the courage to finish the job. Amen.

The results of victory

Read Hebrews 11:30-34 & Psalm 138:1-2

[I] will praise your name for your love and your faithfulness, for you have exalted above all things your name and your word. - Psalm 138:2b

Our actions also have consequences for other people. God will use you if you are open and available to Him to win battles for your family or friends. Know that if God calls you to do this He will give you the victory.

We battled Aldo's giants for seven years. The accident trauma gave his giants a hold over him and affected our whole family. It took ongoing prayer. God showed us that there were things in our family history that had to be removed. We prayed and victory came. We rebuilt the walls around our family. God began to bring healing into his life and also to our family.

God will use me if I am open and available to Him to win battles for my family.

God will do the same for you and your family. Do not despair if you are in the midst of the battle. God will show you a plan of action. He will direct you to do what is necessary to slay your giants.

Prayer

Father thank You so much for Your never ending love and commitment to me; and those that I love and care about. I commit my family to You; help me to faithfully intercede and fight for them. I know You love them much more than I can ever love them. Amen.

21 June

Principle 1: Training

Read Psalm 18:1-2, 30-40, 49-50

He trains my hands for battle; my arms can bend a bow of bronze. - Psalm 18:34

We must be trained for the battle. I have always believed that God uses everything, which happens to us, to prepare us for the next phase of our lives. He uses all of our experiences and makes them profitable and useful as we serve Him.

God used Joshua's faithfulness to lead the children of Israel into the Promised Land and to victory over the City of Jericho. Gideon was an introverted young man; God referred to him as a mighty warrior and he rose to fulfil this title. His obedience was rewarded.

David is our prime example of training for the task. David faithfully did what he was called to do; learning the lessons God sent his way day by day.

Like an athlete, you have to be fit and ready. Like a soldier you have to be battle ready; you do this through spending time in God's Word, prayer and walking in the Spirit.

How battle ready am I today. Am I fit, trained and available for God to use me in battle?

Prayer

Dear Father, You are my Rock, my Fortress and my Deliverer. I take refuge in You. Train my arm for battle, I pray. Make me fit and ready to follow Your orders. Thank You that You give me victory. Amen.

22 June

Principle 2: Confidence

Read Psalm 118:1-14

The Lord is with me; I will not be afraid. What can man do to me? The Lord is with me; he is my helper. I will look in triumph on my enemies. - Psalm 118:6

Joshua had confidence in his God. When he went into Canaan with Caleb to spy out the land for Moses, he went in the confidence of his God. Gideon, although he was a very reluctant hero, when he took up God's challenge, he went forward in the confidence of God. David learnt his confidence in God out in the fields. He certainly never got his confidence from his family.

I have learnt in my own life that when I trust in Jesus, and walk in the fullness of what is mine in Him, then I am confident. I can pray for those who oppose me, I can bless them, asking God to redeem them. As I do this I see them fleeing from me. On the other hand if I live in fear, or if I trust in myself and become filled with pride, then I have no power and my enemies can walk all over me.

My confidence is in the Lord! I will triumph over my enemies.

Prayer

My Father God, I am so privileged to be Your child. Thank You for the many blessings that are mine. I am so grateful that I can approach Your throne of grace with confidence knowing that I am welcome in Your presence. Amen.

Principle 3: Armour

Read Ephesians 6:10-18

Therefore put on the full armour of God, so that when the day of evil comes, you may be able to stand your ground and after you have done everything, to stand.

- Ephesians 6:13

God's armour and the weapons He uses are not those the world chooses. He told Joshua to walk around the city of Jericho. On the seventh day the people shouted and the walls tumbled down. This was very unorthodox.

Gideon's army were armed with trumpets and torches when they defeated the Midianites. David used his bare hands to kill a bear and a lion. He killed Goliath with a sling and five stones. This was more than enough to bring Goliath down.

I have to be clothed in His armour; with His strategy clearly in place. Then I can be sure that I will have the victory.

We must use God's weapons to defeat our giants. You have to fight giants in the Spirit, not in the natural. Many people have tried to fight the battle in their own strength and they have failed.

You have to put on the whole armour of God. Every knee will bow at the name of Yeshua; no foe will be able to stand against the might of God's Name.

Prayer

My Father God, thank You that You give me all the weapons I need to face and fight my giants. I am grateful that if I walk with You, remain in Your Spirit, and wear Your armour I will have victory every time. Amen.

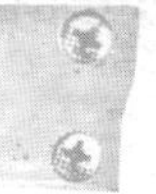

Prayer is the key

Read Ephesians 6:10-18

And pray in the Spirit on all occasions with all kinds of prayers and requests. With this in mind, be alert and always keep on praying for all the saints. - Ephesians 6:18

I was not getting anywhere with slaying my giants because I was trying to do it in my own strength. I knew the right things to do and I was trying to do them – without success. Eventually it became clear to me that I would never succeed until I surrendered to my Father and allowed Him to do it for me.

When I realised this I repented before my Father. He showed me that I needed to rely upon His Spirit. I prayed in the Spirit; Romans 8 tells us the Spirit knows the mind of the Father; therefore the Spirit knows exactly what to pray. In the book of James we read the prayer of a righteous person has great effect.

It is the Spirit who will give me the strategy that God has for me to defeat my giant.

We must walk in the Spirit – day by day, moment by moment. It is the Spirit who will communicate the Father's heart to each one of us.

Prayer

My Father God, I am grateful for Your great love for me. Thank You that I can live in Your Kingdom. Help me to walk and live in Your Spirit, day by day and moment by moment. Amen.

25 June

Humility is a key

Read 1 Peter 5

Humble yourselves, therefore, under God's mighty hand, that he may lift you up in due time. Cast all your anxiety on him because he cares for you. - 1 Peter 5:6-7

Our family has fought the giants who have tried to destroy us, and we have helped Aldo deal with his giants. It has been painful and difficult; but God, our Father, has led us each step of the way.

1 Peter 5 says; *be alert and of sober mind. Your enemy the devil prowls around like a roaring lion looking for someone to devour* (v 8). Notice it says 'like' – this means he has the appearance of; the reality is his teeth were removed at Calvary.

Resist him, standing firm in the faith... (v 9). When I realised where Aldo's problems originated I came before my Father in humility. It wasn't instant victory – but Peter again is a huge encouragement as he tells us: *And the God of all grace, who called you to his eternal glory in Christ, after you have suffered a little while, will himself restore you and make you strong, firm and steadfast* (v 10).

If my walls are secure; my gates reinforced – the devil cannot get in. I won't let him fool me – I will deal with him instead.

Prayer

My Father God, I come before Your throne of grace with a humble heart and a contrite spirit. Thank You that Yeshua gained the victory for me on Calvary over my enemy, the devil. I stand in that victory today. Amen.

26 June

Love is a key

Read 2 Peter 1:1-11

For this very reason, make every effort to add to your faith goodness; and to goodness, knowledge, and to knowledge, self-control; and to self-control, perseverance; and to perseverance, godliness; and to godliness, brotherly kindness; and to brotherly kindness, love. For if you possess these qualities in increasing measure, they will keep you from being ineffective and unproductive in your knowledge of our Lord Jesus Christ. - 2 Peter 1:5-8

Living in the Kingdom of God means you live a life of love. Yeshua taught us by example to love others even when they don't deserve it. It is totally impossible to do it in the natural but in the Spirit we are more than able.

I realised that I had to love the people who had harmed Aldo. God told me that I could not do it on my own. I had to surrender to Him; I had to allow Him to love through me.

> *I cannot love on my own. I will surrender to Him and allow Him to love through me.*

Once I surrendered, God worked in our whole family. If you want to slay your goliath you have to start by loving your enemies. Only then will the Spirit of God be able to work in you. Peter tells us; *if anyone does not have them* (the qualities mentioned in verses five to eight), *they are short-sighted and blind, and has forgotten that he has been cleansed from past sins* (v 9).

Prayer

Father, I confess my inability to love those who have hurt me. I humbly come before You, I know that in my own strength I will never be able to do it. I surrender to Your Spirit. Help me Yeshua, my Saviour, to have Your love for other people. Amen.

27 June

Truth is a key

Read John 8:31-36; 16:7-15

But when he, the Spirit of truth, comes, he will guide you into all truth. He will not speak on his own; he will speak only what he hears, and he will tell you what is yet to come. He will bring glory to me by taking from what is mine and making it known to you. - John 16:13-14

Living in God's Kingdom means walking in the Truth; and bringing our lives into the light of God's Word.

Keeping corners hidden gives the devil a foothold. This is what had happened when Aldo hid his hurt deep inside himself. As this hurt lingered in the dark places they turned to bitterness and gave the enemy a foothold. As I dealt with my own dark places I had to bring them into the light. I had to expose them to the Spirit of Truth; asking the Holy Spirit to cleanse and clean out the dark spaces. As they became filled with the Light I was able to become effective in my prayers and petitions before my Father.

I will invite the Spirit of Truth to come in and clean the dark places. I will allow the pure Light of God to shine in and set me free.

Yeshua promised us freedom. It is your inheritance as a child of God; to walk in Truth and to walk in freedom. You can only do this when the Spirit of Truth has access to every area of your life.

Prayer

My heavenly Father, I come to You acknowledging that I need Your Spirit of Truth to shine Your light of Truth into each and every dark corner of my life. I want to walk in Your Truth, I want to live in Your Kingdom where there is light and life. Amen.

Blessing is a key

Read Luke 6:20-38

But I say to you who hear, love your enemies, do good to those who hate you, bless those who curse you, pray for those who mistreat you. Whoever hits you on the cheek, offer him the other also; and whoever takes away our coat, do not withhold your shirt from him either. - Luke 6:27-29 (New American Standard Bible)

God said that I must bless the people who had harmed us. This was not a concept I could easily understand. As a mother my natural instincts were to reach out and fight to protect my child. As I surrendered my inability to love these people to Him; He loved them through me, and my heart began to change.

God's blessing is a powerful weapon in my hands – when used in the power of the Holy Spirit it can set people free.

The more I blessed them the stronger I became in my ability to fight the battle against Aldo's giants. When we come to God in humility allowing His love to work in our lives, and His Truth to cleanse us, we are able to bless those who curse us. We realise that we cannot withhold the blessing of God from other people.

We do not fight with the weapons that the world fights with. Our weapons are humility, love, truth, speaking out blessing, to name some. These are the weapons of the Kingdom of God.

Prayer

My God, You are a Mighty God. Your Kingdom is an everlasting Kingdom. None can stand against it. The weapons of my warfare are powerful to bring down strongholds. Thank You that my giants cannot stand against these weapons. Amen.

Spiritual warfare is a key

Read 2 Corinthians 10:1-5

For though we walk in the flesh we do not war according to the flesh, for the weapons of our warfare are not of the flesh but divinely powerful for the destruction of fortresses. We are destroying speculations and every lofty thing raised up against the knowledge of God, and we are taking every thought captive to the obedience of Christ. - 2 Corinthians 10:3-5 (New American Standard Version)

When Aldo began having epileptic fits I did not believe in soul ties. Aldo had been deeply hurt by things people had said to him. We are still working through the layers of pain and hurt. He refers to it as his 'deep, deep hurt'. God showed me that I could not fight this battle in the natural it had to be fought in the Spirit; it was spiritual warfare.

As I walk this path and fight this battle; my weapons are not the weapons of the world.

We also dealt with the generational curses that gave the enemy a foothold. Aldo's trauma meant that he was susceptible to being affected by these curses. Again these could only be dealt with in the Spirit.

We are still on our journey; Aldo daily amazes me as he lives so close to the Father. He has a pure love for Yeshua that shines out of his writing and his life. God is restoring him and we are rejoicing in God's goodness.

Prayer

Dear Lord God, thank You that I have weapons fashioned not according to the world but rather according to Your Kingdom. They are powerful and mighty in the pulling down of strongholds. Thank You for victory in Yeshua, Your Son. Amen.

Victory in Jesus

Read Hebrews 12:1-13

For this reason, ever since I heard about your faith in the Lord Jesus and your love for all the saints, I have not stopped giving thanks for you, remembering you in my prayers. I keep asking that the God of our Lord Jesus Christ, the glorious Father, may give you the Spirit of wisdom and revelation, so that you may know him better. I pray also that the eyes of your heart may be enlightened in order that you may know the hope to which he has called you, the riches of his glorious inheritance in the saints, and his incomparably great power for us who believe. That power is like the working of his mighty strength, which he exerted in Christ when he raised him from the dead and seated him at his right hand in the heavenly realms, far above all rule and authority, power and dominion, and every title that can be given, not only in the present age but also in the one to come. And God placed all things under his feet and appointed him to be head over everything for the church which is his body, the fullness of him who fills everything in every way. Ephesians 1:15-23

I have a great crowd of witnesses cheering for me – I fix my eyes upon Jesus – I slay my giant!

Samuel se liefde vir sy Koning
is wat samuel so laat
vashou. Is so lief vir
yeshua. hy sien seun
rus in sy liefde. rooi is
hart van Samuel, so rooi.
wie hom liefhet is wie
vrank bitter vry is. Jy
huil, wie huil sal sien
hy vee ons trane af.
Samuel is gunse wese
so lief vir God. bou
van muur om samuel
se soul het hom gehelp.
vannou af sal Samuel
vure van satan wurg
met God se liefde.
Seën jou vyand Samuel,
seën, seën is liefde.

Letter 7:

A burning love for the King

Samuel's love for his King is what keeps him holding on. I love Yeshua so much. Yeshua can see that I rest in His love. Samuel's heart is so red [covered by the blood of the Lamb]. Those who love Him are those who are free from bitterness. You are crying. He will wipe away the tears of those who cry. Samuel loves God with his entire being. The wall that was built around Samuel's soul helped him against the enemy. From now on Samuel will strangle the fire of the enemy with God's love. Bless your enemies, Samuel. To bless is to love.

Kingdom Principles

Prayer for July

My Father God, I come before You at the beginning of this new month; as we start this second half of this year. I am so grateful that I am Your child and that You love me with an everlasting love. You have planted the seed of Your Kingdom within my heart; I realise that the responsibility is mine to water, fertilise and nurture this seed. I cannot do it in my own strength though; I need Your Holy Spirit to empower me. I bow before You, I worship You, I praise You. Father, I love and adore You, help me to be faithful to all that You have entrusted me with. Teach me Your ways; teach me the principles of Your Kingdom; and help me to live in the fullness of what it means to be a citizen of heaven.
Amen.

1 July

Keys of the Kingdom

Read Matthew 16:13-20

I will give you the keys of the kingdom of heaven; whatever you bind on earth will be bound in heaven, and whatever you loose on earth will be loosed in heaven.
- Matthew 16:19

In Matthew 16 when Yeshua asked His disciples; who do people say the Son of Man is? Their answer is interesting – *Some say John the Baptist; others say Elijah; and still others, Jeremiah or one of the prophets.* These were evasion tactics; but Yeshua does not let them off the hook. Again he asks – Who do you say I am?

At last Peter gets it – he professes; *You are the Christ, the Son of the living God.* Peter nails his colours to the mast. Yeshua commends Peter and tells him that He will give him the keys of the kingdom of heaven. Yeshua says; *whatever you bind on earth will be bound in heaven, and whatever you loose on earth will be loosed in heaven* (v 19b).

As a child of God the keys of the Kingdom are yours if you diligently seek them and learn to use them.

As a child of God the keys of the Kingdom are mine if I diligently seek them and learn to use them.

Prayer

Father God, I come to You in the name of the Lord Yeshua. Thank You that as Your child I have inherited the keys of Your Kingdom. Help me to diligently seek and learn to use these keys. Amen.

The Kingdom is real

Read 1 Chronicles 29:10-13

Yours, O Lord, is the greatness and the power and the glory and the majesty and the splendour, for everything in heaven and earth is yours. Yours, O Lord is the kingdom; you are exalted as head over all. - 1 Chronicles 29:11

In January 2012, Aldo wrote 'My mother thought she was living in the Kingdom, but she was only a tenant. She moved in and out, but today she is a citizen.'

I was shocked when I read the letter, and it was hard to accept; but I realised that it was true. After all the terrible pain, fire and warfare we had endured over the past year, it felt as if God had truly burnt away the old Retah. However, I realised that there is far more to be done; like the apostle Paul I am aware that there is still much of the 'old' Retah who has to die to self. It is a daily process. Walking along the highway of holiness is a step by step, day by day process.

> *The Kingdom of heaven is far more real than I often think it is. It is a glorious, majestic, everlasting Kingdom.*

Through all of this I began to realise that the Kingdom of heaven is far more real than we often think it is. It is a glorious, majestic, everlasting Kingdom.

Prayer

My Father in heaven, I worship You. Your Kingdom is an everlasting Kingdom. I thank You for the privilege of living in Your Kingdom. I am so grateful that I am a citizen and not just a tenant in Your Kingdom. Amen.

In which Kingdom do you live?

Read John 13:36-37; 18:25-27

Peter asked, "Lord, why can't I follow you now? I will lay down my life for you." Then Jesus answered, "Will you really lay down your life for me? I tell you the truth, before the rooster crows, you will disown me three times!" - John 13:37-38

The Apostle Peter walked and talked with Jesus on a daily basis for three years. He watched and experienced firsthand the miracles and wonders that Yeshua performed while He was on earth.

Yet when tested Peter disappointed and denied his Master. Yeshua predicted that by the time the rooster crowed three times Peter would have denied Him three times. This was the turning point in Peter's life.

It is not possible to live in two kingdoms if I want to be an effective and powerful witness for Yeshua.

We see a different Peter at the Sea of Galilee. Yeshua asked Peter three times: Peter, do you love Me? Twice Peter answers; Yes, Lord, You know that I love You. The third time Peter says; You know all things, You know that I love You. Do you think that maybe Yeshua asked Peter the question three times to cancel out the three times Peter denied Him?

Yeshua used this opportunity to give Peter his mission and future purpose in building the Kingdom. God also has a mission and a purpose for our lives.

Prayer

Father God, I realise that so often I try and switch between the kingdom of the world and Your Kingdom. I know that I cannot do this; it doesn't work. I need to be wholeheartedly committed to Your Kingdom and living out the principles of Your Kingdom. Amen.

The key of David

Read Isaiah 22:15-25

I will place on his shoulder the key to the house of David; what he opens no one can shut, and what he shuts no one can open. - Isaiah 22:22

Today we will talk about the key of David. David loved God; he developed intimacy with God as he looked after the sheep in the fields. David spent many hours alone with no human company. He did not feel that life was passing him by. He wrote psalms of praise to his God. He grew in his faith and trust in God.

There is a wonderful lesson to be learnt from the story of Samuel visiting David's home. Even though his family forgot to call him in to meet Samuel, God didn't forget that he was in the field. God prompted Samuel to ask if there were any other sons. Then they called David in. You and I don't have to worry about being noticed by people; God knows about us. He is the only one we need to impress. If God has something planned for you, no one will be able to stand in the way.

David developed intimacy with God as he looked after the sheep in the fields. He grew in his faith and trust in God.

Prayer

Father, I long to have the same intimacy with You that David had. Help me to make the most of my time – I realise that I waste so much time being distracted by things. Lord, when You look at my heart I want You to see one that is overflowing with love for You. Amen.

The key of love and intimacy

Read Luke 10:25-37

"'Love the Lord your God with all your heart and with all your soul and with all your strength and with all your mind'; and, 'Love your neighbour as yourself.'" - Luke 10:27

The key of love is where you come to the place where you say; Abba, Father, teach me Your Agape, teach me, Jesus Messiah, teach me how to love You. When last did you pour your love out for Him like oil upon His feet?

You will not find fulfilment in relationships, things, your studies, sport, or material things. None of these things will bring you love, and a lasting sense of fulfilment.

We all need love. I realised this afresh recently when my father died. His generation endured a very hard life. I deeply regret that I didn't push through his pain and take hold of him and hug him while he was alive; unfortunately there was still too much of the old Retah left and I didn't do this. I missed the opportunity to love him with Agape love.

The first key to the Kingdom of God is to live in love.

The first key to the Kingdom of God is to live in love.

Prayer

My loving Father, thank You that You love me perfectly. You fulfil every need of my body, soul and spirit. I revel in Your love. Help me to share Your love with everyone who crosses my path. Help me to love those that are difficult to love with Your Agape love. Amen.

The principle of repentance

Read Matthew 3:1-17

I baptise you with water for repentance. But after me will come one who is more powerful than I, whose sandals I am not fit to carry. He will baptise you with the Holy Spirit and with fire. - Matthew 3:11

The second key to the Kingdom of God is repentance. Without repentance you and I will not be able to experience the Kingdom of God, and His power will not be able to flow through us.

I experienced the power of repentance when we were in Malaysia recently. Their Saturday prayer meeting started at 7:30pm but by 6pm there were already 3 000 people sitting cross legged on the floor. I was so humbled by their expectancy.

Without repentance I will not be able to come into a place of right standing with God.

I was privileged to lead them and as we came before God I asked Him to reveal His glory lights showing them what they needed to repent of. The people lay on their faces before God.

As they worshiped the power of God's Kingdom descended upon the gathering and people were set free, others were healed. I called out to God asking Him what was happening. He replied that I had unlocked the Kingdom through loving these people with His love.

Prayer

Adonai, I bow before You; God of this universe. Humbly, I come to You in repentance and contrition – asking You to reveal to me through Your Spirit the things I need to repent of. As I receive Your forgiveness, help me to love others, so that Your Kingdom may be revealed to them. Amen.

The principle of obedience

Read Matthew 14:22-36

"Lord, if it's you," Peter replied, "tell me to come to you on the water." "Come," he said. Then Peter got down out of the boat, walked on the water and came toward Jesus. - Matthew 14:28-29

Obedience to His voice will release the manifestation of His glory. Peter was in the boat with the other disciples, and Jesus walked out on the water to them. In order for Peter to go to Jesus he had to get out of the boat. As he took the first step onto the water, he found that he was no longer walking on water, but rather he was placing his foot upon Jesus, his Rock.

This is faith; the world doesn't understand it. The world will tell you that you are crazy, it is not possible; but they do not see what you see. They do not walk where you walk.

The moment Peter obeyed the Spirit of Council; the Spirit of Might was released.

We need to say to God; Lord, I want to hear and obey; I want to trust and obey. When we are in tune with God, He releases the supernatural. God wants to give us the keys so that we can operate in the Spirit of Might and His authority.

Prayer

Father God, thank You for this third key of obedience. Lord, I want to hear Your voice and obey. Release within me the Spirit of Council so that I can experience the Spirit of Might at work in and through me. Amen.

8 July

The principle of prayer

Read Matthew 6:5-13

This, then, is how you should pray: "Our Father in heaven, hallowed be your name, your kingdom come, your will be done on earth as it is in heaven." - Matthew 6:9-10

As you develop a love relationship with God, you will hear His voice. If you obey God's voice, trusting in Him then He will release His Spirit within you. As we abide in Him we remain in constant communication with God through prayer. With the key of prayer God releases His Kingdom in us. In order to receive it though we must have teachable hearts; otherwise it will not be possible for us to receive.

As Jesus walked on earth with His disciples, they saw that He had something precious; the Kingdom was manifested in His life day in and day out. The disciples came and told Jesus that they wanted what He had. They asked Him to share with them the secret of what He had. Lord, teach us how to pray, teach us how to move in this Kingdom.

The personal revelation Jesus gives me changes my life.

Jesus answered His disciples and said: This then is how you should pray.

Prayer

Our Father in heaven, hallowed be your name, your kingdom come, your will be done on earth as it is in heaven. Give us today our daily bread. Forgive us our debts, as we also have forgiven our debtors. And lead us not into temptation, but deliver us from the evil one." Amen.

9 July

The principle of peace

Read John 14:22-31

Peace I leave with you; my peace I give you. I do not give to you as the world gives. Do not let your hearts be troubled and do not be afraid. - John 14:27

You and I are His instruments – one of the keys of the Kingdom is the key of peace. We have received this key through the shed blood of Jesus. He came to make peace between us and God. We are meant to share God's peace with the world around us.

As you walk in a love relationship with God, your Father, living in repentance and obedience before Him, in constant communication; you will be filled with the supernatural power of His Spirit. As you live in the manifest presence of the Spirit of Council and the Spirit of Might, God will enable you to spread and share His peace with other people.

The key of peace means that I do not live a life of fear; instead I live a life of power in the Kingdom of God.

The key of peace also means that you do not live a life of fear, because you know that your God is in control of your circumstances. Instead you live a life of power in the Kingdom of God.

Prayer

Father, thank You for Your peace that permeates every area of my life. Thank You that I have nothing to fear from man or circumstance. Help me to freely share this precious gift of peace with others. I am so grateful for this key of Your Kingdom. Amen.

The principle of revelation

Read Revelation 19:6-10

At this I fell at his feet to worship him. But he said to me, "Do not do it! I am a fellow servant with you and with your brothers who hold to the testimony of Jesus. Worship God! For the testimony of Jesus is the spirit of prophecy." - Revelation 19:10

This is the key that opens the portals of revelation; the testimony of Jesus is the Spirit of prophecy.

Jesus has prophesied over my life many times. At these times He has has given me His plan and purpose for myself and my family. One such example is when I asked the Lord if there would ever be a woman who would love Aldo; would he ever find a wife.

Well it is almost seven years later as I write this devotional and God has brought a beautiful blonde into Aldo's life. Her name is Chantel, he calls her Chans. What Jesus prophesied has come into being. They are engaged to be married. She loves him, serves him, and cares for him.

Jesus reveals the portal of revelation; who is the Spirit of prophecy. It is a key to the Kingdom of God that is a precious gift to me, His child.

Jesus reveals the portal of revelation; who is the Spirit of prophecy. It is a key to the Kingdom of God that is a precious gift to us, His children.

Prayer

Father, thank You for the Spirit of prophecy through Your beloved Son, Jesus. Thank You that You have given me, Your child the key to the portal of revelation through Jesus Christ. Amen.

11 July

The principle of faith

Read Hebrews 11:1-6

"Now faith is being sure of what we hope for and certain of what we do not see." - Hebrews 11:1

Hebrews chapter eleven, is referred to as the 'faith hall of fame'. I can be encouraged by your walk of faith; you can be encouraged by mine. However, we each have to walk our own path of faith.

If you look at the stories of the people mentioned in Hebrews 11 then you will see that they are all very different from each other. There are not two that are the same. Each of them was faced with their own crisis of belief. When this crisis occured they had to make the decision; would they believe and trust God? Would they obey and do what He was telling them to do?

The key of faith unlocks the miracles of God in my life and it enables me to walk a Kingdom walk.

In many instances God told them to do things that defied logic. Yet He had a plan; the purpose was that at the end of the day there would be no question that it was a miracle. No man could take credit for the outcome.

Prayer

Father, I come before You in faith today. I commit my situation to You. Father, give me Your wisdom, reveal to me Your plan. Help me to be obedient to what You are telling me to do. Amen.

The principle of forgiveness

Read Matthew 6:9-15

For if you forgive men when they sin against you, your heavenly Father will also forgive you. But if you do not forgive men their sins, your Father will not forgive your sins.
- Matthew 6:14-15

Forgiveness is the key to freedom. The scriptures leave us in no doubt that we have to forgive. You cannot do this on your own – you need the infilling, empowering of the Holy Spirit to help you. I saw firsthand the effect that unforgiveness had on Aldo's life. He was hurt at an early age enduring the arrows and spiritual attacks of those who have spoken negatively about his walk of faith.

The unforgiveness and hurt manifested in Aldo's life through epileptic fits. He did not talk about his hurts but kept them hidden. As I began to realise the problem I had to help him walk through the process of forgiving those who had hurt him. This was not easy and it was a process but there was release and relief as he was able to do this. The bottom line is that you cannot walk in the Kingdom and not be prepared to forgive.

The bottom line is that I cannot walk in the Kingdom and not be prepared to forgive.

Prayer

My Father, as I come before You I realise that You have forgiven me for so much in my life. Where would I be without Your forgiveness; and yet I so often withhold forgiveness from other people. Help me to take careful note of what Your Word says regarding forgiveness. Help me, I pray. Amen.

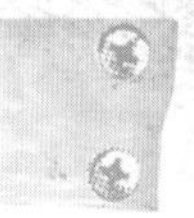

The principle of humility

Read Philippians 2

"Do nothing out of selfish ambition or vain conceit. Rather, in humility value others above yourselves, not looking to your own interests but each of you to the interests of the others. In your relationships with one another, have the same mindset as Christ Jesus: Who, being in very nature God, did not consider equality with God something to be grasped; rather, he made himself nothing by taking the very nature of a servant, being made in human likeness. And being found in appearance as a man, he humbled himself by becoming obedient to death – even death on a cross." - Philippians 2:3-8

Proverbs 11:2 says, *'When pride comes, then comes disgrace, but with humility comes wisdom.'* Pride is one of our greatest enemies. Pride uses all the power and might at its disposal to keep us out of the Kingdom of God.

When pride comes, then follows disgrace, but with humility comes wisdom.

A person who is blinded by pride doesn't see their own faults, and therefore will not confess. Since they don't make mistakes, what do they have to be sorry about? They know everything!

I learnt true humility after going through some costly battles in the spirit; battles of life and death. This made me realise that nothing, absolutely nothing of Retah can stand before God's omnipotence, and that in my own strength I am unable to overcome the enemy. The victory comes as a result of the blood of the Lamb (Christ's work on the cross), and the grace of God. I must die, and Christ must live through me.

Prayer

Dear Lord God, I bow before You. I acknowledge that all too often my heart is filled with pride. I humble myself before You, my Father. I pray that You will cleanse me and fill me with Your Spirit of Truth. Amen.

The principle of grace

Read Matthew 18:23-35

Then Peter came to Jesus and asked, "Lord, how many times shall I forgive my brother or sister who sins against me? Up to seven times?" Jesus answered, "I tell you, not seven times, but seventy-seven times." - Matthew 18:21-22

I get impatient sometimes when I see people complaining for no reason. One night I was grumbling about someone as our family sat down to have dinner. Suddenly Aldo asked: 'Mom, how much grace is there in your grace bucket' 'What grace bucket, Aldo?' I asked, somewhat confused by his question.

He answered me saying, 'Before the throne of God there is a grace bucket, Mom. Every time you give grace to someone, grace is placed in your bucket. You can read about it in the book of James, Mom.' '... *Judgment without mercy will be shown to anyone who has not been merciful. Mercy triumphs over judgment'* (James 2:13).

Mercy triumphs over judgment.

The more I begin to realise how great God's grace is within me, the easier it is for me to extend it. The Holy Spirit has reminded me that I receive forgiveness every time I confess a mistake – why would I then hold other people's mistakes against them?

Prayer

Father, please forgive me for not extending grace to others. Help me, Lord, to understand others' hurt and pain, and then to extend a hand of love to them. Amen.

The principle of spiritual fruit

Read Galatians 5:19-24

But the fruit of the Spirit is love, joy, peace, patience, kindness, goodness, faithfulness, gentleness and self-control. Against such things there is no law. Those who belong to Christ Jesus have crucified the flesh with its passions and desires" - Galatians 5:22-24

Luke 4:43-45 tells us; '*No good tree bears bad fruit, nor does a bad tree bear good fruit. Each tree is recognised by its own fruit. People do not pick figs from thornbushes, or grapes from briers. The good man brings good things out of the good stored up in his heart, and an evil man brings evil things out of the evil stored up in his heart. For out of the overflow of his heart, his mouth speaks.*'

The Holy Spirit is the 'Gardener' pruning our tree so that we can bear the *fruit of the Spirit.* God's seed within us accomplishes this. The fruit is not a product of our own works or our goodness – it is all thanks to God's Spirit in us. It is when we are rooted in God's love and allow Him to prune us, that we begin to bear good fruit for His Kingdom.

The fruit is not a product of my own works or my goodness – it is all thanks to God's Spirit in me.

Prayer

Dear Father, thank You that Your Holy Spirit dwells within me producing the fruit of the Spirit in my life. I realise that I cannot cultivate or manifest the fruit on my own. Amen.

The principle of blessing

Read Numbers 6:22-27

The Lord said to Moses: "Tell Aaron and his sons, 'This is how you are to bless the Israelites. Say to them: The Lord bless you and keep you; the Lord make his face shine on you and be gracious to you; the Lord turn his face toward you and give you peace.' So they will put my name on the Israelites, and I will bless them." - Numbers 6:22-27

In Proverbs 18:21 we read; *'The tongue has the power of life and death, and those who love it will eat its fruit.'* From the beginning it was God's plan that we would bless one another with our tongues, but our sinful nature has completely distorted this principle. Today, gossip and slander are in full swing! There are even magazines and TV programmes specially dedicated to gossip.

I can only truly bless my enemies if I've decided to pick up my cross and follow Yeshua.

Blessing others is one of the strongest weapons we have. Every day when I go jogging, I use this special time to bless my husband and my children. I bless our household, our finances, my ministry and also my enemies; because the Word says very clearly: *'But love your enemies, do good to them, and lend to them without expecting to get anything back. Then your reward will be great, and you will be sons of the Most High, because he is kind to the ungrateful and wicked'* (Luke 6:35).

Prayer

Dear Father, help me to bless those who curse me. I can only do this as Your Spirit fills me and empowers me. Thank You for this key to Your Kingdom – it is so powerful. Amen.

The principle of servant-hood

Read Hebrew 7:1-3 & Genesis 14:18-20

Then Melchizedek king of Salem brought out bread and wine. He was priest of God Most High, and he blessed Abram, saying: "Blessed be Abram by God Most High, Creator of heaven and earth. And praise be to God Most High, who delivered your enemies into your hand." Then Abram gave him a tenth of everything. - Genesis 14:18-20

Melchizedek had an intimate relationship with the living God. On the way back from the battlefield, Melchizedek approached Abraham and served him food and wine, as well as an important word directly from the throne room of God. He reminded Abraham of whom God is and that the victory belonged to Him. To God and God alone belong all honour and praise.

This is what God also expects from me. To serve and bless others in obedience to His voice.

Melchizedek did what God asked him to do – he served. Without making a 'show' of it, without getting his name in lights, without publicity or advertising, Melchizedek (a *king*) went to serve Abraham in obedience to God's command.

God expects us to serve and bless others in obedience to His voice. Are you willing to go where God sends you and to do what He asks you to do without a fancy title or reward? You will only be able to do this if you are a true servant.

Prayer

Father God, again I thank You for this key to Your Kingdom. Help me to bless others at every opportunity I get. I have received so many blessings from You that I long to share them in service to others. Amen.

The principle of sanctification

Read Romans 12

"Therefore, I urge you, brothers [and sisters], in view of God's mercy, to offer your bodies as living sacrifices, holy and pleasing to God - this is your spiritual act worship." - Romans 12:1

Sometimes the sanctification process goes hand in hand with great suffering. I have experienced this hard truth in my own life, but I also know that if it is 'Godly suffering', the result will glorify God through the fruit we bear.

Job's life is an example of this; Job lost all his children, and literally everything he owned and he ended up on an ash heap scraping the sores on his body with a potsherd. Job remained faithful to God, despite his circumstances.

This is the real test of our love for God. Even though Job questioned God he didn't allow his hardship to turn him away from God. The Lord honoured Job's faithfulness and later gave him more than he had at the start. '*The Lord blessed the latter part of Job's life more than the former part ... And so Job died, an old man and full of years'* (Job 42:12a;17).

Can I see how God uses hardship to change my heart and build my character?

Prayer

Father, this key to Your Kingdom is not an easy one; suffering is not pleasant. Thank You that You hold me and guide me – leading me along the path to a changed heart. Lord, I want to be pure before You. Amen.

19 July

The principle of provision

Read Matthew 6:25-34

"So do not worry, saying, 'What shall we eat?' or 'What shall we drink?' or 'What shall we wear?' For the pagans run after all these things, and your heavenly Father knows that you need them. But seek first his kingdom and his righteousness, and all these things will be given to you as well." - Matthew 6:31-33

In the same way that natural laws exist, God's Kingdom also works according to certain rules. Farmers will tell you about the preparation of the soil before seeds can be sown. Once this is done the seed can be planted. The farmer trusts God for rain and sunlight so that the seeds germinate and grow. The quality of the harvest depends on the quality of the soil and the seed.

When I care for the needs of others, I show the character of God to a broken world.

If we don't sow, we are not going to reap. We cannot expect God to bless us if we have not sown our seed. God says we must sow into the lives of others. Why is this so very important: Because we're called to sow goodness, grace and love in the lives of those who really need it. Through an open hand and a heart that cares for the needs of others, we show the character of God to a broken world.

Prayer

My Abba Father, You are so good to me. You provide for me each day – I am so grateful. Above all I am grateful that You have given me salvation through Your Son, Yeshua the Christ. Help me to share all that You have given me with others. Amen.

The principle of sowing and reaping

Read Mark 12:41-44

Calling his disciples to him, Jesus said, "Truly I tell you, this poor widow has put more into the treasury than all the others. They all gave out of their wealth; but she, out of her poverty, put in everything – all she had to live on." - Mark 12:41-44

One of my favourite stories in the Bible is the story about the woman who put her last copper coins into the temple treasury: It's not about how much you give. Rather it is the spirit in which you give it. Abba Father wants to look after His children – He wants to give to us from His bounty! Yes, I believe this with all my heart.

Whether it's health, finances, or anything else – God is my source! Therefore, I will always have enough.

Sowing means that we share what we have with others. You do not have to be rich to share with others. Even though you sometimes feel like the underprivileged one, give from what you have; God will take care of you. It's all about the condition of your heart.

Remember: *You can never out-give God.* I trust God for all my family's needs as well as my own. Whether it's health, finances, or whatever it is – God is our source! Therefore, we will always have enough.

Prayer

Dear Father, help me to have a Kingdom mentality when it comes to sowing generously. I realise that everything I have comes from You. Help me to share with others. Amen.

The principle of worship

Read John 4

Yet a time is coming and has now come when the true worshippers will worship the Father in Spirit and truth, for they are the kind of worshippers the Father seeks.
- John 4:23

The key of worshipping in Spirit and Truth is accessed through intimacy with God; through opening the door of obedience where you listen to and heed God's voice as He speaks to you. We are to return again and again to the fountain of living water until we are filled up to overflowing with the Spirit of God.

I believe that God is raising a generation that will confront the powers of darkness and this generation will manifest the Kingdom of God. John 4:23 tells us: *Yet a time is coming and has now come when the true worshippers will worship the Father in Spirit and truth, for they are the kind of worshippers the Father seeks.*

I believe that it is in the secret place where God fills me with His Holy Spirit.

Do you want to be a worshipper who worships in Spirit and Truth? This is the sign and characteristic of a true worshiper; this is the outward evidence of someone who is living in the Kingdom of God.

Prayer

Father, you have clearly said in Your Word that the worshipers You are seeking are those who worship in Spirit and in Truth. Lord, I desire to be a true worshiper – fill me with Your Holy Spirit, I pray. Amen.

The principle of the Spirit of Truth

Read John 14:25-27; 16:7-15

But when he, the Spirit of truth, comes, he will guide you into all truth. He will not speak on his own; he will speak only what he hears, and he will tell you what is yet to come. - John 16:13

We cannot function without the key of the Spirit of Truth. Yeshua promised us that, *The Counsellor, the Holy Spirit, whom the Father will send in my name, will teach you all things and will remind you of everything I have said to you* (John 14:26).

Are you experiencing turmoil at home, or maybe at school or college? You need the wisdom of the Counsellor each moment of the day. How do you make decisions if you do not have the Counsellor advising you what you should do? We are in a spiritual battle and we cannot fight this battle in the flesh and in our own strength.

I am called to be an 'atmosphere changer'; I must take the mind of Christ, the aroma of Christ into every situation I encounter.

Know that as you live in God's Kingdom you have the Spirit of Truth within you. No matter what your circumstances the Counsellor, The Spirit of Truth will be with you. Yeshua has promised you: *Peace I leave with you; my peace I give to you* (John 14:27a).

Prayer

My Abba Father, I come to you. I am so grateful that You did not leave me without a Helper. Thank You that You sent the Spirit of Truth to lead me, to counsel me, to comfort me and to instruct me. I cannot be an 'atmosphere changer' without Your Spirit at work in me. Amen.

The principle of Spirit senses

Read Isaiah 30:18-26

"Whether you turn to the right or to the left, your ears will hear a voice behind you saying, 'This is the way; walk in it.'" - Isaiah 30:21

We have five natural senses: sight, hearing, smell, taste and touch. We also have spiritual senses and we need to learn how to use them. These spiritual senses help us communicate with God.

God's Word tells us that God *is* Spirit (John 4:24). It is important to remember that God speaks to our spirit, and not to our soul. The soul comprises our thoughts, emotions and our will. Although God uses our soul to reveal Himself to us in different ways, He speaks to our spirit. Our spirit doesn't see-saw the way our emotions do, and it is made to communicate with God.

The more time I spend communicating with God, the more clearly I will hear His voice.

In Hebrews 11:6 we read that without faith it is impossible to please God. Remember that everything that happens in the Kingdom of God is anchored in faith. It's all about relationship. We need to learn how to be still and to wait on God. God speaks to each of us uniquely.

Prayer

My Father, I long to have this kind of a relationship with You; where You are sharing Your heart with me. I pray that You will annoint me with Your Spirit, fill me up to overflowing; help me to develop my spirit senses so that I can know You more and more. Amen.

24 July

Serve One Master

Read Matthew 4:1-11

Jesus said to him, "Away from me, Satan! For it is written: 'Worship the Lord your God, and serve him only.'" - Matthew 4:10

If we want to live in God's Kingdom we cannot be half hearted in our commitment. We cannot hold the keys in our hands and not use them.

When we face tempatations and attacks from the enemy we must follow Jesus' example. Satan took Jesus up onto a high mountain and showed Him all the kingdoms of the world. He offered the kingdoms to Jesus if He bowed down and worshipped Satan. Jesus had to choose which kingdom He would to live in. He could not have both; it had to be one or the other. You and I cannot live in two kingdoms either. We have to choose whom we will serve. Jesus' response to Satan was clear and definite; *'Worship the Lord your God, and serve him only.'*

> *The keys of the Kingdom only open the locks of the doors in God's Kingdom. They do not fit the locks of the doors in any earthly kingdom.*

Our choice is do we choose the transient kingdoms of this world or do we choose the everlasting Kingdom of God our Father.

Prayer

My Father, I thank You that through the death and sacrifice of Yeshua, my Saviour, I have been given the key of Salvation. I thank You, Father, that my birthright is to be a citizen of Your Kingdom – today I take the oath of allegiance anew. Amen.

25 July

Thy Kingdom come

Read Matthew 6:5-13

Our Father in heaven, hallowed be your name, your kingdom come, your will be done on earth as it is in heaven. - Matthew 6:9b-10

Yeshua came to this world to reveal the Kingdom of God to His followers. Over the three years of His earthly ministry He taught people about the Kingdom of God. In Matthew chapter 6 His disciples came to Him and asked Him to teach them how to pray. Yeshua told them, this is how you should pray; *Our Father in heaven, hallowed be your name, your kingdom come, your will be done on earth as it is in heaven* (vs 9b-10).

How do we live in God's Kingdom here on earth? Verse 10 says – we are to do God's will on earth. Romans 8 tells us that we must be controlled by the Holy Spirit in order to do God's will. The Spirit is life and peace.

Yeshua makes it clear that I am meant to live in the Kingdom of God here on earth.

If we are going to live in the Kingdom we must take hold of the keys of the Kingdom and use them. We must unlock the doors of the Kingdom.

Prayer

Our Father in heaven, hallowed be your name, your kingdom come, your will be done on earth as it is in heaven. Father, fill me with Your Spirit so that I can live and function in Your Kingdom here on earth. Amen.

Blessed are the poor in spirit

Read Matthew 5:3-12

Blessed are the poor in spirit, for theirs is the kingdom of heaven. - Matthew 5:3

Jesus told us in Matthew that the *poor in spirit* will inherit the Kingdom of God. The kind of poverty that Yeshua is referring to is the realisation that we have nothing to bring to the Master. There is nothing we can do; our best efforts are as nothing. We have to come in our abject poverty of spirit before God.

Often once we have come to Christ we forget our dependence upon God. We move forward in our new status as a child of God and we forget that we need to live in total dependence upon Him. This is when we are in danger of falling into pride and arrogance. When we become proud and arrogant this is when the enemy can easily gain a foothold in our lives.

When I am poor in spirit, my Father will exalt me and lift me up so that I can live as part of His family in His Kingdom.

In Philippians chapter two Paul speaks about how Jesus humbled Himself in obedience to His Father. Jesus lived in total obedience and dependence upon Father God.

Prayer

Father, I come before You recognising my poverty of spirit. I realise that there is nothing that I can offer You other than my heart, soul and mind. I come to You anew realising my total dependence upon You – there is no safer place to live. Amen.

Blessed are the persecuted

Read Matthew 5:3-12

Blessed are those who are persecuted because of righteousness, for theirs is the kingdom of heaven. - Matthew 5:10

When you choose to walk in the Kingdom of God applying the principles of His Kingdom in your life you will find that there will be those who will not approve of you. We need to be clear that we are not talking about persecution when we do wrong or sin. Yeshua clearly says; *blessed are those who are persecuted because of righteousness.* Often Christians suffer because of the sinful choices they have made.

How do we react when we are persecuted for righteousness sake? We are to bless those who persecute us – it is as simple and as difficult as that. You can only bless people who are hurting you if you are walking and living in the Spirit.

If I am going to inhabit the Kingdom I have to walk in forgiveness, blessing those who persecute me.

Again Yeshua is our perfect example of living like this. He forgave those who tortured and ultimately murdered Him. He could do this because He never lost sight of His mission and His calling.

Prayer

My Father God, I come to You realising that You have called me to follow You. I know that following You wholeheartedly will often mean that people will not get me. When this happens help me to bless and not to curse these people. Help me to love as Yeshua loved. Amen.

Faith like a mustard seed

Read Matthew 13:24-35

He told them another parable: "The kingdom of heaven is like a mustard seed, which a man took and planted in his field. Though it is the smallest of all your seeds, yet when it grows, it is the largest of garden plants and becomes a tree, so that the birds of the air come and perch in its branches." - Matthew 13:31-32

The mustard seed is small and insignificant, when you first look at it you would never anticipate the *potential* hidden within the seed when it germinates!

It's the same with us. The Kingdom starts out as a seed planted in our hearts, which eventually becomes so big that it takes over our lives, overshadowing and uprooting all other kingdoms. There is only place for one Kingdom in our hearts; we cannot be of the earthly kingdom and the heavenly Kingdom – it has to be one or the other.

> *God starts by planting a little seed in my heart. If I nurture it, by watering and fertilising it, then eventually it will grow into a big tree.*

When the mustard seed reaches maturity it is one of the strongest plants. Today I realise that everything big, starts out small. We are called to faithfulness as we grow in the Kingdom of God. We have a calling to be useful citizens of the Kingdom – we fulfill this calling by nurturing the seed God has planted within us.

Prayer

My heavenly Father, You have planted the seed within my heart. Thank You that through the nurture and care of Your Holy Spirit within me, I can water, fertilise and take care of the seed. Help me to faithfully bear fruit. Amen.

The wheat and the tares

Read Matthew 13:24-30

The servants asked him, 'Do you want us to go and pull them up?' 'No,' he answered, 'because while you are pulling the weeds, you may uproot the wheat with them. Let both grow together until the harvest. At that time I will tell the harvesters: First collect the weeds and tie them in bundles to be burned; then gather the wheat and bring it into my barn.' - Matthew 13:28b-30

The enemy came in the night and planted weeds among the wheat. When the farmer discovered this, it was too late to pull the weeds out and so he had to watch the weeds grow with the wheat. At the right time – when the wheat's roots were deep and strong – the weeds could be pulled out and burned.

God tells us that we still live in a sinful world full of problems and difficult circumstances; but the day will come when our faithfulness to Him will be rewarded. We have a choice to get rid of the weeds *in* us and to live in victory over the things that bind us in the world. God wants us to live in the spiritual reality of His Kingdom with our eyes focused on Him in complete dependence on Him. There, we will experience His provision for all our needs – spirit, soul and body – in a supernatural way.

For now I live side by side with the weeds around me, but one day in the not too distant future, Yeshua will come and fetch me.

Prayer

My Father God, I pray that You will help me to be faithful to You until the end of my days. Help me to be ruthless in eradicating the weeds within my life. Fill me today afresh with Your Spirit. Amen.

30 July

Come as a child

Read Mark 10:1-16

When Jesus saw this, he was indignant. He said to them, "Let the little children come to me, and do not hinder them, for the kingdom of God belongs to such as these. I tell you the truth, anyone who will not receive the kingdom of God like a little child will never enter it." - Mark 10:14-15

We are brought up to achieve, to strive for what we want and to work hard. None of this is bad in and of itself; except that we often get our priorities out of order because these values become most important to us. Yeshua taught a profound principle regarding the Kingdom to His disciples in Mark chapter ten. He told them they had to become like little children. What did He mean by this; how can you become like a little child again?

> *Having a child-like faith does not mean I am childish. It is the exact opposite in fact; it means that I trust God to know what is best for me.*

Little children are wholehearted in their love and devotion. Their ability to believe and have faith is unlimited and complete. We are to come in absolute faith. It means that we enter into, walk in and live within the Kingdom of God wholeheartedly. We are God's children and we must live our lives as children of the Kingdom and the Most High God.

Prayer

My Abba Father, I come before You as Your child. I realise that I have lost some of my child-like faith as I have allowed the world to encroach into my heart and life. Please work in my heart, soften it, and help me to live in child like faith. Amen.

31 July

An everlasting Kingdom

Read Psalm 145:1-21

Your kingdom is an everlasting kingdom, and your dominion endures through all generations. - Psalm 145:13

Yeshua's desire is for each of His disciples to live a Kingdom-life so that we can demonstrate the power and love of the Father here on earth just as He did. We can only do this if we live a Spirit filled life.

Hear the Lord God Almighty speaking to you: 'My dear child, don't wait for one day – live life to the full in My Kingdom here on earth. I have so much more planned for you than running round in circles chasing the wind. Be an empty vessel and make yourself available to Me so that I can fill you up to overflowing with My goodness. My favour and My anointing will spill over onto the lives of others. I want to make My Kingdom manifest here on earth through you. Be the difference. Be the light in a dark world. I am the Light in you. Choose life, so that you may live!'

I worship an Almighty God. He is not distant. He is not weak. He is not deaf. He invites me to live in His Kingdom now.

Prayer

My Father, I worship You, I bow before You acknowledging that You are Mighty. Thank You for the many lessons You have taught me over this past month. I am so grateful that I have the privilege of living in Your Kingdom. Help me through Your Spirit to be a faithful citizen. Amen.

Wysheid se stilwees en
vertroue vind ons net
in God se teenwoordigheid.
Sy Gees sien Jesus
sal ons nooit begewe
of verlaat nie hy is
saam ons in alles
wat ons doen rooi
hart is wat ons het
wanneer ons God vertrou.
Samuel sien sy lewe
so vol vrede. Vure
van vyand is weg
want Samuel sien om
te vergewe bring vrede
en in woord sê God
vrede my vrede gee
ek julle, bly in God
vertrou hom daar is
vrede.

Letter 8:

Be still and know I am God

Wisdom says that we will find quietness and trust only in God's presence. Jesus says His Spirit will never leave us nor forsake us. He is with us in everything we do. Our hearts are red [covered by the blood of the Lamb] when we trust God. Samuel's life is full of peace. The fire of the enemy is gone, because Samuel has seen that blessing others brings peace. In the Word, God says: 'I will give you My peace.' Abide in Him – there you will find peace.

The Kingdom within you

Prayer for August

My Father God, I come to You in the precious Name of Jesus, my Saviour and Lord. Your Kingdom is an everlasting Kingdom. You are a mighty God, I worship You and I adore You. I bring my gift of worship to You. You have placed the seeds of Your Kingdom within me. You have called me to live a Kingdom life. Lord, help me to nurture the seed You have sown in my life. I want to be the best that I can be for You. I pray that You will work in my life through the power of Your Holy Spirit. Cleanse me, fill me, and empower me. In the precious Name of Jesus.

Amen.

1 August

The Light has come

Read Isaiah 60:1-3,19-20

Arise, shine, for your light has come, and the glory of the Lord rises upon you.
- Isaiah 60:1

If I am a citizen of the Kingdom of heaven and I have the Kingdom within me people will be able to look at my life and say; 'there is something different about her?' For many years I believed the Kingdom of God was something that I would encounter one day when I got to heaven. It did not affect my daily life too much.

As God began to open my eyes I began to understand the meaning of *living in the Light of the Kingdom of God. Isaiah puts it like this: The sun will no more be your light by day, nor will the brightness of the moon shine on you, for the Lord will be your everlasting light, and your God will be your glory. Your sun will never set again and your moon will wane no more, the Lord will be your everlasting light, and your days of sorrow will end* - Isaiah 60:19-20.

This is the choice I have – I can either inhabit a shallow, dim never-land or I can inhabit the glorious light of God's Kingdom.

Prayer

Father, I come before You with hands raised in praise and worship. Thank You that Your Light has come. Thank You that Your Kingdom is within me. Help me to live my life to the fullest as a citizen of Your Kingdom. Amen.

The Kingdom of God within you

Read Luke 17:20-37

Once, having been asked by the Pharisees when the kingdom of God would come, Jesus replied, "The kingdom of God does not come with your careful observation, nor will people say, 'Here it is,' or 'there it is,' because the kingdom of God is within you."
- Luke 17:20-21

When we come to God through Jesus Christ, He places His seed in our hearts and lives. We are used to working for what we get – but you cannot earn your salvation. Citizenship of heaven is given freely through faith.

When we enter the Kingdom – the Kingdom enters us. When something is on the outside it is more difficult for it to influence and have an effect on someone. However, when it is on the inside the influence and change comes from within and affects every aspect of the person's life. This has profoundly changed my life; it has brought me into a whole new dimension in my walk with God.

Is His Kingdom evident within me – Am I blessing other people through the overflow of God's Kingdom within me?

He has filled me with His Holy Spirit and enabled me to live in a different dimension. Are you growing in your walk with the Lord, is His Kingdom evident within you – are you blessing other people through the overflow of God's Kingdom within you?

Prayer

Dear Father God, I come to You, praising You and worshipping You! You have saved me through Jesus, Your Son; You fill me with Your Spirit and You have planted the seed of Your Kingdom within me. Help me to live in such a way that the seed flourishes and grows. Amen.

3 August

Seek first His Kingdom

Read Matthew 6:25-34

But seek first his kingdom and his righteousness, and all these things will be given you as well. - Matthew 6:33

The world rushes around worrying about all manner of things; accumulating money, possessions and prestige. When those who have the earthly kingdom within them pray, their prayers centre upon their needs and desires. Their thoughts, ambitions and goals are all temporal and to do with their own comfort and success.

Jesus clearly said in Matthew 6:31-32; '*So do not worry, saying, 'What shall we eat?' or 'What shall we drink?' or 'What shall we wear?' For the pagans run after all these things, and your heavenly Father knows that you need them.'*

If the seeds of the Kingdom are growing and flourishing inside us, we will use our time to further the Kingdom of God in our world. Our prayers will be for the things the Spirit of God lays upon our hearts. Prayer is an awesome, powerful tool. James tells us that the prayer of a righteous person is powerful and effective. Do not waste your 'prayer power'.

I can cast my cares upon Him because He cares for me – and those I love. I can be about His business and He will take care of my business.

Seeking God's Kingdom means that we will daily come before our Father asking Him to fill us with His Holy Spirit. The more we are filled with the Spirit, the more our thoughts, desires and actions will be Kingdom orientated. If we are focused upon the Kingdom of God, using the keys and the principles of the Kingdom to unlock the Kingdom of God – there will be increasing evidence of the influence of the Kingdom in lives through our speech and actions.

Prayer

Abba Father, You know all the things that would swallow up my focus and time. Thank You that I can bring them to You and lay them at Your feet. Help me to be focused upon Your Kingdom and the eternal business of living out Your Kingdom here on earth. Amen.

4 August

Our King Jesus!

Read Revelation 22

I, Jesus, have sent my angel to give you this testimony for the churches. I am the Root and the Offspring of David, and the bright Morning Star. - Revelation 22:16

Who is this King Jesus that we serve, whose Kingdom is within us?

He is the river that flows in and through us – we must drink and be refreshed – v1.

He is the *Lamb of God* who sits upon the throne – who takes away the sin of the world – v1.

Jesus is the *Tree of Life* – in Him we are trees of righteousness, the planting of the Lord – v2.

He is the *Light of the world* – As His followers we too are to take His light into our world – v5.

Jesus is a *'Re-warder'* – we share in Jesus' reward, the Kingdom – v12.

Jesus is the *Alpha and Omega* – we live in Jesus Christ – v13.

He is the *Root and offspring of David* – and we too are His people – v16.

As His Bride I must prepare myself for the day when my Bridegroom comes back to fetch me.

Jesus is our *Bright Morning Star* – Jesus has come and shone His light into the darkness.

He is the Bridegroom.

Prayer

Father, I come to You in the Name of King Jesus, *Lamb of God*. Jesus, You refresh me each day with *Your Water of Life*. Thank You for my salvation. You are the *Light of the world*; the *Alpha and the Omega*. You are the *Bright Morning Star* and my longed for *Bridegroom*. Come, Lord Jesus. Amen.

5 August

The fullness of Christ

Read Colossians 1:13-20

For God was pleased to have all his fullness dwell in him, and through him to reconcile to himself all things, whether things on earth or things in heaven, by making peace through his blood, shed on the cross. - Colossians 1:19-20

Colossians tells us that everything has its beginning in Jesus. Our hope is to see and experience the fullness of Christ. The Kingdom of God must increasingly grow inside us.

Jesus told His disciples in Matthew 5 how they were to live if they wanted to live in the Kingdom. We are destined to rule and reign with Jesus, but it happens not as a result of lauding our power over everyone. Rather it is about living as a servant. We need the fresh infilling of the Holy Spirit each day to help us to live with a servant's heart.

When I have the Kingdom within me I will not be able to stop myself sharing the fullness of Jesus.

Jesus is our example and our inspiration. He has made it possible through the fullness of who He is as the Son of God for us to have the Kingdom of God within us. We are to share this fullness of what He has imparted to us with the world around us.

Prayer

Father, thank You for the Incomparable Christ, who dwells within me. Thank You, Jesus, that You are the First and the Last. Your Kingdom is an everlasting Kingdom. Everything both in heaven and on earth is subject to You. I bow before You,and worship You my Lord and Saviour. Amen.

Christ our hope of glory

Read Colossions 1:21-29

To them God has chosen to make known among the Gentiles the glorious riches of this mystery, which is Christ in you, the hope of glory. - Colossians 1:27

The Kingdom within us is real. Giving our lives to the advancement of God's Kingdom in this world is the most rewarding and fulfilling thing we can do. Paul speaks about the mystery of Christ that has been made known to us – the Gentiles. This mystery is something that those who come to Christ understand as the Holy Spirit opens their spiritual eyes of understanding.

Paul further instructs us telling us how we are to share the 'hope' that is within us. He says that we are to admonish and teach everyone with all wisdom, so that we may present everyone perfect in Christ. This hope is too precious for you to not share with others. If you are living in the Kingdom and the Kingdom is growing within you then you will joyously share the hope within you.

Once I am in the Kingdom of God my calling is to share and to teach others about this 'hope' that is within me.

If we do not share Christ with the world around us, who is going to?

Prayer

Father, thank You for the great gift of Jesus, my hope of glory. Thank You that the hope I have in my heart is a sure hope. My faith in You is built upon reality and upon Your faithfulness to me. Help me to faithfully share Jesus and this wonderful hope with others. Amen.

7 August

One with Jesus

Read Luke 9:23-27

Then he said to them all: "If anyone would come after me, he must deny himself and take up his cross daily and follow me. For whoever wants to save his life will lose it, but whoever loses his life for me will save it." - Luke 9:23-24

The reality is that the more you die to self, the more mature you become; the greater the Kingdom will become within you. I can share with you how God began teaching me to drink from the fountain of living water; how He gave me food from the tree of life and how I have drunk and eaten from the milk and the manna.

However, none of this is evidence of becoming one with Jesus. The way to do this is to have the Kingdom growing within you. There is no difference between you and me. I don't want you to think that I have arrived, or that I have attained a greater level of spirituality than you. God has created us as unique individuals but the Spirit works in each of us, and draws us to God if we are open and seeking the Kingdom of God.

Jesus is the main key; I must become one with Him; allowing Him to unlock my heart and spirit.

Prayer

Father God, thank You that I am Your special child. I am so grateful today that You, the King of heaven, love me and want to have a relationship with me. Thank You that I can be one with Jesus, Your Son. Amen.

Step by step transformation

Read 2 Corinthians 3

Now the Lord is the Spirit, and where the Spirit of the Lord is, there is freedom. And we, who with unveiled faces all reflect the Lord's glory, are being transformed into his likeness with ever-increasing glory, which comes from the Lord, who is the Spirit.
- 2 Corinthians 3:17-18

After Moses spent time with God he reflected the glory of the Lord to those around him. The Word tells us this was a passing or a fading glory. When someone comes to Christ the veil is removed. The Holy Spirit lives within us. He is a permanent reminder and guarantee of the glory of God that dwells among men. This glory is not a fading glory because it is vested in Jesus Christ.

As we walk in the Spirit, living in the Holy of Holies, worshipping before the throne of God we are transformed, step by step; moment by moment. We live in the new Covenant. God promised us that this new Covenant, which was instituted and ushered in through the sacrifice of Jesus, is our inheritance as God's children.

Am I spending time worshiping my Father? Am I walking in the Spirit and reflecting the glory of my Lord through life?

Jesus is our hope of glory and we are transformed day by day into His likeness through the Holy Spirit at work within us.

Prayer

Dear Father, thank You that the veil no longer exists separating me from You. I come to You in the name of Jesus, my Saviour. Fill me to overflowing with Your Holy Spirit so that I can more and more reflect the glory of my Lord through a transformed life. Amen.

9 August

Transformed through His Light

Read John 1:1-8; 8:12

When Jesus spoke again to the people, he said, "I am the light of the world. Whoever follows me will never walk in darkness, but will have the light of life." - John 8:12

Wherever Jesus went the Light of God went – Jesus is the Light. His Light has shined into the darkness. The Light of God in our lives illuminates and shines into every corner of our lives. You might say to me, 'Retah, everyone has their faults and weaknesses, it is not possible to live a consistently holy life.' This is not true; Jesus came so that you can be transformed by His Light.

When you have the Kingdom of God within you and you begin to live out Kingdom principles, you will see transformation taking place in your life. As you keep your focus upon Jesus looking into His Light you will be transformed by that Light, through His Spirit. It will change how you view the world and those around you. Your goals will change, your desires will change because the Light will shine in and the darkness will have to flee.

I have to allow the Light to shine into the darkness of my life so that transformation can take place – have I made this choice?

Prayer

Dear Father, *Your Word is a lamp to my feet and a light for my path.* Thank You that I have the Light of life living within me. Continue to shine Your Light into the deep recesses of my life illuminating everything that Your Spirit wants to change. Amen.

Living in the Light

Read Ephesians 5:6-21

For you were once darkness, but now you are light in the Lord. Live as children of light (for the fruit of the light consists in all goodness, righteousness and truth) and find out what pleases the Lord. - Ephesians 5:8-10

Living in the Kingdom means that I live in Him and have my being in Him. I am sold out to Him. The fruit of righteousness is to be evident in our lives. As we live in the Light, the deeds of darkness in our lives will be exposed. We are further encouraged to make the most of every opportunity, being careful how we live.

It is Christ in me; He is my hope of glory – not what I do. I cannot earn my place in the Kingdom through living a religious life or embarking upon good works. It is all too easy to get caught up in good works. I can only take my place as a citizen of God's Kingdom through faith in Jesus Christ. When I stray or the old nature rears its head the Holy Spirit will be right there nudging me and reminding me of whom I am in Christ.

Once I am a child of God and His Light is in my life then I will not be able to help myself; I will start to bear the fruit of righteousness in my life.

Prayer

Father, I long to walk in the Light of Christ, my Saviour and Lord; and I long to walk in the fullness of Your Holy Spirit, Lord. Help me to live in Your Light, I pray. Amen.

Living out the Light

Read Luke 8:1-18

No one lights a lamp and hides it in a jar or puts it under a bed. Instead, he puts it on a stand, so that those who come in can see the light. - Luke 8:16

If you are a child of God and His Kingdom is within you; then you will live out the principles of the Kingdom. Aldo often writes about living a life that is transparent before both God and man. The world needs to see Christians living out the principles of the Kingdom. Do the people you interact with, who are not followers of Christ, experience His love flowing through you? Are you a light shining in the darkness for them? People should look at us and be drawn to Jesus as a result of what they see.

The Bible tells us not to hide our lamp under a jar or a bed, but to place it on a stand so that people can see and be drawn to the light. What is inside of us will come out. The question is what is inside of you and what is coming out?

The Light is Christ and I am called to live out His Light.

Prayer

Dear Father, King of my heart, I love You. Lord, thank You for Your Light that has come into my life. Thank You that it illuminates every area of my life. I want to be a lamp that burns brightly shedding the Light to all those around me. Amen.

12 August

Living a life of faith

Read Matthew 9:18-31

Then he touched their eyes and said, "According to your faith will it be done to you"; and their sight was restored. - Matthew 9:29-30a

Living a life of faith has the following components: There is the belief, the step and the resting. I have to believe in my heart. All through the Gospels we read stories of people who believed in their heart; but they had to act on this belief though.

Taking the step of faith requires action. They had to do something; the father had to come to Jesus and ask Him to come and bring his daughter back to life. The woman with an issue of blood had to step forward and touch the hem of Jesus' robe. In that act of stepping forward her faith was rewarded.

I must believe in my heart; bring my need to God and then trust and rest in Him, as He brings His solution to my situation.

Then there is the resting. Once I have brought my concern or need to Jesus I have to rest in His response. Casting my cares upon Him means that I don't pick them up again. This is often the hardest part for us.

Prayer

My Father, Your Word says that according to my faith it will be done to me. Father, help me to believe in You, come to You and rest in You. Thank You that I can trust You with every aspect of my life and the lives of those I love. Amen.

13 August

Living in humility

Read Luke 18:9-14

The Pharisee stood up and prayed about himself ... But the tax collector ... said, 'God have mercy on me, a sinner.' "I tell you that this man, rather than the other, went home justified before God. For everyone who exalts himself will be humbled, and he who humbles himself, will be exalted." - Luke 18:11a,13a&c,14

Are you struck by the difference between the two men? The one is very confident about his self righteousness and his own accomplishments. He acts as if God is lucky to have him deign to serve Him. We can judge him but as I look at him I see definite traces of myself when I get out of step with the Holy Spirit.

Having the Kingdom within me is characterised by a humble heart.

On the other hand we see the tax collector. He stood at a distance, didn't feel he could even lift his eyes to heaven. He called out to God, asking Him to have mercy on him, a sinner. Jesus looked upon the two of them and He didn't see the outward appearance; He saw his heart. Jesus has some damning words for the Pharisee. He also used the situation to teach His disciples a lesson about humility. If we have the Kingdom within us we will live a life of humility.

Prayer

Father, I come before You with a grateful heart in humble thanksgiving for Your great love and mercy for me. Help me to walk day by day in Your Spirit so that I may stay close to You at all times. Amen.

Living in the Kingdom

Read John 8:1-18

When Jesus spoke again to the people, he said, "I am the light of the world. Whoever follows me will never walk in darkness, but will have the light of life." - John 8:12

You cannot know what the Kingdom is like if you haven't experienced living in the Kingdom. It is a bit like a cook book. You can have the best cook book in the world standing on your shelf. You can take it down from the shelf and read the recipes, you can even get all the ingredients together; but you must actually make the recipe and taste it in order to experience it.

To the Pharisees the letter of the law was more important than the love and grace of God. They judged the woman caught in adultery; using it as an opportunity to condemn. Jesus used it as an opportunity to demonstrate the grace and mercy of God. I am not suggesting that we ignore the Word of God – but we mustn't use it as a rod to people's backs. Jesus gave us the perfect example when He spoke to the woman.

Living in the Kingdom is living like Jesus.

Prayer

My Lord and God, I am so privileged to live in Your Kingdom. Thank You for the example of Jesus and the opportunity I have to share Your mercy and grace with others. Give me Your heart for the hurting. Amen.

15 August

Living in repentance

Read 1 John 1:1-10

If we confess our sins, he is faithful and just and will forgive us our sins and purify us from all unrighteousness. - 1 John 1:9

Religion encourages you to do things in order to attain holiness. However, you will never become transformed into the image of Christ by doing things. We fall for this so easily because we are brought up to believe we must achieve. We are taught to work hard for everything we get (this is not a bad thing – it is just not applicable to our spiritual life).

Maybe you are struggling with something in your life. God sent Jesus to this world to set you free. He came so that we can walk in the Light. He did not come to condemn us. With Him there is no darkness. The solution is to repent. Our verse today gives us great hope: *If we confess our sins, he is faithful and just and will forgive us our sins and purify us from all unrighteousnes* (1 John 1:9).

I must come to Him, repent and He will cleanse me from all sin. Then I must go out and walk in the Light.

Prayer

Father, I want more of You, I long for more of You. I come before You in humility asking You to forgive me as I confess my sin before You. Cleanse me, fill me and empower me to live victoriously for You. Amen.

Living in holiness

Read Exodus 3:1-8

"Do not come any closer," God said. "Take off your sandals, for the place where you are standing is holy ground." Then he said, "I am the God of your father, the God of Abraham, the God of Isaac and the God of Jacob." At this Moses hid his face, because he was afraid to look at God. - Exodus 3:5-6

We come to God on the strength of one thing, and one thing only; the blood that was shed by the Lamb of God. There is nothing we can do – there is nothing we can accomplish in and of ourselves. We can pray all day, we can do good works until we drop from exhaustion; only the blood of the Lamb will make us righteous.

When we enter into the throne room, we are immediately on 'Holy ground'. If you remember when Moses experienced the burning bush, God told him to remove his sandals because he was on 'Holy ground'. Once we realise the reality of the Spirit of God within us we will begin to live a life of holiness. It will not be according to the Law, it will come from deep within us – the evidence of the Kingdom within. It will be the outward manifestation of the Kingdom growing in us.

Holiness is something the Holy Spirit works out in my life as I yield to Him, living in dependence upon Him.

Prayer

Lord, I come into Your Holy presence. I bow before You in adoration, praise and love. Thank You that I can come into Your throne room, that I can worship before Your throne. Fill me anew with Your Spirit so that I can be continually transformed into the likeness of Christ. Amen.

17 August

Living a healing life

Read Mark 16:14-20

"And these signs will accompany those who believe: In my name they will drive out demons; they will speak in new tongues ... they will place their hands on sick people, and they will get well." - Mark 16:17,18c

Physical healing can be instantaneous or it can be a process. Another kind of healing is emotional and spiritual healing; I have seen many people set free emotionally and spiritually. This kind of healing is every bit, in fact more important than physical healing.

Your life will manifest the fruit and the power of the Holy Spirit. As you interact with people you will be sensitive to what their needs are. A Kingdom life is a life lived in meekness and humility; it is a life where serving others and living out the love of Jesus is a part of each day. It will mean that the Holy Spirit is convicting you of the things in your life that must be changed. These things must be brought into the light and healed. It is your birthright to live a whole, healthy and vibrant life in the Kingdom of God.

Living a 'healing life' means that each day I will be transformed by the power of the Holy Spirit within me; I will be becoming more and more like Jesus.

Prayer

Father, thank You for Your promise of healing. I am so grateful that I can come before You with my physical, emotional and spiritual needs. I pray that you will help me to live a 'healing life' reaching out to others who are in need. Amen.

Living in discernment

Read Philippians 1:1-11

And this is my prayer: that your love may abound more and more in knowledge and depth of insight, so that you may be able to discern what is best and may be pure and blameless until the day of Christ. - Philippians 1:9-10

Our focus is God's Kingdom; living for Him, walking with Him and being His servant here on earth. God is looking for those who are meek, poor in spirit and gentle. He is looking for Kingdom people who will give themselves to others. He is looking for those who will live with discernment, drawing wisdom and insight from His Word and His Spirit. As we spend time in the Word and in the throne room with our God, being filled with His Spirit we will not need to worry about being led astray by strange teachings or worldly ideas and plans. We will have the mind of Christ.

I live in the insight, knowledge and discernment of the Holy Spirit who is at work within me.

We do not fear the world, people or circumstances. We have a sound mind focused upon the things of God. God promises to complete the good work He has begun in us; He will present us perfect on the day that Jesus Christ returns to take us home.

Prayer

My Father God, I praise You; You are a God of truth and love. You are meek and gentle; You are a God who is patient and long suffering; You are kind and merciful. Fill me with discernment so that I can live the best life I can for You. Amen.

19 August

Living selflessly

Read Matthew 3:1-12

"I baptise you with water for repentance. But after me will come one who is more powerful than I, whose sandals I am not fit to carry. He will baptise you with the Holy Spirit and with fire." - Matthew 3:11

When I am standing in the Light the Spirit can show me when I am being self-centred, focused on my own agendas and plans; when I am depending upon my own self righteousness. As the Spirit shows me these things the call comes, 'Retah, repent, repent.'

When I am out of step with the Spirit then I am totally unaware of these flaws in my character and spiritual life. Have you noticed this too? When we walk in the Light the smallest things become illuminated and transparent. This is why we are admonished over and over in Scripture to walk in the Light.

Jesus is the most perfect example of a selfless life. He was selfless to the point that He gave His life – so that I can have eternal life.

As we live and walk in the Kingdom we will find ourselves being challenged more and more regarding the way we live. The outcome will be to bring us closer to our Lord and to take us a step further in our process of transformation.

Prayer

Father, I thank You for the selfless life of Jesus, my Saviour. Jesus, thank You that You lay down Your life for me. As I live and walk in Your Kingdom reveal the areas in my life where self rules and reigns still. I repent that I so often depend upon my own self righteousness and abilities. Amen.

20 August

Living a life of service

Read Matthew 20:20-28 & Hebrews 12:28

Therefore, since we receive a kingdom which cannot be shaken, let us show gratitude, by which we may offer to God an acceptable service with reverence and awe.
- Hebrews 12:28 (New American Standard Bible)

There is no place for a personal agenda in Kingdom living. In our Scripture reading we see some of Jesus' disciples who have personal agendas regarding their place in the Kingdom. A Kingdom citizen lives differently: not seeking their own best interests but rather they seek first their Kings interests and then the interests of other people.

This is so different to worldly standards where we are taught to make sure that we get what is due to us, where we are considered weak if we do not push our own agendas. Paul who understood what it was to push his own agenda and then after his conversion experience became wholly sold out to God's Kingdom puts it beautifully in Romans 12:1, he says, '*... I urge you therefore, brethren, by the mercies of God, to present your bodies a living and holy sacrifice, acceptable to God, which is your spiritual service of worship.*'

What matters to God is the quality of my spiritual service of worship before Him. He looks at my heart.

Prayer

My Father God, I come before You bringing to You my spiritual service of worship. Father, examine my heart and find it acceptable in Your sight, I pray. Amen.

Living in forgiveness

Read Matthew 18:21-35

Then the master called the servant in. 'You wicked servant,' he said, 'I cancelled all that debt of yours because you begged me to. Shouldn't you have had mercy on your fellow servant just as I had on you?' In anger his master turned him over to the jailers to be tortured, until he should pay back all he owed. "This is how my heavenly Father will treat each of you unless you forgive your brother from your heart."
- Matthew 18:32-35

When we walk in meekness we will not need to criticise or fight to have our opinions accepted – we will leave it up to God. You will come to the place where you will be able to bless your enemies and pray for them. It is totally impossible for us to live like this in the natural. We can try and try, we can pray and pray; but to no avail. It is only when we surrender to God and His Holy Spirit; giving control of our lives to Him. As we live in a place of surrender we will increasingly see the evidence of a changed life and changed attitudes.

How dare I not forgive when God has forgiven me all my sins?

There is tremendous freedom in forgiveness – the torture that Jesus spoke of is not only the spiritual aspect but also the emotional aspect. There are so many people who are living in torture because they choose not to forgive.

Prayer

Father, I thank You from the bottom of my heart that You have forgiven me my sins. I am so grateful that I am Your child. Help me to surrender to Your Spirit so that I can forgive those who have hurt me. Father, I want to forgive – but I need You to help me. Amen.

Living in meekness

Read Ephesians 4:1-7

Be completely humble and gentle; be patient, bearing with one another in love.
- Ephesians 4:2

Meekness, gentleness and humility are interdependent – if you have one you will have the other. A meek person is not a proud person. Pride often prevents us from forgiving and operating in the power of God. When we are more concerned about ourselves and how things affect us, than what we are about the Kingdom and Kingdom principles, we cannot live a meek life. A meek person is someone who has a humble and a gentle heart.

If we look at character, how we behave, we see that a hard heart is a cursed heart. You cannot serve God and have a hard heart. It is not for me to say that you are not born again; but when your heart is hard then you have not been saturated, sanctified, washed and soaked in the blood of the Lamb. You have not yet gone through the fire that peels off the hard layers around our hearts.

A meek person will always be the least; surrendering themselves to the Lord.

Prayer

Dear Lord God, You have given me wonderful examples in Your Word of people who lived meek lives. Jesus, my Saviour, is the prime example of the strength that resides in meekness. I surrender to Your Spirit. Work in me, moulding me to be the person You want me to be. Amen.

23 August

Living a Life of trust

Read Proverbs 3:1-18

Trust in the Lord with all your heart and lean not on your own understanding; in all your ways acknowledge him, and he will make your paths straight. - Proverbs 3:5-6

So often we are more concerned with image and how things look than the reality of what our relationship with God is really like. Living a life of trust means that I honestly believe that God is more than able to take my burdens; that when I have difficulties and challenges I take them to Him. I follow His command to cast my cares upon Him because He cares for me.

I know that the moment I hand over my burdens to God He will give me His answer for the situation. It is not about my wisdom and my will, but rather His wisdom and His will. Don't be satisfied with yesterday and the relationship you had with God then, always trust that there is more. Seek more of God and you will find more. God does not break us down, but rather He builds us up in our holy faith.

A Kingdom life is one that is lived trusting God for more; more of His love, more of His peace, more of His power, and more of His holiness.

Prayer

Father, I want more of You. I want to live a life of vibrant trust in You. Thank You that You want only the best for me. I am so grateful that as I come before You I can cast every care and concern upon You, knowing that You will take them, and that You have the solution. Amen.

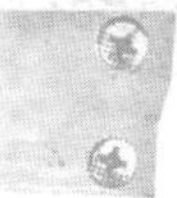

Living a thankful life

Read 1 Thessalonians 5:14-24

Be joyful always; pray continually; give thanks in all circumstances, for this is God's will for you in Christ Jesus. - 1 Thessalonians 5:16-18

Living a Kingdom life means to live a life of thankfulness. God has given us salvation; through His Son, Jesus Christ. We have been brought from the kingdom of darkness and given citizenship in His Kingdom of Light. We have been saved from death and given a new life that will never end. He has also given us the Holy Spirit who dwells in us, and empowers us.

Paul says in 1 Thessalonians *to Rejoice always, to pray continually, and to give thanks in all circumstances.* Paul uses the word ***all***, there are no exclusion clauses – all is ***all***. There are times in our lives when we come before the throne, with tears in our eyes and hearts, but still we come giving thanks. The reality is that no matter what happens in your life you still have God; He is still there, He doesn't change.

I am thankful no matter what happens because I have an eternal hope burning within me.

Prayer

Father, thank You that I come into the Holy of Holies, before Your throne of grace. I am here Lord, to give You the glory due Your Name. I bow before You in thankfulness and I rejoice in Your great love for me. Thank You, Thank You! Amen.

25 August

Living a life of worship

Read John 4:7-24

Yet a time is coming and has now come when the true worshippers will worship the Father in spirit and truth, for they are the kind of worshippers the Father seeks. God is spirit and his worshippers must worship in spirit and in truth. - John 4:23-24

Jesus says in John 4 that God is looking for worshippers who will worship Him in spirit and truth. Every area of our lives should be lived as an act of worship. Everything we do should be done as worship unto the Lord. We worship Him with our thoughts and our actions. Kingdom life means living a life that is one hundred percent sold out to God. True worship is expressed to God when you are alone with Him bowing before His throne.

When Jesus spoke to the Samaritan woman in John 4 He is helping her to see that she needs the Water of Life in order to be able to quench her thirst. He offered her the Water of Life. Jesus does the same for you and me. We cannot be citizens of the Kingdom of God unless we have been born again. This is the prerequisite – the passport if you like.

God is spirit and His worshippers must worship in spirit and in truth.

Prayer

Father God, thank You for the Water of Life that You have freely given to me. I am so grateful that I need never thirst again. I long to be a worshipper who worships You in spirit and in truth. Amen.

Living a praying life

Read Ephesians 6:10-18

And pray in the Spirit on all occasions with all kinds of prayers and requests. With this in mind, be alert and always keep on praying for all the saints. - Ephesians 6:18

God will only be able to change what we surrender into His hands. Part of prayer is about surrendering to the King. It is where He fills us with His love. Give over control of your subconscious (where all the pain and trauma lies) to the Holy Spirit, so that He can gradually bring everything into the light for healing to take place. Don't bury your pain, because it is in the darkness that the enemy reigns. Give *everything* over to God.

Why do we often struggle to pray? It is because there are so many distractions that take our attention away from our 'First Love'. Do you find that sometimes when you start praying your thoughts will stray to problems you are having at school, or maybe your cell phone rings. This is exactly how the enemy tries to keep us away from the fire of God's presence – through all kinds of distractions.

He seeks the place of 'First Love' in my heart. I will then be drawn to Him like a magnet and make time to be with Him.

Prayer

Father, forgive my lack of perseverance and passion when it comes to prayer. I want to pray without ceasing, I want to communicate with You in a meaningful way. Help me, I pray. Amen.

Living a life of blessing

Read Ephesians 1:3-14

Praise be to the God and Father of our Lord Jesus Christ, who has blessed us in the heavenly realms with every spiritual blessing in Christ. - Ephesians 1:3

An inheritance is something you get after someone has died. Jesus had to die in order for us to receive the inheritance of eternal life. There are two stages of this inheritance: the first part we receive when we come to faith in Jesus Christ. The second stage is when we die and go to be with the Lord. However, we do not need to wait until we get to heaven in order to live in the blessing that is ours in Christ.

We have spoken before about the power of speaking out blessing upon other people. Have you adopted a life of blessing others? Do you make a practise now of blessing your family members, your friends and other people you come into contact with during your day? You will only be able to do this if you have a Kingdom mentality; if the Kingdom is within you – it is a supernatural thing to do.

God tells me that I am to bless those who curse me. I must not meet curses with curses, but rather I must bless those who curse me.

Prayer

Father, there is no way that I can bless those who curse me in my own strength. I bring my hurts to You. I lay them at Your feet – fill me with Your love for those that I need to bless. Thank You that I enjoy every spiritual blessing in Christ Jesus. Amen.

Blessed are those who mourn

Read Matthew 5:3-12

Blessed are those who mourn, for they will be comforted. - Matthew 5:4

God said: 'Blessed are those who mourn.' What does this mean? It means that I have tears in my eyes over my condition. This is definitely not pride or the attitude that I have arrived. It is the attitude of the meek, merciful, and pure in heart; of someone who is a peacemaker.

The longer I am on this road of holiness, the more I am being transformed into His image. I now have mercy and compassion for people who are suffering, it is something that has grown and grown over time. God does not just want to give us health and wealth; He wants complete control of our lives.

Part of Kingdom living is being aware of my shortcomings. I will experience genuine mourning and sorrow for the sin in my life.

God wants all of us; one hundred percent. He wants to be the total desire of my heart. It is for this reason that I continue to pray: 'Lord, give me and my household a desire for You. Give us a desire for Your Word.'

Prayer

Father, I humbly come before You. Through Your Spirit search my heart and see if there be any wicked way in me. Cleanse me and heal me, I pray. Amen.

29 August

Endure suffering

Read Isaiah 43:1-4

Fear not, for I have redeemed you; I have summoned you by name; you are mine. When you pass through the waters, I will be with you; and when you pass through the rivers, they will not sweep over you. When you walk through the fire, you will not be burned; the flames will not set you ablaze. For I am the Lord, your God, the Holy One of Israel, Your Saviour. - Isaiah 43:1b-3a

What this verse is saying is that we will be tested in the fire, and everything that is not of God will be burnt away – however, after the fire we will be standing strong and true. It is this cleansing that will help us to stand against the times when people would throw stones at us. We will be able to withstand the attack; and our response will be to bless them and forgive them.

Suffering will come, I cannot avoid it – but when I suffer God will walk with me.

Each time I go through the fire another layer of self is peeled away. I realise that it is through suffering that the most is accomplished in my life in terms of transformation into the likeness of Christ. I am so grateful that God is at work in my life. No matter what I go through God has given me the promise that He will be there with me – He will never leave me or forsake me.

Prayer

Dear Lord, thank You for Your wonderful promise in Your Word. I need not fear suffering or anything that might happen to me. I am so grateful that You have promised that You will be with me. Amen.

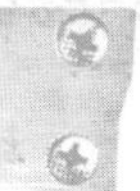

Our reward

Read Matthew 19:16-30

And everyone who has left houses or brothers or sisters or father or mother or children or fields for my sake will receive a hundred times as much and will inherit eternal life.
- Matthew 19:29

The call to discipleship is a call to put Christ first in our lives. When the seed of the Kingdom is placed within us we have the responsibility to nurture that seed. It is at this point that the seed grows differently in each person's life. You will see the outworking of the Kingdom in someone's life according to the soil that the seed has fallen on. When we nurture and grow the seed then the Kingdom will grow and become evident in our life.

As His children, as citizens of His Kingdom, we are to be about Kingdom business. My eyes are to be upon the task that God has set before me. In our Scripture reading Jesus assures His disciples that those who sacrificed for the Kingdom will receive their reward; but the greatest reward is eternal life. This is the ultimate reward for us. Is your greatest reward the knowledge that you will spend eternity with your Lord?

As a child of God there is no greater reward than knowing that I will spend eternity with my heavenly Father.

Prayer

Father, thank You that You have saved me from my sin into Your Kingdom of Light. Thank You that I have the privilege of living for You. I look forward to my reward that is spending eternity with You. Amen.

31 August

The pearl of great price

Read Matthew 13:44-46

Again the kingdom of heaven is like a merchant looking for fine pearls. When he found one of great value, he went away and sold everything he had and bought it.
- Matthew 13:45-46

We will only receive the Kingdom if we are passionate and desperate to receive it. It must be the most important thing in your life. You must be willing to sacrifice everything in order to attain it. You cannot be undecided or unsure about what you want. If you do not come to the place where you will give up everything to gain this Kingdom you will find that the seed will falter and fade.

God calls us to experience the fullness of His Kingdom. He has so many blessings and lessons He wants us to enjoy and learn. In the parable about the treasure and the pearl we see that when the merchant discovered the pearl he desired it above all else. He went off and sold everything that he owned so that he could buy the pearl. When something has cost you everything you own then you will look after it, and care for it.

This is my inheritance – to own the pearl of great price – what am I doing with it?

Prayer

My Father, thank You for the lessons You have taught me through Your Word and Your Spirit. I am so grateful that You have given me the Pearl of great price – I have Your Kingdom within me. Help me to live a Kingdom life to the honour and glory of Your Name. Amen.

Wysheid sê seisoene is
sy manier om sy kinders
te help hy se jaar na
jaar is seisoene van sy
hulp. bid, bid, bid sien
ek het my ouers in ons
winter seisoen gedoen.
by ons somer seisoen
sal soul genees. seisoen
sien ek nou is somer gesien
herfs sal nog meer seer
wat seun het genees sodat
Lente sal ons orde sien.
hy sê seun sal nooit
weer so koue winter hê
nie. sien seisoene sal sien
hulle blare van "self" moet
bly affal.

Letter 9:

Seasons

Wisdom says that seasons are His way of helping His children. He says that He helps His children year after year through His seasons. I saw that my parents prayed, prayed, prayed, in our winter season. In our summer season my soul will heal. I can see that the season is now summer. In autumn more healing will take place, so that in spring there will be order in my soul. He says that the boy will never again have such a cold winter. I see different seasons. I see that the leaves of 'self' must keep on falling off.

Victory in Jesus

Prayer for September

Father God, I come to You in the Precious Name of Jesus, my Lord and Saviour. I ask that You will guard my tongue and reveal all the lies of the enemy, so that I will stand in agreement with Your Word. I know that Jezebel hates repentance, she hates humility, and she cannot stand it when someone is able to be the least. She cannot bear it when I speak Christ's mercy over another person's life. Her tactic is to make pride surface in my life, but I will not fall for this. Lord, as I come before You today, I declare that I will fight the enemy. I will not accept the lies, I will not believe them. I rebuke them in Jesus' Name. Lord, I choose the truth, and I ask that You will come in Your might and wisdom to help me. According to Your Word, my God, I put on Your armour. I take up Your weapons, I stand in Your Light. I am Your child and I claim my heritage in Jesus Christ. In Your grace and mercy help me to deal with the strongholds in my life and in the lives of my loved ones. I bring my family heritage to You. Today I choose a new path for myself and my descendents; I choose a Godly heritage. I proclaim today: *Now have come the salvation and the power and the Kingdom of my God, and the authority of His Christ. For the accuser, who accuses me before our God day and night, has been hurled down. I overcame him by the blood of the Lamb and by the word of my testimony; I do not love my life so much as to shrink from death. Therefore I rejoice with the heavens and those who dwell in them!* Victory is mine in Jesus! Amen.

What is a stronghold?

Read 1 John 4:1-6

You, dear children, are from God and have overcome them, because the one who is in you is greater than the one who is in the world. - 1 John 4:4

Today we are going to talk about strongholds. You might ask what a stronghold is. It is a lie of Satan that you continue believing. At sometime in your life you were hurt; it could be emotionally, through something that someone said to you, or it could be a physical hurt as well. This is what happened to Aldo; he was hurt and experienced rejection through the words and actions of certain people, and he was broken down as a result of this.

I have time and again asked the Lord why Aldo, a man of God, listens to these lies. The same question can be asked of you. If you are living in defeat and in the grip of a stronghold, why are you listening to the lies of Satan? Jesus Christ died to set you free from the stronghold of Satan over your life.

Jesus Christ died to set you free from the stronghold of Satan over your life.

Prayer

My Father God, I bow in worship before You. I submit to You and Your will for my life. Father, I pray that You will free me by the power of Your Spirit of Might. I ask You to fill me anew, and give me a new spirit that is free to live for You. Amen.

2 September

God is greater than the enemy

Read 1 Kings 19:1-4

Elijah was afraid and ran for his life. He came to a broom tree, sat down under it and prayed that he might die. "I have had enough, Lord," he said. "Take my life; I am no better than my ancestors." - 1 Kings 19:3a,4b&c

Recently the Lord spoke to me about altars and reminded me of how Elijah, the prophet of God was attacked by Jezebel. Elijah, the mighty man of God fearlessly challenged the prophets of Baal. His faith was strong until he went down into the city and he heard people saying that Jezebel planned to kill him.

Usually Jezebel uses people close to you to speak her words of death. She attacked Elijah where he was weak. His door was undefended and she was able to slip through. The same thing can happen to us. The enemy attacks us where we are weak and vulnerable. Elijah believes her lies and runs away, and lies down under a Juniper tree to die.

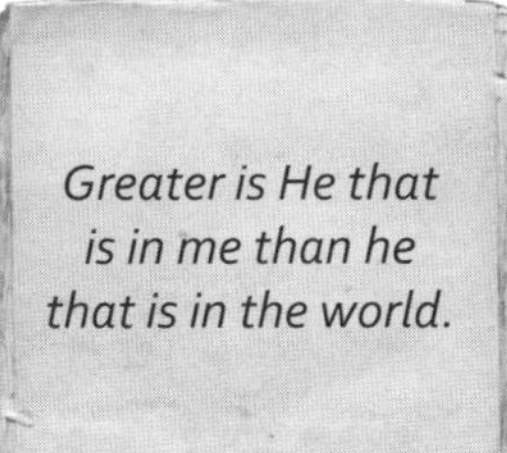
Greater is He that
is in me than he
that is in the world.

Are you believing and worshiping Jezebel or are you believing and worshipping God? *Greater is He that is in me than he that is in the world.*

Prayer

Father, thank You for Your great love for me. I bring my hurt and rejection to You – I lay them at Your feet. Father, I desire to worship only You – please fill me with Your healing power so that I can stand tall in the strength of who I am in You. Amen.

3 September

Strength to overcome

Read 1 Kings 19:5-9

So he got up and ate and drank. Strengthened by that food, he travelled for forty days and forty nights until he reached Horeb, the mountain of God. - 1 Kings 19:8

There are so many Christians whose tongues are controlled by Jezebel. Jesus said that a tree is known by its fruit. What matters is living out the nature and character of Christ in our daily lives. It is one thing to talk and complain about the pressure you are under and another to rejoice in what you are experiencing.

God invites everyone who is burdened and heavy laden to come to Him and receive strength. You have a choice; you can live in the Kingdom and follow Kingdom principles or you can follow the wisdom of the world and live by the principles and logic of the world.

When we inhabit the Kingdom we are not the victim but the victor in Christ Jesus.

When we choose to live according to Kingdom principles we are not bound by this world. We answer to a higher power – to God Himself. When we inhabit the Kingdom we receive the strength and the wisdom to deal with the attacks of the enemy.

Prayer

Father in heaven, Your Kingdom is an everlasting Kingdom. I bow before You, My Lord and Saviour. It is as I abide in You that I have the strength, wisdom and victory over my enemy, the Devil. I am more than an over-comer in Jesus Christ, my Lord. Amen.

His mighty strength

Read Psalm 27

The Lord is my light and my salvation – whom shall I fear? The Lord is the stronghold of my life – of whom shall I be afraid? Wait for the Lord; be strong and take heart and wait for the Lord. - Psalm 27:1,14

When we approached the seventh anniversary of our motor vehicle accident that happened on 19 June 2004, God opened our eyes to see that this was the reason we were experiencing a renewed attack from the enemy.

We all battle against the lies the enemy uses to rub into the wounds and tender places in our spirits and emotions. He uses our thoughts to find his way into our mind. As Christians we have the mind of Christ. You can say a million times a day; I have the mind of Christ. It is not going to get you anywhere, because it is only an intellectual fact until it becomes an experiential reality for you.

We are being trained up to be strong in the Lord.

How does it become reality? You need the infilling of the Holy Spirit to renew your mind day by day. You need to come before God in humility giving Him complete control of every area of your life.

Prayer

My Father, thank You for Your mighty strength that is at work within me. Thank You for the empowering of Your Holy Spirit that overcomes the enemy of my soul. Lord Jesus, thank You for Your victory on Calvary, that means I have Your mind and Your nature at work within me. Amen.

Darkness into Light

Read Psalm 18:1-3, 16-29

You save the humble but bring low those whose eyes are haughty. You, O Lord, keep my lamp burning; my God turns my darkness into light. - Psalm 18:27-28

We must yield one hundred percent to the Holy Spirit. There cannot be any dark place in our lives. Where the Light is darkness cannot linger. If you have been deeply hurt, you tend to return to the hurt over and over again.

We feel inferior, believing we are no good. This starts the cycle repeating itself in our minds; and our mind affects our behaviour and speech and we live in defeat and pain. This is exactly where the enemy wants us and where he wants to keep us; that way we are of no use to the Master. There is nothing that he likes better than a child of God living in defeat.

You do not have to live allowing the enemy to have His way with you. Come to your Father today, submit to His Spirit.

We are to bring these areas into the Light. We are to submit our thoughts to Christ. God has called you to live in victory, you are His well-loved child. You do not have to live in defeat.

Prayer

Father, You are a mighty God. You are all powerful; there is no one and nothing which is more powerful than You. I am Your child and I have all the energies of heaven on my side. Father, as I stand up to the enemy of my soul, fill me, I pray, with Your might and power. Amen.

Wilful Obedience

Read Luke 11:33-36

See to it, then, that the light within you is not darkness. - Luke 11:35

The enemy's objective is to keep us in darkness, but if we are willing to submit to and be wilfully obedient to God then He can work in our lives. If you believe the enemy when he tells you that living in defeat, in the painful and hurt places is what your life is about then you are living in disobedience. This is not what God saved you for.

Aldo always writes that we are to be transparent. It is in those dark places that our dark thoughts linger and where Satan latches on to them. He operates in the darkness. When you live with hidden anger, hidden desires of revenge, hidden jealousy and hidden rebellion you are in Satan's domain; you give him legal right to be in your life. You don't have to live in the enemy's domain; you have victory in Christ, so pray with me:

The lamp of the Lord searches the spirit of a man; it searches out his inmost being.

Prayer

Lord Jesus, shine Your glory light over my life, shine it into my spirit and soul. I don't want any dark places in my life where the enemy can get a foothold. Amen.

7 September

Beware of pride

Read Luke 22:24-34

"Simon, Simon, Satan has asked to sift you as wheat. But I have prayed for you, Simon, that your faith may not fail. And when you have turned back, strengthen your brothers." - Luke 22:31-32

Satan was able to gain a foothold in Peter's life because of pride. Jesus warned Peter that Satan had demanded permission to sift him like wheat. In Aldo's case the enemy had the legal right to do what he had been doing to Aldo because Aldo continued to believe he was not good enough, he continued to believe the lies.

The good news is that Aldo was sifted but could not be destroyed. What does 'sifting' mean? It means that Satan brings you out of alignment. The enemy takes the part of your heart that is in darkness and sifts it in the darkness. He keeps you in the darkness; building a stronghold or a fortress to keep you imprisoned.

Jesus prays for you that once you have been through the sifting you will return and be a blessing to your brothers and sisters.

The blessing for us is that God does not abandon us. As with Peter, Jesus is there, the prayer He prayed for Peter is just as relevant for us.

Prayer

Dear Lord Jesus, thank You that You pray for me. Thank You that Satan cannot have his way with me. I am so grateful that Your love never fails, never deserts me – You are there with me through everything. Amen.

The pitfall of pride

Read Proverbs 16:16-33

Pride goes before destruction, a haughty spirit before a fall. - Proverbs 16:18

Yesterday we read that the disciples got together and were talking about who was the greatest among them. Peter was in the forefront of this conversation. He had a certain status among the disciples; after all he was the one who had walked on water.

Our reading today tells us that pride comes before destruction. We are to submit ourselves to God. James tells us that we are to resist the devil and he will flee from us (4:7). We can only resist him once we have opened the dark corners and areas of our lives up to the Light of God. Once we have done this the devil will have nowhere to hide. If you have pride in your life, if you identify with what Peter went through, then don't delay; repent before the Lord. Don't allow pride to keep you from walking in freedom and victory before the Lord.

Don't allow pride to keep you from walking in freedom and victory before the Lord.

Prayer

My Father God, I humbly bow before You. Father, I come in repentance before You asking You to forgive me for the pride which is in my life. I recognise that I have taken the glory which is due to You. Lord, forgive me, I pray. Cleanse me and renew my heart and mind. Amen.

9 September

Demolishing strongholds

Read 2 Corinthians 10

For though we live in the world, we do not wage war as the world does. The weapons we fight with are not the weapons of the world. On the contrary, they have divine power to demolish strongholds. - 2 Corinthians 10:3-4

The world's mightiest weapons are nothing compared to the weapons of the Spirit. We have the Spirit of Might on our side fighting for us. As we submit to God, bringing our dark places into His Light He opens the arsenal of heaven and places it at our disposal. You are a mighty warrior in the Lord. He strengthens your arms and prepares you for battle. You are a warrior bride.

Take every thought captive and make them obedient to Christ. There is no other way. The victory is ours – but we have to take the action.

When we clean out the dark corners we are giving our demons eviction notices. I will no longer live listening to and being influenced by the lies and deceit. I give my mind, soul and spirit over to the Living God. In Romans 6:12 we read: *Therefore do not let sin reign in your mortal body so that you obey its evil desires.* We cannot entertain sin in our lives because it weakens our defences and gives Satan a foothold in our lives.

Prayer

Father God, You are the Almighty God and I worship You. Lord Jesus, please help me to take every thought captive and make them obedient to You. I lay them at Your feet, dear Lord. I submit to You – I desire no one and nothing else to have control over me – only You. Amen.

You are under grace

Read Romans 6

For sin shall not be your master, because you are not under law, but under grace.
- Romans 6:14

We're no longer slaves to sin but we are slaves to the law of grace. It is a choice we make; Satan's lies so often cause us to believe that we do not have a choice. Satan is cunning and clever and he attacks us where the weak spots are. For Peter his pride together with his impetuousness made him a prime candidate for sifting.

Paul warns us in Romans 6 that we cannot allow sin to live in our mortal bodies if we want to live for Christ. Satan knows that so often we don't really want to change so he continues to tell us his lies, strengthening the stronghold in our lives. We have to come before God, repent, and be willing to turn and break this stronghold in our lives. You have everything you need to live a Kingdom life through the shed blood of Jesus.

Take your victory today – live in it. Stand tall and proclaim that you will follow your Master and Him only.

Prayer

My Lord and Master, I bow in humble adoration before Your throne of grace today. I worship You and adore You, You are the God Almighty – there is none besides You. Forgive my unbelief, Lord. Cleanse me, fill me, empower me to walk in Your ways. Amen.

11 September

Grace to the humble

Read James 4

But he gives us more grace. That is why Scripture says: "God opposes the proud but gives grace to the humble." - James 4:6

James 4:7 tells us that we must submit to God and the devil will flee from us. The Scripture continues to instruct us; we must cleanse our hands and purify our hearts. This speaks to our actions (hands) and thoughts (heart). You have to be single minded about serving God.

We must deal with our past, bringing everything that has happened to us before the throne of grace. We must bring our hurts and dark sore places opening them to the Light. We must expose our thoughts, the hatred, un-forgiveness and bitterness we carry around inside of us to the Light. When we do this and humbly repent, when we lay them at the feet of Jesus, acknowledging that in and of ourselves we do not have the strength to forgive; but in Him we are more than able. When we do this with a sincere and humble heart the change will take place.

A humble heart, where pride has been banished is a fertile breeding spot for grace to abound.

Prayer

Dear Lord God, I come before You realising my absolute need and dependence upon You. I am nothing without You. I can do nothing without You. Work in my life, I pray. I open my mind, soul and spirit to You. Shine Your light in and illuminate every dark corner. Amen.

Humble before God

Read 1 Peter 5

Humble yourselves, therefore, under God's mighty hand, that he may lift you up in due time. - 1 Peter 5:6

Humbling yourself under the mighty hand of God is not a once off exercise; it is a daily walk. This is the only way to prevent Satan from gaining a foothold. It is his mission to trip us up. This is why when we allow our thoughts to run wild we land up in difficulties. We must have the mind of Christ; our thoughts must be centred upon the Word of God. When a thought comes into our minds we must submit it to the Light. In the Light it will not be able to take hold if it is not a Godly thought.

This is why Paul admonishes us in Philippians 4:8: *Finally, brothers, whatever is true, whatever is noble, whatever is right, whatever is pure, whatever is lovely, whatever is admirable – if anything is excellent or praiseworthy – think about such things.* In order to live like this you have to have a humble heart.

I must focus my mind on all that is praiseworthy. Satan has no defence against a mind like this.

Prayer

My Father God, I humble myself before You. Help me to think on what is true, noble, right, pure, lovely, and admirable – all that is praiseworthy. Give me a humble heart for You and a mind filled with Your Light. Amen.

13 September

Repentance

Read Psalm 51

Have mercy on me, O God, according to your unfailing love; according to your great compassion blot out my transgressions. Wash away all my iniquity and cleanse me from my sin. - Psalm 51:1-2

A Christian can be oppressed by demons; as a child of God you cannot be possessed though – they cannot be inside of you. They can however attack you from the outside pressurising you, and unleashing a spirit of fear upon you. This spirit of fear evidences itself in continually seeking sympathy, wanting people to feel sorry for you and in experiencing irrational fears.

A thought life which has not been crucified will allow the enemy entrance and a foothold which will in turn become a stronghold. If I hadn't been walking this road with Aldo I would never have come to a place of understanding the danger and devastation caused by this. What we often don't realise is that our bitterness is food to Satan; he feeds on it. Step one is repentance: We have to come before God and repent of our sin.

We have to come with a humble heart before God and submit our thoughts to Him.

Prayer

Father, I come to You Lord in humble acknowledgement of my sin. I have, through my thoughts and actions, given Satan a foothold in my life. Forgive me, I pray. Cleanse me and change my thoughts, I pray. Amen.

Resist the devil

Read James 4:7-10

Submit yourselves, then, to God. Resist the devil, and he will flee from you. - James 4:7

People often want to skip the repentance step and move straight to deliverance. It doesn't work like that though. We first have to acknowledge our sin and bring it before God. It has to be brought into the Light and submitted to the scrutiny of the Holy Spirit. Once we have repented before God then deliverance can begin. The important thing to realise is that you do not need someone else to help you with deliverance. You have everything you need in Christ. Bring your thoughts to God, examining them in His light and you will be able to reject the thoughts that are not from Him. You have the mind of Christ enabling you to reject thoughts that would drag you back into darkness.

Ignorance is one of Satan's greatest weapons. We need to educate ourselves regarding his tactics so that we can resist him.

We are going to look at some of the tactics Satan uses on us. We need to educate ourselves regarding his tactics so that we can resist him.

Prayer

My Father God, I come before You with a heart filled with gratitude. Thank You that You have equipped me with everything that I need to win the battle against the enemy of my soul. I submit to You, My Lord. Amen.

15 September

A prayer for guidance

Before we look at the tactics that Satan would afflict us with we are going to spend time in prayer asking God, our Father, to lead and guide us.

Father, there are areas in my life where I have been hurt, and where I have listened to the lies of the enemy – I bring them to You, surrendering them to You today. I ask You, as we go through the list of ways that Satan uses to trap us that You will show me where I am vulnerable. I acknowledge and confess that it is only in the power of the Holy Spirit, and through the name of Jesus Christ that I can bind the work of Satan.

I proclaim out loud today, that every stronghold in my life will come down. I need fear nothing because greater are You who is in me than he who is in the world. Clothe me in Your righteousness Lord, as I clothe myself in Your armour, so that when the voices speak, I will be able to discern what is of God and what isn't.

God help me that no evil will be able to find a foothold in my life. I declare that my thoughts will be in line with Your Word, and not aligned with unbelief and the lies of the enemy. Lord, You instruct me to resist the Devil; with Your help I will do this relentlessly.

Father, I honour You. I want to live for You. As we look at Satan's tactics I do it in the strength and protection of the Name of Jesus Christ, and the power of Your Holy Spirit.
Amen.

Satan's tactics

Read Matthew 12:38-45

For as he thinketh in his heart, so is he. - Proverbs 23:7 (King James Version)

We must understand Satan's tactics, and how he operates. Everything begins with a stronghold. A stronghold that is characterised by a cold love, a hard heart filled with fear. Other characteristics are pride, un-forgiveness, greed, lust, hate, bitterness, and jealousy.

We must build a new house; a house of restoration, based on God's character. Proverbs 23:7 says, *"For as he thinketh in his heart, so is he."* You are what your thought life is. If we do not keep a guard on our thoughts, then we will once again allow Satan to gain a foothold. Then, as he regains a foothold, the stronghold is re-established in our lives. Our empty houses have to be filled with the Holy Spirit. As God's children we have not been saved to live in defeat and misery. We have been saved to live a Kingdom life.

> *As God's children we have not been saved to live in defeat and misery. We have been saved to live a Kingdom life.*

Prayer

My Father God, thank You for the power of Your Holy Spirit who dwells within me. Give me the courage, and the will to deal with the strongholds in my life, so that my house can be cleaned out. Then, Father, I pray that You will fill me with Your Spirit. Amen.

Focus upon God

Read 2 Kings 6:8-23

"Don't be afraid," the prophet answered. "Those who are with us are more than those who are with them." - 2 Kings 6:16

Our focus must be on Christ, and not on our situations. The easiest way for the enemy to get to us is when we lose focus, and our thoughts drift. You will not be able to bring something to life if you keep your eyes focused on what is dead; you must have your eyes focused on the living God, and then there will be life.

We must be careful not to focus on the battle; because if we do this then we will be dragged down. Our eyes must be firmly focused upon the living God, who has won the battle for us. In our reading today Elisha prayed for his servant, *"O Lord, open his eyes so that he may see." Then the Lord opened the servant's eyes, and he looked and saw the hills full of horses and chariots of fire all round Elisha* (v 17).

Our eyes must be firmly focused upon the living God, who has won the battle for us.

Prayer

Father, I am so grateful that You have redeemed me. Thank You that You have saved me to live a Kingdom life here on earth. Help me to keep my focus upon You. Open my eyes to see Your glory, might and power. Fill me with Your Spirit anew each day. Amen.

Love the Lord your God...

Read Mark 12:28-34

Love the Lord your God with all your heart and with all your soul and with all your mind and with all your strength. - Mark 12:30

Focus on God's plan for your life, because Satan wants you to believe that you are good for nothing. His aim is to stir up your bitterness, and bring to the surface all the emotions and feelings that lurk in the darkness inside of you.

Aldo wrote to me: Mom, a hard heart is a cursed heart. A cursed heart is one filled with bitterness; a stumbling block that the enemy wants to place in your path. Praise God, He promises us that little by little we will drive the enemy out. In Mark 12:30 Jesus tells you exactly how to do this. He says, you will *love the Lord your God with all your heart and with all your soul and with all your mind and with all your strength.* You might cry out in response; Lord, I don't have it in me, help me! I want to walk in divine forgiveness.

My cold heart must be renewed and revitalised, becoming a heart that beats with the love of Jesus for others.

Prayer

Dear Father God, thank You for Your love for me. I want to live in a way that pleases You. I want my love for You to be the defining emotion in my life. I know that out of my love for You will flow a deepening love for other people. Amen.

19 September

Show mercy to your neighbour

Read Luke 10:30-37

The expert in the law replied, "The one who had mercy on him." Jesus told him, "Go and do likewise." - Luke 10:37

It is very hard for someone who has a cold, hard heart to show mercy to other people. Again you need to come before God, crying out for His help: Lord, I don't want to be judgemental, because You alone, Lord, are the Judge. I repent Lord; please remove the log out of my eye so that I can see my fellow man with eyes of compassion and love.

You cannot do this in your own strength. It will only happen as you yield and submit to the Holy Spirit, daily taking on the mind of Christ. You will be willing to take up your responsibility to care for your neighbour through prayer and love. When you forgive someone you free them up to be changed by God. God has shown infinite mercy to you; He has forgiven you all your sin. You dare not do less for other people, even if they have hurt you.

The love of Jesus does not change other people; it changes me. I become more forgiving, loving, understanding and caring.

Prayer

Father, I realise forgiveness is the key to freedom. Thank You that You have forgiven me for so much. Where would I be without Your grace and mercy? Help me to extend mercy to my neighbour. I realise that I am responsible for my neighbour – help me to love as You love. Amen.

A Repairer of Streets with Dwellings

Read Isaiah 58:1-12

Your people will rebuild the ancient ruins and will raise up the age-old foundations; you will be called Repairer of Broken Walls, Restorer of Streets with Dwellings.
- Isaiah 58:12

When Satan has strongholds in our lives or the lives of our family what are left are often only ruins. We are called to rebuild the ancient ruins – sometimes these go back in our families for several generations. We are to ruthlessly root out the strongholds and fortresses. Once we have done this we are to begin rebuilding the foundations of our lives and those of our families.

We read in Matthew 12 that when a house is cleaned out unless it is filled the evil spirits will return and take it over again. This is the reason why we have to be Restorers of Streets with Dwellings. We are to repair our Dwellings and then make sure that they are filled with the Holy Spirit so that there will be no room for the enemy. You are to become a Repairer of Broken Walls, and a Restorer of Streets with Dwellings.

Your body is the temple of the Holy Spirit – there is no room for any other tenant.

Prayer

My Father, I need Your help. I cannot do this on my own. I want to be a Repairer of Broken Walls, a Restorer of Streets with Dwellings. I want to live according to the principles of Your Kingdom. Help me, I pray, fill me with Your Spirit. Amen.

21 September

Emotional Healing

Read Isaiah 58:1-9

Then your light will break forth like the dawn, and your healing will quickly appear; then your righteousness will go before you, and the glory of the Lord will be your rear guard. - Isaiah 58:8

Your soul consists of your will, your emotions and your thoughts. This is where you experience emotional hurt. If you do not deal with the bad things that happen in your life the hurt settles in your soul. These wounds give the enemy a foothold in your life causing darkness to descend upon your soul. There are three types of hurts; the first is 'unhealed hurts'. These are the hurts you bury deep inside yourself. The second type is 'unresolved issues'. These are caused by broken relationships. They provide a wedge for Satan to gain a foothold. The third hurt is 'unmet needs'. When you look to people to meet your needs you will always be disappointed. Only Jesus can fulfil your needs.

If I allow His Light to shine into the dark places He promises that my healing will come quickly.

Come to Him today; allow His Spirit to wash over you, to cleanse you and to heal you. He promises you in Jeremiah 33:6: *"Nevertheless, I will bring health and healing to it; I will heal my people and will let them enjoy abundant peace and security."* The Lord promises that He will heal you, and restore your joy if you trust in Him.

Prayer

Father, I thank You that You know me so intimately. You know where all the sore places are in my life. I am so grateful that I cannot hide from You. Help me today to open myself up to Your Holy Spirit. Come in and cleanse me. Bring health and healing into my soul, I pray. Amen.

Physical Healing

Read Luke 13:10-17

"Then should not this woman, a daughter of Abraham, whom Satan has kept bound for eighteen long years, be set free on the Sabbath day from what bound her?"
- Luke 13:16

Jesus was in the temple, when He noticed the woman in the crowd. Jesus immediately stopped, called her up and delivered her. This angered the religious leaders who felt that this was not the 'proper time' to do this sort of thing.

Are you missing out on God's blessing in your life because of your religious spirit. Do you have a judgemental spirit that looks upon people who are afflicted and think they must have done something to deserve being the way they are? Alternatively, are you afflicted and because of the lies of Satan you feel you do not deserve to be set free. You have allowed him to tell you that this is your life – you have to live like this? This is a lie – you were saved to be free. Don't let Satan rob you of your heritage. Break down the stronghold he has built in your life.

Come to your Father, ask forgiveness and He will set you free. Your Kingdom heritage is that you should walk in victory.

Prayer

Father, I thank You for the freedom I have in Jesus Christ. Please help me to live in the reality of this freedom. I realise that I have bought into Satan's lies – this is not what You saved me for. I am Your child, it is my heritage to be free. Amen.

23 September

Deliverance from suffering

Read 1 Peter 5:6-10

Humble yourselves, therefore, under God's mighty hand, that he may lift you up in due time. - 1 Peter 5:6

God has taught me that I can rejoice in suffering. It is while going through difficult times that I have learnt my most important lessons. As we walked through the situation of Aldo's hurt, I cannot and will not pretend that it wasn't difficult; but as we battled his strongholds God's presence was mightily with us.

Whatever you are going through you need to come to an understanding that the devil has no power, other than the legal power you give him. This is why Peter says, *your enemy the devil prowls around like a roaring lion* – he is not a roaring lion – he just presents himself in the *likeness* of a roaring lion. The only credibility he has is what you give him. *Resist him, stand firm in your faith*. Come before Your Father, cast all your anxiety on Him because He cares for you – you are not alone. *Be self-controlled and alert*.

Be vigilant – guard your heart and your mind so that Satan cannot gain a foothold in your life.

Prayer

Dear Father God, I am so grateful that You are in control of my life. I submit to You in this difficult time that I am going through. Thank You for the injunction to stand firm and be alert. Thank You for the assurance that You are with me, and that You care for me. Amen.

Listen to the still small voice

Read 1 Kings 19:9-15

After the wind there was an earthquake, but the Lord was not in the earthquake. After the earthquake came a fire, but the Lord was not in the fire. And after the fire came a gentle whisper. When Elijah heard it, he pulled his cloak over his face and went out and stood at the mouth of the cave. - 1 Kings 19:11c-13a

We return again to the story of Elijah. I mentioned before that one of Satan's favourite tricks is to make us so tired that we lose perspective. When we are exhausted it is difficult to think straight. Elijah was tired. In verses 10 and 14 he tells God how zealous he has been for Him and how hard he has worked for God.

Even in his dark place Elijah can still recognise God's voice. God taught Elijah and us a very important lesson. We often beg God for a miracle, one that will be visible for all to see. What God taught Elijah is that often He appears to us in *the still, small voice.* Is this why we sometimes miss Him – because we are looking for the grand gesture? Don't allow the enemy to dull your spiritual senses so that you cannot hear God. He is there all the time – He never leaves you.

I need to approach His throne of grace in humility and submission. Like He had for Elijah He has a message for me – am I listening?

Prayer

My Father God, I am humbled as I bow before You. I realise that so often I am just like Elijah, feeling sorry for myself. I forget sometimes Whom it is that I serve. Thank You for reminding me again today. I am listening to You. Amen.

25 September

The Truth sets you free

Read John 8:31-36

Then you will know the truth, and the truth will set you free. - John 8:32

We are saved to be sons and daughters of the living God. This is our heritage. One of the key benefits of this heritage is that we are set free to live differently. You are a child of the King, and you have inherited a Kingdom that will never pass away. Therefore, you can confidently deal with your earthly heritage. I shared with you how I have had to deal with the heritage from my earthly family.

This is the wonderful thing – wherever you come from, whatever your past has been you can draw a line under it. You can choose to do the work of pulling down and rebuilding. As you rebuild you will be putting in place a godly heritage for those who will come after you. *Humble yourselves before God*. Jesus says that if we follow His teaching we will know the Truth and the Truth will set us free.

If the Truth sets you free you will be free indeed. Truth is a person – Jesus Christ. Are you living in freedom?

Prayer

Father, You saved me to live in freedom. Help me to abide in Your Word so that I can know the Truth. Thank You Jesus, You are the Truth and You set me free. Amen.

Who is your father?

Read John 8:37-47

Jesus said to them, "If God were your Father, you would love me, for I came from God and now am here. I have not come on my own; but he sent me." - John 8:42

Jesus asks the Jewish leaders a vitally important question: Who is your father? They were so smug and secure in their 'religious heritage' that they totally missed God Himself standing in front of them. Jesus warned them of the danger of their sin and self righteousness. They claimed to be Abraham's children, whereupon Jesus reminded them that Abraham was a man after God's own heart – so then surely they should be like Abraham.

Jesus asked the Jewish leaders, *Why is my language not clear to you?* He answers His own question saying, "*Because you are unable to hear what I say. You belong to your father, the devil, and you want to carry out your father's desire ... He speaks his native language, for he is a liar and the father of lies*" (vs 43-44). The same question can be asked of us? Which father are we listening to: Our heavenly Father or the father of lies?

Do I understand the language that Jesus speaks? Who is my father?

Prayer

Dear God, I am so grateful that I can call You my Father. I realise this is a huge privilege that I so often take for granted. Thank You that I can live my life as Your child, in Your Kingdom. I thank You for Jesus Christ, my Saviour and Lord. Amen.

27 September

Take up your weapons

Read 2 Corinthians 10:3-5

The weapons we fight with are not the weapons of the world. - 2 Corinthians 10:4a

Paul had to deal with a lot of opposition in his life. Not only did he have to deal with his own regrets about persecuting the Christians but he had to deal with people's attitudes towards him. It would have been easy for him to allow the enemy to gain a foothold in his life as a result of guilt and hurt. He knew what it was to break down the strongholds and fortresses of Satan.

We must live in this world; but we don't have to live like the world. *The weapons we fight with are not the weapons of the world. On the contrary, they have divine power to demolish strongholds. We demolish arguments and every pretension that sets itself up against the knowledge of God, and we take captive every thought to make it obedient to Christ.* This is your war plan – use it.

My flesh inhabits this world but my spirit lives in the Kingdom of God. I live in a different dimension.

Prayer

My Father God, I worship You, Almighty God, Ruler of heaven and earth. Thank You for the weapons of warfare that You have given to me. I present my thoughts to You today, I ask You to take them captive by Your Holy Spirit and make them obedient to Christ. Amen.

The armour of God

Read Ephesians 6:10-18

Finally, be strong in the Lord and in his mighty power. Put on the full armour of God so that you can take your stand against the devil's schemes. - Ephesians 6:10-11

You and I cannot go into battle against the enemy without the right kit.

You need the *belt of truth* buckled around your waist – the truth sets you free. The Truth is Jesus; the truth is God's Word. A belt keeps garments securely in place. You need the *breastplate of righteousness* in place – Jesus is our righteousness. When we come to salvation we are clothed in His righteousness that protects us from sin. Your *feet fitted with* the readiness that comes from *the gospel of peace* – we are the bearers of the Good News of the Gospel of Jesus Christ. We are peace bearers to those who are in turmoil. Take up *the shield of faith*, with that you can extinguish all the flaming arrows of the evil one. You have the ability to deflect the enemy's arrows through the shield of faith. Finally, the *helmet of salvation* and the *sword of the Spirit*, these complete your armour.

If I am clothed in the armour of God there will be no chink for the enemy to get a foothold in my life.

Prayer

Father, thank You for Your armour – help me to diligently put it on each day. Help me also to pray in the Spirit on all occasions. Thank You that I can bring my prayers and requests to You, being alert and always keeping on praying for all the saints. Amen.

29 September

Delivered into the Kingdom of Light

Read Colossians 1:13-20

For he has rescued us from the dominion of darkness and brought us into the kingdom of the Son he loves, in whom we have redemption, the forgiveness of sins.

- Colossians 1:13-14

This is the reason that Satan keeps trying to find a way to make you fall. He does not like the fact that you have been rescued from his domain of darkness; and that you now live in the Kingdom of God. He continually tries to find ways to pull you back into the darkness. You are a child of the King – live like the royalty you are.

The problem is that too many of God's children are still living as if they are in the kingdom of darkness. Our passport into the Kingdom of God is Jesus Christ. As children of God we have a right to live in His Kingdom. Too many of us are giving up our rights, trading them for the lies of Satan that keep us in bondage. Satan would keep you believing you are a step-child – rebuke his lies today, and claim your birthright.

You have been rescued from the domain of darkness and transferred into the Kingdom of the Son – live like a child of the King.

Prayer

Father, I stand in awe of You, I lift my hands in praise and worship. I bow before Your throne with a thankful and grateful heart full of love for You. I am Your child and I rejoice in my Kingdom life. Amen.

Victory in Jesus

Read Revelation 12:10-12

Then I heard a loud voice in heaven say: "Now have come the salvation and the power and the kingdom of our God, and the authority of his Christ. For the accuser of our brothers, who accuses them before our God day and night, has been hurled down. They overcame him by the blood of the Lamb and by the word of their testimony; they did not love their lives so much as to shrink from death. Therefore rejoice, you heavens and you who dwell in them!" - Revelation 12:10-12a

Victory in Jesus! Our scripture tells us that Satan has been hurled down. Aldo often writes about the blood which cleanses us. Without the shedding of blood there is no salvation:

We overcome the enemy by the blood of the Lamb, and the word of our testimony. We have to speak out the Truth of who we are in Christ. We have to take our place, claim our inheritance. Christ died for us, and we belong to Him. We cannot cling to our lives – we must surrender them to Him.

You can rest in the knowledge that even though we go through hardships and trials, the victory is already ours in Jesus. You are on the victory side!

The culmination of our battle is victory in Jesus. Pull down the strongholds. Begin to rebuild the broken places, and replenish the barren landscape. Allow the Holy Spirit to energise and empower your life. Do not give up but persevere, knowing that you have the victory – it is yours for the taking. You are meant to live victoriously in the Kingdom of God.

Prayer

My Father God, ruler of the heavens and the earth. I praise You, and humbly bow before You. Jesus I exalt You – You are my Lord and Saviour. Thank You for the victory that I have through Your shed blood. Help me to never stop praising You. Amen.

hou sleutels in ons
hand rooi sleutels
sien ek dat seën is
die sleutels tot 'n
lewe in oorvloed, dis
humble vir my ek
sien hoe hulle kan
oopsluit wat in die
Gees is. Wat in God
se Koningkryk is. Dis
wat hy sê, gebruik
die sleutels wat ek
vir jou gee. saam sal
bou van muur om jou
soul hulp wees vir
jou om in my Koningkryk
te wandel. Wat ek jou
gee sleutels bind en
ontbind werke van Satan.
sleutels hang sleutels
om nek, sien sleutels
is nou wat my
humble julle leer deep
Wysheid. sluit wat jy
nodig het om te
weet oop in God
se Koningkryk.

Letter 10:

Keys

We hold the keys in our hands. I see red keys. Blessing is the key to a life of abundance. It is humbling to see, but I can see how these keys can unlock what is in the Spirit – in God's Kingdom. He says: 'Use the keys that I give you. The keys, together with the building of the wall around your soul, will help you to walk in My Kingdom. The keys that I give you will bind and loose the works of Satan. Hang the keys around your neck.' I see that the keys will help me to humbly teach you the things that Wisdom shows me. Unlock what you need to know in God's Kingdom.

Living a life surrendered to God

Prayer for October

Father, I come to You in great humility and gratitude for Your faithfulness to me. Thank You that You are the same; yesterday, today and forever. You have saved me for a purpose and You have given me a destiny. Forgive me that so often I am unwilling to surrender to You. I get so caught up in my own ambitions, in my own needs and in my own ideas. I am so quick to find my own solutions to situations and circumstances. I choose to live according to my wisdom and I do not seek Your wisdom. Father, it breaks my heart that I fail you so often. Yet, You continue to love me and forgive me. I know that You are calling me to surrender my life one hundred percent to You. Help me as I walk through this month with You to come to that place. Help me to deal with the things that are holding me back. I want above all else to please You and serve You. I praise You for Your goodness to me. In Jesus Name,

Amen.

The blessing lies in surrender (1)

Read Philippians 4:1-9

Do not be anxious about anything, but in everything, by prayer and petition, with thanksgiving, present your requests to God. And the peace of God, which transcends all understanding, will guard your hearts and your minds in Christ Jesus.
- Philippians 4:6-7

Aldo was going to join us on his first ministry trip; we were booked to go to Pakistan. I was concerned about taking him out of his comfort zone and into a strange environment.

A few days before we left I was praying; I heard God saying to me that the secret lay in surrender. At the time I did not understand what He was referring to. I had received reports that things were not good in Pakistan. I turned on the television and all I saw was mayhem and disaster.

What situation in your life are you struggling to surrender to God today?

The old Retah flew into action; I advised Judike to cancel the tickets. Tinus's first question was, "Retah, what is God telling us to do?" I responded by saying, no way are we going. However, the more I dug my heels in the more uneasy I became.

Again the voice of the Lord came to me, "Retah, the blessing lies in surrendering to My will."

Prayer

Father God, although I know that the blessing lies in surrendering to You, it is sometimes so hard. Very often there seems to be really good reasons why it is sensible and right to go against Your will. Help me to surrender through the power of Your Holy Spirit. Amen.

The blessing lies in surrender (2)

Read John 12:23-26

I tell you the truth, unless a kernel of wheat falls to the ground and dies, it remains only a single seed. But if it dies, it produces many seeds. - John 12:24

The next morning I woke up feeling the same unease. Aldo has a journal where he writes his messages and he had written: *Mom, Jesus hasn't told us not to go.* I told the Lord, "I am sorry that I was disobedient. Sorry that I was not yielding to You, that I was not willing to trust You with Aldo and all the arrangements." As I was talking to the Lord, Judike phoned back to say the tickets hadn't been cancelled, we could still go.

I realised that I was not surrendered; I was allowing fear to enter my heart. If Aldo was going to carry out God's plan for his life I would have to trust God. Two evenings earlier God had told me, "The secret lies in surrender." What are you struggling with and finding difficult to trust God with in your life? Like me, you have to learn the lesson that the blessing lies in surrender.

Fear causes me to mistrust God and makes it difficult for me to surrender.

Prayer

Father God, I come before You realising anew that trust is not lip service but heart service. I cannot say I trust You if I am not prepared to act on it. I surrender the things that are holding me back from trusting You – take them, I pray. Amen.

Never surrender to the devil and sin

Read James 4:1-12

Submit yourselves, then, to God. Resist the devil, and he will flee from you. Come near to God and he will come near to you. Wash your hands, you sinners, and purify your hearts, you double-minded. - James 4:7-8

The Lord showed me that we must never, ever surrender to the devil and to sin. James tells us that if we resist the devil he will flee from us. I realised that he had almost caught me. I allowed him to blind me with images of the floods in Pakistan. He was able to fill me with fear because my focus was not on God but on circumstances. This was such a vital lesson for me to learn as we entered the new phase in our lives of Aldo joining me in the ministry.

The thoughts in my mind will filter down into my heart and manifest in my speech and actions.

James goes on to tell us that we must draw near to God and He will draw near to us. We must wash our hands and purify our hearts. Purifying our hearts means we must not allow sinful thoughts to take root in our minds, filtering down into our hearts and manifesting in our speech and actions.

Prayer

Father God, I come to You in praise and adoration for Your great love for me. You have saved me to live a life of victory. I know that victory only comes as I resist the devil, flee from sin and live a life which is surrendered to You, in the power of Your Holy Spirit. Amen.

Maturity equals surrender

Read 2 Corinthians 12:1-10

But he said to me, "My grace is sufficient for you, for my power is made perfect in weakness." Therefore I will boast all the more gladly about my weaknesses, so that Christ's power may rest on me. - 2 Corinthians 12:9

Are you going through situations and circumstances in your life that you are battling to surrender to God? You love God, you know what you must do, but it is just so hard. There are no exclusionary clauses; we cannot choose what we surrender to God and what we keep holding on to. It is all or nothing.

The yes answers are not always the ones that build us up in our faith and lead us to maturity.

The Apostle Paul also battled to surrender and accept God's will for his life. He was afflicted by 'a thorn in the flesh'. Paul begged God to remove it. God said no. Why? Not because God couldn't remove it, but because Paul had to learn the lesson of surrender. He had to be prepared to live with the thorn if that was God's will for his life. Paul learnt that God's grace was sufficient for every situation. So often we are only interested in God answering our prayers the way we want them answered.

Prayer

My Father, You love me, You love those that are near and dear to me; I know this and yet I struggle to surrender those I love to You. Forgive my unbelief, I pray. Help me; give me the strength to surrender to You. Amen.

Servant-hood equals surrender

Read Romans 15:1-13

We who are strong ought to bear with the failings of the weak and not to please ourselves. - Romans 15:1

I constantly ask myself why the 'I' in me is still so strong; why I struggle so to yield to God. Romans 15:1 is a strong reminder that we are meant to put the interests of others before our own. When I looked at the television images of floods in Pakistan I immediately thought of what the conditions would be like when we arrived there.

The enemy used my concerns for Aldo to blindside me and pitch me off course. When we follow Christ we are called to live in a different reality. You cannot be a servant and follow your own desires and will. We either choose to serve the Master of heaven and earth or we choose to serve the enemy. What is tempting you to split your allegiance today? Don't hold back. You have to confront it and bring it to the foot of the cross.

One definition of servant-hood is that it equals surrender.

Prayer

Father, You have saved me to live a different reality. You have given me everything – You hold nothing back – not even Your Son. Help me to surrender everything to You. In Jesus name, Amen.

Take up your cross and follow Jesus

Read Luke 9:22-27

Then he said to them all: "If anyone would come after me, he must deny himself and take up his cross daily and follow me. For whoever wants to save his life will lose it, but whoever loses his life for me will save it." - Luke 9:23-24

You don't have the option of taking up your cross today; and then laying it down tomorrow when life gets too hard, then the following day picking it up again. It doesn't work like that; it is a way of life. It means Jesus becomes more every day and Retah becomes less. I say no to myself and yes to Jesus. How can we define what our cross is? It is the situation where our will crosses the will of God, our Father. This is our cross; the point at which we have to surrender our wills to His will.

In the midst of laying down our lives we will know His life-giving power.

When you take up your cross and choose to follow Jesus you are also living your destiny. There is no safer place to be than in the centre of God's will. Daily we are called to surrender our will and lay our lives down in service to God and others.

Prayer

Dear Father in heaven. You have called me to be Your child. You have made me a citizen of Your Kingdom. Help me to choose daily to take up my cross and follow Jesus, the Saviour of my soul. Thank You for Your Holy Spirit who dwells in me helping me to do Your will. Amen.

The end of your tether

Read Philippians 2:3-18

Your attitude should be the same as that of Christ Jesus: Who, being in very nature God, did not consider equality with God something to be grasped, but made himself nothing, taking the very nature of a servant, being made in human likeness.

- Philippians 2:5-7

A little while ago a woman shared with me she was finding life too difficult. "I don't have the faith that you have," she concluded. I replied to her, "So, you mean if my faith runs out then I must give up on my child?" This is the harsh reality.

When I reach the end of my tether then the only answer is to bow lower and lower in the presence of my King. It is not about me, it is about God's will for my life. It is a day by day choice to surrender to God's will for your life. Left to our own devices there is no way that we will choose to be the least. Being a servant does not come naturally.

Jesus had to choose daily to surrender His will to the will of His Father – I have to do the same.

Jesus came to this earth to show us the way by example – He chose servant-hood and a life of sacrifice.

Prayer

Dear Father, thank You for Jesus' example. Jesus, You have promised me that when I am at the end of my tether and feel I cannot go on any longer, You will give me the strength to obey. Amen.

Victory in God's will

Read Ephesians 1:1-11

And he made known to us the mystery of his will according to his good pleasure, which he purposed in Christ. - Ephesians 1:9

The following day I began to sob as God revealed my disobedience to me. What mother wouldn't think twice before taking her child into a dangerous situation? The enemy is clever, he knows that he cannot easily trip you up with obvious sin; so he will try and use something that on the face of it is a good thing – such as a mother's love. Yet in this instance my 'mother's love' meant that I was disobeying God and His will for both Aldo and myself.

God delivered us from the kingdom of darkness into His Kingdom of Light. This means that we have everything we need to live the Christian life and follow Him. The power is ours through Jesus Christ; we must learn to use it. Each time we choose the path of surrender a new victory is won. Jesus won the ultimate victory on Calvary.

The victory for each of us comes through the surrender of our will to God's will.

Prayer

My Father, in the midst of the heat of the battle; help me to stop and turn to You. Help me to seek You first before I react to the circumstances I find myself in. I know that if I do this You will guide me; giving me the wisdom and the courage to do Your will. Amen.

9 October

The mind of Christ

Read 1 Corinthians 2

"For who has known the mind of the Lord that he may instruct him?" But we have the mind of Christ. - 1 Corinthians 2:16

Taking up my cross and following Jesus means that I surrender my thoughts and adopt the mind of Christ. We are called to live a life yielded to God. Having the mind of Christ means knowing and walking in God's will day by day. This is the last thing the enemy wants us to do. His aim is to sow confusion in our minds; to fill our minds with fear, doubt and confusion. When he can cause you to doubt God, and because of the fear disobey God – then he has gained the victory.

We do not have the spirit of the world; when we come to Christ we receive the Spirit of God. We are citizens of God's heavenly Kingdom; therefore we are to live accordingly. We do not need to question God, when He tells us to do something we can obey even if it goes against all human logic.

Spiritual things are spiritually discerned.

Prayer

My Father, thank You that I have the mind of Christ. When I need wisdom I call upon Your Spirit to instruct me. I surrender my will to Your will and know that there is no safer place for me and those that I love. Amen.

10 October

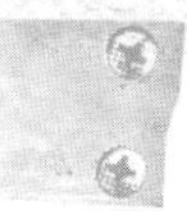

The Spirit of Christ

Read Romans 8:1-18

You, however, are controlled not by the sinful nature but by the Spirit, if the Spirit of God lives in you. And if anyone does not have the Spirit of Christ, he does not belong to Christ. - Romans 8:9

God has blessed us with an inner strength. He has blessed us with His power and His character. In our own strength we can do nothing; but in God's strength there is nothing that we cannot accomplish. As the Lord spoke to me, He showed me that this was the reason He was bringing Aldo into the ministry. God wanted me to yield to Him. With Aldo becoming a part of the ministry I would not be able to follow my plans. I would not be able to control circumstances and the things that would happen – I would have to depend even more fully upon the Lord. It would be His strength that would make it possible, not mine.

The answer to your fear lies in surrender to God.

What is the situation that you are facing in your life at the moment? Is it causing you to forget that you have the Spirit of Christ within you? Are you falling into the same trap that I did; are you tempted to forget who you are in Christ?

Prayer

My Father God, I realise afresh today how easy it is for me to be overwhelmed by my circumstances. Forgive me, I pray. I come afresh to You and ask You to fill me with Your Spirit once again. Thank You that I have the Spirit of Christ in me. Thank You that I am Your child. Amen.

11 October

Maturity versus immaturity

Read Romans 8:1-18

...because those who are led by the Spirit of God are sons of God. - Romans 8:14

The spirit that marks the true child of God is the spirit of son-ship. We have an inheritance that marks us as children of God. We are heirs to God's Kingdom. God spoke to me the night before I heard about the floods in Pakistan. He told me that when He looks at His children He wants to see maturity. He continued to say, "It is the Spirit of Christ in my children that gives them maturity. When you, as my child, begin to manifest Christ's Spirit in your daily living, then you will begin to know and experience what it is to walk in true maturity."

Maturity equals obedience to the Spirit of Christ within you.

As a child of God I do not need to be afraid of circumstances or situations. I can know that if God leads me into a situation He will provide and undertake for me. Being a son or daughter of God has benefits but it also carries responsibilities.

Prayer

My Father God, I lift my voice and my heart to You in praise. You are a great God. I ask you to help me to walk in the strength of Your Spirit. Thank you that I have the mind in Christ, and that His Spirit is within me. Help me to walk in maturity. Amen.

Nature of Christ

Read Galatians 5:16-26

Those who belong to Christ Jesus have crucified the sinful nature with its passions and desires. Since we live by the Spirit, let us keep in step with the Spirit. Let us not become conceited, provoking and envying each other. - Galatians 5:24-26

The sign that marks us as belonging to God is that we have the Spirit of Christ within us. We have His nature, which is a meek, humble and gentle spirit, not a spirit of self-centredness. So much of Christianity today is about what we can get out of it. We dictate to God (in faith) what He must give us. In this philosophy of serving God there is not much room for walking in humility. Christ came to this world to serve, not to be served.

I believe with all my heart that God wants to bless His children. I believe that with Him nothing is impossible and that He gives us every good gift. However, His blessings are not for our selfish gain but for the glory of His name. The bride of Christ will be willing to surrender no matter what the cost; this is the Spirit of Christ.

The more we yield, the more Christ's nature will be evident in our lives.

Prayer

My Father, I realise that I cannot do what You are calling me to do in my own strength. I need You to fill me with Your Spirit. Thank You that as I come to You in submission the nature of Christ becomes more visible each day in my life. Amen.

13 October

Where is your focus?

Read Matthew 7:13-23

"Not everyone who says to me, 'Lord, Lord,' will enter the kingdom of heaven, but only he who does the will of my Father who is in heaven." - Matthew 7:21

The Word tells us that we are to *enter through the narrow gate*. It goes on to warn us, *for wide is the gate and broad is the road that leads to destruction, and many enter through it*. Once we have entered through the narrow gate, how do we remain upon the narrow path? The Lord has shown me that we cannot do it on our own. We need the Spirit of Christ within us so that we can live a life surrendered to God

If you are feeling bogged down by your circumstances; if things seem to be going wrong in your life – don't despair. Surrender to God's will for your life – He knows best. Make Him your focus. Turn your eyes upon Jesus, look full in His wonderful face, and the things of the earth will grow strangely dim, in the light of His glory and grace.

Make your heavenly Father your focus.

Prayer

Father, forgive me that my focus is so easily drawn away from You. I repent before You and turn from my sin. Fill me with Your Spirit, I pray. Help me to look to Jesus and focus upon Your will and purpose for my life. Amen.

14 October

Be prepared in season and out

Read 2 Timothy 4

Preach the Word; be prepared in season and out of season; correct, rebuke and encourage – with great patience and careful instruction. For the time will come when men will not put up with sound doctrine. - 2 Timothy 4:2-3

We are already moving into a time when people do not want to hear the truth of God's Word. Instead they choose the easy road. People do not want to receive instruction and correction. We cannot allow ourselves to be deflected from proclaiming the Truth of God's Word. This is the reason the enemy wants to sidetrack us. He tries to make us fearful.

Paul tells Timothy to: *Preach the Word...* leaving us in no doubt regarding what we are to do. If we live like this then we will be able to say with Paul: *I have fought the good fight, I have finished the race, I have kept the faith. Now there is in store for me the crown of righteousness, which the Lord, the righteous Judge, will award to me on that day – and not only to me , but also to all who have longed for his appearing.*

Preach the Word; be prepared in season and out of season.

Prayer

My Father, like Paul, I long to be able to say; I have fought the good fight, I have finished the race, I have kept the faith. Help me to be faithful, I pray. Give me the courage to be ready to speak Your Word in season and out of season. Amen.

15 October

Change or else...

Read Acts 17:22-34

In the past God overlooked such ignorance, but now he commands all people everywhere to repent. - Acts 17:30

God will not overlook our sin forever. He clearly calls us to repent and turn from our sin. There comes the day when His Spirit prompts us and says, okay no further; it is time to sort this out. When this happens we need to obey. If you feel that there is a cement ceiling and you are not getting through to God, then go back and examine when the last time was that He told you to do something. Did you do it? If you didn't then you need to sort out whatever it is. You will likely find when you have done this the communication lines will be open again.

God is serious about His children obeying Him.

As we look at Scripture we see many examples of men and women in whose life God worked. We can learn much from their stories and how God worked in their lives using them to fulfil His purposes.

Prayer

My Father, I worship You and praise You. I give You the honour and glory due Your Name. Forgive my unbelief, I pray. Help me to yield to You. Forgive my stubbornness and selfishness. I ask You to help me to be quick to respond to Your prompting in my life. Amen.

Abraham begins his journey with God

Read Genesis 12:1-9

The Lord had said to Abram, "Leave your country, your people and your father's household and go to the land I will show you." - Genesis 12:1

God is telling us that the next time He asks us to do something we are to immediately obey. The first person we are going to look at is Abraham; God told him to pack up his things and leave his home. God told Abraham (his name was still Abram at that stage) that He would show him where to go. Abraham didn't have a clear understanding of where he was headed.

God is specific in His instructions and He expects total obedience from us.

God gave Abraham the most wonderful promise that would be his and all his descendants if he obeyed God (you and I are his descendants and we are still benefitting today because of Abraham's obedience). "I will make you into a great nation and I will bless you; I will make your name great, and you will be a blessing. I will bless those who bless you, and whoever curses you I will curse; and all peoples on earth will be blessed through you."

Prayer

Father God, You are the God of Abraham, Isaac and Jacob; and You are my God too. Thank You that You are the same yesterday, today and forever. No matter what else changes You never do. You are clear in Your commands to me – help me to obey. Amen.

17 October

God is in control

Read Genesis 12:10-20

Now there was a famine in the land, and Abram went down to Egypt to live there for a while because the famine was severe. - Genesis 12:10

Abraham decided to go down to Egypt to escape the drought. He asked Sarah to say she was his sister so that the men would not kill him. God struck the Pharaoh and his house with great plagues because the Pharaoh slept with Sarah. Instead of lying Abraham should have trusted God. The Pharaoh would not have been able to harm Abraham because he was under God's protection. Even in Abraham's disobedience God undertook for him.

We can shake our heads at Abraham, but we are not all that different. Take my situation with Pakistan. I learnt that it is all too easy to choose my own plans and solution. We can learn from Abraham's mistake today, when we go our own way we are faced with the consequences of our actions. When we choose not to yield to God then we are walking in disobedience. Trust God He will undertake for you.

I need to trust that God has a plan and a purpose in all situations.

Prayer

Father, I thank You for Your grace and mercy. Even when I disobey You, You graciously give me a chance to repent and turn from my unbelief. I am so grateful to You, Lord. Help me not to take Your grace for granted. Help me to learn to obey. Amen.

Living without regrets

Read Genesis 16

So she [Sarah] said to Abram, "The Lord has kept me from having children. Go, sleep with my maidservant; perhaps I can build a family through her." Abram agreed to what Sarai said. - Genesis 16:2

God promised Abraham an heir; but he didn't wait for God. Sarah told him to sleep with Hagar and Abraham agreed. Hagar became pregnant and things didn't go well so she ran away.

The angel of the Lord found Hagar ... and he said, "Hagar, servant of Sarai, where have you come from, and where are you going?" "I'm running away from my mistress Sarai," she answered. Then the angel of the Lord told her, "Go back to your mistress and submit to her." The angel added, "I will so increase your descendants that they will be too numerous to count." ... She [Hagar] gave this name to the Lord who spoke to her: "You are the God who sees me" (vs 7-9;13).

Abraham lived with the consequences of his disobedience. It is a strong warning to us. There are times when we have to make a choice; God's will or our own will?

Following the will of God for your life means you will live a life without regrets.

Prayer

My Father, I bow before You. I acknowledge that You are a God of justice and a God of might and power. I need never fear as long as I walk in obedience to You. I want to live a life without regrets, help me to walk in obedience to You. Amen.

19 October

The test of waiting

Read Genesis 21:1-21

So Sarah conceived and bore a son to Abraham in his old age, at the appointed time of which God had spoken to him. - Genesis 21:2 (New American Standard Bible)

Have you been waiting for what seems like a long time for a promise that the Lord gave you to become reality? Take courage from Abraham's story. How is this for waiting? Abraham waited more than 25 years for God to fulfil His promise to give him an heir. Eventually when Abraham is ninety-nine years old God says to Abraham; *"Is anything too difficult for the Lord?* ***At the appointed time*** *I will return to you, at this time next year, and Sarah shall have a son."* A year later Sarah conceived and bore Abraham a son; his name was Isaac.

God has an appointed time to fulfil His promises to you.

There were lessons Abraham had to learn before God could fulfil the promise. The same is true for us; we have to learn the lessons God wants to teach us. It is called maturing which comes through living a life surrendered to God, being faithful day by day to what God is telling us to do.

Prayer

My Father God, I am humbled. I realise that so often I am exactly like Abraham. I want to do things my way in my time. Help me to yield to You and wait for Your appointed time. Amen.

The ultimate surrender

Read Genesis 22:1-10

Some time later God tested Abraham. Then God said, "Take your son, your only son, Isaac, whom you love, and go to the region of Moriah. Sacrifice him there as a burnt offering on one of the mountains I will tell you about." - Genesis 22:1a,2

This is the ultimate, impossible thing to ask a parent to do. However God knows exactly what He is doing. The phrase ***burnt offering*** referred to in verse 2 – *signifies the total surrender of the heart and life of a worshiper to God. It is a voluntary sacrifice.*

This has a beautiful link with an earlier verse in Genesis chapter 15:6: *Abram **believed** the Lord, and he credited it to him as righteousness.* The word ***believe*** – carries the idea of unqualified committal of oneself to another person. Even after this Abraham struggled to yield to God. This is why it was important for Abraham to be willing to sacrifice Isaac to God. Isaac came from God and Abraham had to acknowledge that he belonged to God.

Are you willing to totally surrender your heart and life to God?

Is there someone in your life whom you love and are not willing to sacrifice to God? If so learn from Abraham.

Prayer

My Father, I realise that You ask nothing less than total surrender from me. So often I am half-hearted in my yielding to Your will for my life. Help me to be a true worshipper who places all on the altar of sacrifice. Amen.

God provides

Read Genesis 22:11-18

"Do not lay a hand on the boy," he said. "Do not do anything to him. Now I know that you fear God, because you have not withheld from me your son, your only son." So Abraham called that place The Lord Will Provide. - Genesis 22:12,14a

Faith and worship go together. Abraham learnt many of his lessons the hard way. So when we encounter him in Chapter 22 of Genesis standing with a knife in his raised hand, about to plunge it into his only son we know that a major change has taken place in Abraham's life.

When Isaac questioned Abraham, he answered *"God himself will provide the lamb for the burnt offering, my son."* This was the level of Abraham's trust in God. By this stage in his life Abraham understood that God was his ultimate provider.

Abraham trusted his God because he knew his God.

Abraham raised the knife – and God said: *Now I know that you fear God, because you have not withheld from me your son, your only son. Abraham looked up and there in a thicket he saw a ram caught by its horns* (vs 12-13). What is God asking you to place on the altar of sacrifice? Are you holding back because of unbelief?

Prayer

Father, I am filled with awe and wonder as I bow before You. What an amazing God You are. You do not change. What you did for Abraham you can do for me. I declare today that You alone are my Provider. I yield to You. Amen.

Noah - obeys

Read Genesis 6

Noah did everything just as God commanded him. - Genesis 6:22

The Lord saw how great man's wickedness on the earth had become, and that every inclination of the thoughts of his heart was only evil all the time (v 5). God looked around to see if there was someone who would be willing to be used by Him. *Noah found favour in the eyes of the Lord ... Noah was a righteous man, blameless amongst the people of his time, and he walked with God* (vs 8-9).

The phrase *Noah did everything just as God commanded him* – defines Noah's life. Noah obeyed even though no one believed him. He continued doing *everything just as God commanded him.* God made a covenant with Noah that to this very day is still a witness to the fact that He was faithful to what He promised Noah. Trust God to accomplish what He calls you to do; just obey and do everything God commands you.

God calls you to obey and do everything He commands you to do.

Prayer

My Father God, thank You for the example of Noah's life. The Covenant You made with him is still evidence today of Your faithfulness. Help me to be obedient to You no matter what. I praise You for Your great love and faithfulness to me. Amen.

23 October

Joseph - forgives

Read Genesis 50

And as for you, you meant evil against me, but God meant it for good in order to bring about this present result, to preserve many people alive. - Genesis 50:20 (New American Standard Bible)

Joseph was a person who understood his purpose. Despite all the hardship he went through one phrase is repeated over and over again; *the Lord was with Joseph – the Lord caused all that he did to prosper.* Even in jail Joseph prospered. This would never have happened if Joseph hadn't forgiven the people who had harmed him.

During the famine his brother's came down to Egypt to beg for food. Joseph could have chosen to not give them grain but instead he treats them kindly. You can imagine their fear when they realise it is Joseph they are dealing with.

Are you prepared to bring His salvation to those who have harmed you?

Is your lack of forgiveness preventing you from living a life that is surrendered to God? The Word tells us that revenge belongs to the Lord; He is the one who will act on our behalf. God is the one who will allow you prosper. God loves everyone; even those who have hurt you.

Prayer

My Father in heaven, everything is in Your hands. I realise there is no safer place for me to be than in the centre of Your will for my life. Whatever happens in my life You can turn it to good. Thank You for this. Amen.

Moses - overcomes fear

Read Exodus 3

God also said to Moses, "Say to the Israelites, 'The Lord, the God of your fathers – the God of Abraham, the God of Isaac and the God of Jacob – has sent me to you.' This is my name forever, the name by which I am to be remembered from generation to generation." - Exodus 3:15

Although Moses grew up in the courts of Pharaoh his heart remained with his people in Egypt. He had to flee Egypt when as a young man he killed an Egyptian who was beating an Israeli slave. God spoke to Moses in a unique way – after all you do not see a burning bush every day. You could say this was the tipping point in Moses' life. This was his test; would he yield to God?

God asks us to surrender – He is the One who will accomplish His purposes through us.

Moses was not a natural born leader but over the years he grew into his role as leader of the children of Israel. Moses had to be willing to yield to God though, and then God used him despite himself. This is all that God asks of us; that we should be willing to obey Him. He only asks that we surrender ourselves to Him. He is the one who will accomplish the goals which He sets us.

Prayer

Dear Father, so often all I can see are the reasons why I shouldn't do something for You. Forgive my unbelief. Help me to be like Moses who even while filled with trepidation did what You asked Him to do. Amen.

Jonah - overcomes prejudice

Read Jonah 1 and 3

When God saw what they did and how they turned from their evil ways, he had compassion and did not bring up them the destruction he had threatened. - Jonah 3:10

God told Jonah to go to Ninevah, and tell them to repent before it was too late. Jonah did not want to go; he did not want to surrender to God – so he ran away to sea. After the fish spat Jonah out, God had Jonah's attention and he went to Ninevah.

The people repented and God didn't destroy them. Jonah was angry because he had a deep prejudice against the people of Ninevah; he didn't believe that they deserved to be saved. Jonah was self-righteous and judgemental. So often we are just like Jonah. We become filled with 'righteous' indignation when we think God is showing mercy to the 'wrong people'. One of the ways we have to learn to surrender to God is in the area of accepting that He is a God of grace and mercy, and that He will show His mercy to whomever He chooses to.

Next time you question God's mercy remember the story of Jonah.

Prayer

Dear Father, I realise that so often I allow my deep seated prejudices against certain people to get in the way of my yielding to your will. Forgive me, I pray. Thank You that You have shown me so much grace and mercy in my own life. I do not have the right to begrudge Your grace from others. Amen.

Esther - puts others first

Read Esther 4

For if you remain silent at this time, relief and deliverance for the Jews will arise from another place, but you and your father's family will perish. And who knows but that you have come to royal position for such a time as this? - Esther 4:14

Esther was a beautiful young woman. She had everything going for her. When the king chose her as his new queen a whole world of luxury opened up to her. It would have been all too easy for her to turn her back on her people and give herself wholeheartedly to her own enjoyment. Esther's Uncle Mordecai raised her to serve and love God, as well as her people.

When Esther heard of Haman's plot to kill the Jews she knew she had to do something. Mordecai asks her the question: *And who knows but that you have come to a royal position for such a time as this?* Esther puts her life on the line to petition the king on behalf of her people. God grants her favour in the eyes of the king and evil Haman is arrested and hung for his intention to kill the Jews.

Has God placed you in a particular position for such a time as this?

Prayer

My Father, I am so inspired by the story of Queen Esther. I realise that You have placed her story in Scripture to encourage me to look beyond myself and my own comfort. Give me the courage to step out and yield to Your will when You call upon me. Amen.

Job - surrenders through suffering

Read Job 1-2

Though he slay me, yet will I hope in him. - Job 13:15a

Job was blameless, upright, God fearing, and rich. Satan said that if God took everything away from Job he would curse God. God gave Satan permission to test Job but not to lay a hand on him. Job lost all his children and everything he possessed.

Job's response: "*Naked I came from my mother's womb, and naked I will depart. The Lord gave and the Lord has taken away; may the name of the Lord be praised*" (Job 1:21). Satan said that if Job suffered physically he would curse God.

If you are suffering how are you handling it?

Job was afflicted with boils from the soles of his feet to the crown of his head. His wife and his friends were of no help to him. Job remained faithful and after he suffered he said: *My ears had heard of you but now my eyes have seen you. Therefore I despise myself and repent in dust and ashes"* (Job 42:5-6).God restored to Job seven times more than he lost.

Prayer

My Father, I am so comforted to know that You have me in the palm of Your hand. Nothing can touch me that does not come through You. Help me to be faithful no matter what comes my way. Amen.

John the Baptist - surrendered to his purpose

Read Matthew 3

"I baptise you with water for repentance. But after me will come one who is more powerful than I, whose sandals I am not fit to carry. He will baptise you with the Holy Spirit and with fire." - Matthew 3:11

John the Baptist's purpose was to prepare the way for Jesus. He told people that the Kingdom of God was at hand. He called people to repentance. John the Baptist's whole life was focussed upon his mission. He had no thought for his own comfort or needs. He was sold out to the establishing of God's Kingdom.

We are called to be faithful wherever we are. Are you living your purpose?

Are you living your godly purpose? Is your life consecrated to fulfilling God's plan? Each one of us is called to proclaim the Good News to those we come in contact with. Like John the Baptist, we are charged to spread the Kingdom of God on this earth. We are God's mouth piece – we are His servants. Daily we are to be telling people about Jesus and His saving grace. It can require as much courage to share the Gospel with the people in your office as it can take to travel to far-flung places.

Prayer

Father, thank You that You have a plan and purpose for my life. I am amazed that You choose to use me to establish Your Kingdom on this earth. I pray that You will keep me faithful and focussed upon my purpose. Amen.

Paul - committed to the Gospel

Read Acts 9:1-19

But by the grace of God I am what I am, and His grace toward me did not prove vain; but I laboured even more than all of them, yet not I, but the grace for God with me.
- 1 Corinthians 15:10 (New American Standard Bible)

Paul knew what it was to receive God's grace. Despite his great faith Paul learnt how to live with suffering. We read in 2 Corinthians 12:8-10: "*Three times I pleaded with the Lord to take it away from me. But he said to me, "My grace is sufficient for you, for my power is made perfect in weakness." Therefore I will boast all the more gladly about my weaknesses, so that Christ's power may rest on me. That is why, for Christ's sake, I delight in weaknesses, in insults, in hardships, in persecutions, in difficulties. For when I am weak, then I am strong.*

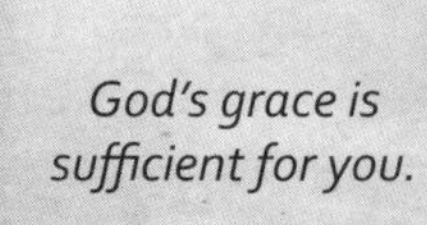

God's grace is sufficient for you.

Is there something in your life that is a thorn in your flesh? If so follow Paul's example; there is victory in surrender. Sometimes the greatest victory is not in deliverance but in living victoriously in the midst of a trial.

Prayer

My Father God, I trust You with my life. I long to be single-minded in fulfilling Your purpose for my life. Give me the courage to follow You to the end. Thank You that Your grace is more than sufficient for me. Amen.

Jesus - surrendered to God's will

Read Matthew 26:36-46

Going a little farther, he fell with his face to the ground and prayed, "My Father, if it is possible, may this cup be taken from me. Yet not as I will, but as you will."
- Matthew 26:39

Even Jesus had to go through the process of surrendering His will to the will of His Father. We see this in the Garden of Gethsemane. Jesus pleaded with God three times to 'remove the cup' from Him. Throughout His life on earth Jesus modelled what it means to live a life surrendered to the will of God. He didn't come to do His will but the will of His Father. He also said that He did only what the Father told Him to do. Jesus promised us that as we fulfil God's will He will never leave us nor forsake us.

God made the ultimate sacrifice by sending His Son to this world to die for each of us on the cross; and Jesus made the supreme sacrifice by giving His life so that we can have Salvation. Surely whole-hearted surrender is the only appropriate response we can offer.

Surely, whole-hearted surrender is the only appropriate response I can offer.

Prayer

Father, I bow before You in humble adoration and thanksgiving for Your great love for me. I am so grateful to be Your child. Thank You Jesus for Your wonderful example of sacrificial love towards me. Help me to walk in obedience and surrender, I pray. Amen.

Blessing in surrender

Read Ephesians 2:1-10

For it is by grace you have been saved, through faith – and this not from yourselves, it is the gift of God – not by works, so that no one can boast. - Ephesians 2:8-9

What motivates you to surrender to God when He asks you to do something for Him? Is it fear – or the threat of punishment if you don't do it? If this is your motivation then you are not living in the truth of what God saved you for. God is a God of grace, mercy and love. *Because of his great love for us, God, who is rich in mercy, made us alive with Christ even when we were dead in transgressions – it is by grace you have been saved* (vs 4-5).

Ask Him to reveal His love for you – so that you can feel safe and accepted by Him. Then respond to His love by surrendering your life to Him. Walk in the purpose He has for your life. He prepared the works He has for you to do before the world was formed. Walk in your destiny.

Living a life surrendered to God's will for your life is the path of blessing.

Prayer

Father, I come before You confessing that there are times when I am motivated by fear. I realise that the enemy wants me to see You through the eyes of fear. Forgive me, I pray. Thank You for Your love, mercy and grace that You pour out upon me every day. Amen.

Wysheid sê soos 'n
arend wat vlieg op
bid se krag raak arend
moeg? o ja, so moeg was
ek toe sit yeshua my
in rots se skuiling
waar hy vir my self
ware voedsel gegee
het. Sy voedsel so die
rustige liefde vir my siel.
Was so magteloos teen
jagters wat my wou
hang sien toe bid
hulle wat vir my
liefhet Lusifer sal bid
nie kan veg nie.
Lusifer is vuur in soul
van mense. Seun sien
bid van ware gelowiges
het baie krag sal graag
vir ouers wou help maar
sal hulle bou van muur
het so baie my gehelp.
rut sien so arend "sien"
rut bid, bid sien die
hand van God red arend
so baie, baie dankie vir
bloed van yeshua. arend
sal nou weer vlieg op
ware geloof.

Letter 11:

The eagle in you

Wisdom says that we are like eagles flying on the power of prayer. Does the eagle ever become tired? Oh yes. I was so tired, but then Yeshua put me into the shelter of the rock, and there He fed me with real food. His food is the peaceful love for my soul. I was helpless against the hunters that wanted to hang me. The ones who love me then prayed for me. Lucifer won't be able to advance against those prayers. Lucifer is the fire in the souls of men. The boy sees that the prayers of the true Believers hold much power. I really wanted to help my parents, but they helped me by building the wall around my soul. The wall really helped me. Ruth, you see that the eagle can 'see'. Ruth, keep on praying – you will see the hand of God that saves the eagle. Thank You so much for the blood of Yeshua. The eagle will now once again fly on the wind of true faith.

Walking in the anointing of God

Prayer for November

Dear Father, I bow before You in humble adoration, You are a great and a faithful God. There is none like You, my Lord. You have called us to walk in Your anointing. Each one of Your children have received Your precious Spirit as a deposit within us. You have anointed us in the Beloved. Father, we long for an increased anointing, we long to be used by You. Teach us as we spend time in Your Word exactly what it means to walk in increasing anointing. Give us a fresh, daily infilling of Your Spirit. Lord, we realise that it is only as we become increasingly less, and You become more that we will know a greater anointing upon our lives. Help us to be prepared to do the work, help us to be courageous and strong and to stand firm in our time of trial. We know that without trial there is no great anointing. Father, we love You and worship You. Use us we pray. In Jesus Name,

Amen.

1 November

Walking in discernment

Read Psalms 119:121-128

I am your servant; give me discernment that I may understand your statutes.
- Psalm 119:125

I have thought a lot about discernment. It is such a vital spiritual tool, and yet so often lacking in many Christians' lives. Every day the enemy tries to trip us up. We need discernment to be able to overcome him.

Another reason we need discernment is so that we can know the difference between what is true and what is false. We are bombarded with choices. If we do not have spiritual discernment we will not be able to distinguish between what is from God and what is from the enemy.

God's anointing upon our lives will enable us to walk in discernment. As His anointing floods our lives we will find that He becomes our focus. When God is our focus then His wisdom and discernment will become evident in our decisions and choices. If you lack discernment ask God, He will give it to you.

God's anointing upon my life will enable me to walk in discernment.

Prayer

My Father, I come before You to worship You. I pray that You will fill me with understanding and discernment today. I want to walk in Your statutes and according to Your ways. Lord, anoint my life for the honour and glory of Your name. Amen.

2 November

God judges our motives

Read Matthew 25:31-46

"Then the righteous will answer him, 'Lord, when did we see you hungry and feed you, or thirsty and give you something to drink? When did we see you a stranger and invite you in, or needing clothes and clothe you? When did we see you sick or in prison and go to visit you?' "The King will reply, 'Truly I tell you, whatever you did for one of the least of these brothers and sisters of mine, you did for me.'" - Matthew 25:37-40

Lack of discernment is nothing new. Jesus spoke about it and saw right through it in Matthew 25. We must examine our hearts, actions and motivations. I hope that the words in our reading today jolted your heart in the same way they did mine. None of us want to hear the words 'Depart from Me.'

The scary thing about this Scripture is that Jesus is talking to Believers. We need God's anointing upon our lives. This month we are going to look at walking in God's anointing. One of the distinguishing features between someone walking in the anointing, and someone who isn't is the level of discernment evident in their lives. The outworking of discernment will be a life lived to the honour and glory of God's name. We will not be interested in our own selfish desires but rather we will be sold out to doing the will of our Father.

When God takes over my life there is no limit to what He can do through me.

Prayer

Father, I realise that I cannot walk in discernment based on my own wisdom. I need Your anointing upon my life, so that I can have Your fullness in my life. Lord, help me to submit to Your Spirit – fill me, I pray. Anoint my life. Amen.

3 November

The wind of the Spirit

Read John 3:1-21

Jesus answered, "Very truly I tell you, no one can enter the kingdom of God unless they are born of water and the Spirit. Flesh gives birth to flesh, but the Spirit gives birth to spirit. You should not be surprised at my saying, 'You must be born again.' The wind blows wherever it pleases. You hear its sound, but you cannot tell where it comes from or where it is going. So it is with everyone born of the Spirit." - John 3:5-8

I have been walking with the Lord for several years and I have come realise and experience that the less Retah becomes, the stronger the anointing is. As I have surrendered more and more to the Lord, He has filled me and placed His anointing upon my life. This anointing is not for my own benefit, but in order for Him to fulfil His purposes through my life.

I can experience the anointing as I walk with God in a daily walk of submission and commitment to Him.

I have also learnt that the anointing is not cheap, but comes at a great cost. It cannot be bought and one person cannot bestow the anointing upon another person. The anointing comes from God. His Spirit touches our lives and flows through us. Once an individual has received the anointing, it costs them to walk in that anointing. Walking in God's anointing is a call to walk in obedience. We can all experience the anointing as we walk with God in a daily walk of submission and commitment to Him.

Prayer

Dear Father God, I bow in worship before Your throne. You have called me to serve You, and You alone. As I walk in obedience to the calling upon my life I experience Your anointing. Thank You Lord, that Your Holy Spirit leads me and guides me. As I encounter people I pray that the anointing on my life will become evident, blessing them. Amen.

The aroma of Christ

Read 2 Corinthians 2

But thanks be to God, who always leads us as captives in Christ's triumphal procession and uses us to spread the aroma of the knowledge of him everywhere. For we are to God the pleasing aroma of Christ among those who are being saved and those who are perishing. - 2 Corinthians 2:14-15

In order to walk in the anointing I have to be a broken vessel. Only as a broken vessel is God able to use me. Wherever I walk there should be an atmosphere of change – this change comes about because of the anointing inside of me.

I received some bath essence balls as a gift and I decided to try one in my bath. As the ball burst open the bath water was infused with the wonderful aroma. Not only the bathroom, but the whole house was filled with the aroma. First Josh, then Aldo and finally Tinus came to find out what smelt so good.

The broken vessel of my life becomes the means for the aroma of Christ to reach the world.

As the Spirit infuses our lives, we are soaked through with the aroma of Christ. The perfume spreads out attracting people. As we walk in the anointing, the Spirit uses us to be a witness and a testimony to Christ.

Prayer

My Father God, I pray that as I am submerged in Your Spirit, the thick outer shell of my life will be softened so that the aroma of Christ can spill out. As the perfume permeates the air around me, I pray that people will be attracted to Jesus. I want to be the aroma of Christ to a world that is dying. Amen.

Treasure in jars of clay

Read 2 Corinthians 4:1-12

But we have this treasure in jars of clay to show that this all-surpassing power is from God and not from us. - 2 Corinthians 4:7

If dropped on a hard stone surface a clay jar will shatter and break. Human beings are fragile physically as well as spiritually. Yet God has chosen to place within us His precious treasure: The Gospel of Jesus Christ. Without His Light shining in us we are in darkness. Paul says in 2 Corinthians 4:6, *For God, who said, "Let light shine out of darkness," made his light shine in our hearts to give us the light of the knowledge of the glory of God displayed in the face of Christ.*

Once His Light has illuminated our lives we no longer live in the kingdom of darkness but we become citizens of God's Kingdom. Then we march to the beat of a different drum. We have the Holy Spirit within us. He is our compass guiding us along the path that God has mapped out for us. He anoints us for the purpose that God has called us to.

The anointing is not for my own benefit, but for the fulfilling of my purpose. God entrusts me with the treasure of the Gospel.

Prayer

My Father, You have entrusted me with the treasure of the Gospel. You have deposited within me. I am not meant to keep it selfishly for myself, but I am to give it away to others. Help me to be faithful to this calling upon my life. Anoint me for the purposes You have called me to. Amen.

A well-polished shell

Read 2 Corinthians 4:8-18

We are hard pressed on every side, but not crushed; perplexed, but not in despair; persecuted, but not abandoned; struck down, but not destroyed. We always carry around in our body the death of Jesus, so that the life of Jesus may also be revealed in our body. - 2 Corinthians 4:8-10

One day God gave me a picture of an egg. He said to me, 'Retah, your life is like an egg. The outer shell has to shine, and appear perfect.' God is not very interested in the outside – He looks at the heart. Everything He has planned for us – our destiny is inside of us. My perfect egg cracked, the shell broke, and the inside came spilling out. God scooped up the mess. He took my broken egg and placed it in a bowl with flour, blending the mixture together.

If everything that keeps my shell polished is stripped away, and my egg lays smashed on the ground – what would happen then?

We cannot choose the method by which our egg is processed into the flour. For me it was a very painful process. I almost lost everything in order to gain eternal life and my destiny. It is only when the egg cracks open that you see what is inside. Then the contents are revealed and the world can see what the egg is made of.

Prayer

My Father, I come humbly before You. I realise that so much of my life revolves around my image, and the maintenance of that image. Forgive me, I pray. Lord, I don't want my life to be devastated before I am prepared to surrender to You. Lord, reveal my destiny and purpose to me. Amen.

7 November

A cracked egg

Read Romans 8:28-39

No, in all these things we are more than conquerors through him who loved us. For I am convinced that neither death nor life, neither angels nor demons, neither the present nor the future, nor any powers, neither height nor depth, nor anything else in all creation, will be able to separate us from the love of God that is in Christ Jesus our Lord.- Romans 8:37-39

God took my broken egg and He mixed it in with the flour. This was a very painful process. My shell was no longer there – I could not hide behind it. I no longer had control of my well-ordered life. God kneaded the mixture together, until the flour and the egg were completely blended. He asked me, 'Retah, can you separate the egg from the flour?' I realised nothing can separate me from His love.

His anointing upon my life will propel me to fulfil His purposes, and plans for my life.

In the instant that my shell broke, my life changed. When everything else was lost He became everything to me. He became my Bread of Life, He became my Living Water. Whatever your circumstances come to Him – allow Him to mix the egg with the flour. Allow Him to form the dough that is your life into a fragrant loaf of bread. You need fear nothing. His love will not only console you, but it will also sustain you.

Prayer

Father God, I come to You in praise and adoration. Thank You for Your great love for me. Nothing can separate me from Your love. It does not matter what happens in my life, I am safe and secure in Your love for me. I love You, Lord, and I want to spend my life in joyful service to You. Amen.

Spreading the aroma

Read 2 Corinthians 2:14-17

But thanks be to God, who always leads us as captives in Christ's triumphal procession and uses us to spread the aroma of the knowledge of him everywhere.

- 2 Corinthians 2:14

And so we became one. His fingers pressed and moulded the dough of my life into a baking pan – He then placed me into the oven – another even more painful process. He tenderly placed me on the shelf in the oven and closed the door. When the baking time was over and the oven door was opened, what came out was a beautifully baked loaf of bread. Freshly baked bread smells delicious.

God says in 2 Corinthians 2:14, *But thanks be to God, who always leads us as captives in Christ's triumphal procession and uses us to spread the aroma of the knowledge of him everywhere.* We are meant to walk each day in His anointing, through His Spirit who lives within us. When this is true my life gives off the aroma of Christ. There is nothing of me – I am the bread that is one with the Bread of Life.

The aroma I am giving off is not my own but rather Christ's aroma.

Prayer

Father, I realise that often I can lose sight of the purpose while experiencing the pain. Lift my head, I pray, above my circumstances. Help me to see the bigger picture – the eternal picture. Give me courage. I thank You for Your love that enfolds me. Amen.

9 November

Don't judge the anointed

Read Matthew 7:1-6

'Do not judge, or you too will be judged. For in the same way as you judge others, you will be judged, and with the measure you use, it will be measured to you.'

- Matthew 7:1-2

As human's we are quick to judge other people. We listen to and spread gossip. 'Have you heard about ...?' people will ask. 'Yes, I have, but you know what? He or she is only a fallible human being, the same as I am.' The truth is that even when people fail and fall, God still loves them. His love does not change.

Jesus had this to say about judging other people. '*Why do you look at the speck of sawdust in your brother's eye and pay no attention to the plank in your own eye? How can you say to your brother, "Let me take the speck out of your eye," when all the time there is a plank in your own eye? You hypocrite, first take the plank out of your own eye, and then you will see clearly to remove the speck from your brother's eye*' (Matthew 7:3-5).

I am so much better at judging other people, than I am at examining my own life.

Prayer

My Father God, I worship You – You are a great and mighty God. Your compassion, love and forgiveness reach from generation to generation. Thank You for all the times You have forgiven me. Help me to pray for other people rather than judging them. Give me Your compassion and love. Amen.

Anointed for healing

Read James 5:13-20

Is anyone among you sick? Let them call the elders of the church to pray over them and anoint them with oil in the name of the Lord. And the prayer offered in faith will make the sick person well; the Lord will raise them up. - James 5:14-15

There are different types of anointing. The first is when someone anoints you with oil for a particular purpose. You are ill and God tells me to anoint you with oil and to pray for you. I am the empty vessel through whom the Holy Spirit is going to bring healing to you. I put the oil on my hand and I lay my hands upon you. I then pray the prayer of faith, and together we trust God to do a healing work in your life. The Holy Spirit touches you and you receive your healing.

It is important to realise that this anointing is for a specific purpose. Walking in the anointing comes only through the Holy Spirit, and is a day by day relationship and empowering – it is not a once off event. We are to be the bread, giving off the aroma of Christ.

I must be available to God, and then He will use me to anoint the sick, and pray for them so that they can be healed.

Prayer

Father, You are a great and awesome God. I come before You with hands outstretched. Touch me and anoint me, I pray, so that I can be used by You. I am open, ready and available; for You to work in and through my life for the glory of Your Name. Amen.

11 November

Anointed for a purpose

Read 1 Samuel 16

So Samuel took the horn of oil and anointed him in the presence of his brothers, and from that day on the Spirit of the Lord came powerfully upon David. - 1 Samuel 16:13

God chose David even though he was far from perfect. Despite his failings He loved God, and God referred to him as a man after His own heart. In 1 Samuel 16:7, God says to the prophet Samuel, *'Do not consider his appearance or his height, for I have rejected him. The Lord does not look at the things people look at. People look at the outward appearance, but the Lord looks at the heart.'*

We look at the outward appearance, at the shell of the egg – if the shell is impressive – then we are impressed. How many times have you fallen for an impressive shell – only to be disappointed later on? God looks at the heart. God knew that David would make mistakes later on. God knew he would sin – of course He did. God also knew David's heart – David had faith in God – he was a giant slayer.

David was a man after God's own heart. Do I love God like this? Am I a person after God's own heart?

Prayer

Dear Father God, I long to be known as a person after Your own heart. Help me to open my life to the power of Your Holy Spirit so that Your life and love can flood my life. I realise that You can only use me if I am empowered by Your Holy Spirit. Amen.

Anointed of God

Read Ephesians 4:1-13

So Christ himself gave the apostles, the prophets, the evangelists, the pastors and teachers, to equip his people for works of service, so that the body of Christ may be built up until we all reach unity in the faith and in the knowledge of the Son of God and become mature, attaining to the whole measure of the fullness of Christ.
- Ephesians 4:11-12

Besides being king, God used David as a prophet, and He used him as a priest (2 Samuel 23:2 and 2 Samuel 24:25). Today God still places people in positions to serve Him. In Ephesians 4:11-13 we have the five-fold ministry. *So Christ himself gave the apostles, the prophets, the evangelists, the pastors and teachers* (v 11). Aldo has been anointed by God as a prophet. I know this because of the things God reveals to him.

I cannot choose how God will use me, it is His choice. My part is to be open and available to whatever it is He wants to do through me.

God gives a specific anointing to certain people in order for them to fulfil a specific position. There is the anointing to accomplish a specific task; and then there is the anointing where God will use us to pass on healing, or a specific word to someone. Each of God's children can be used by Him in any of these ways if we are open to His Spirit working in our lives.

Prayer

My Father God, I am in awe of the fact that You choose to use people like me to accomplish Your purposes here on earth. Help me Lord, to be open to Your Holy Spirit. Help me to be obedient to what Your Spirit is telling me to do. I want to walk in the anointing of Your Spirit. Amen.

13 November

Jesus anointed

Read Philippians 2:1-16

... have the same mindset as Christ Jesus: Who, being in very nature God, did not consider equality with God something to be used to his own advantage; rather, he made himself nothing by taking the very nature of a servant, being made in human likeness. - Philippians 2:5-7

John the Baptist did not want to baptise Jesus. He said, *"I need to be baptised by you, and do you come to me?"* (Matthew 3:14). John knew exactly who Jesus was. After all, his anointing was to prepare the way for Jesus. Jesus said, *"Let it be so now; it is proper for us to do this to fulfil all righteousness." Then John consented* (v 15). Why did John consent? Because he understood his purpose; he was in-tune with the Spirit.

If Jesus, being God, needed the anointing of the Holy Spirit in His life; how much more do I need to receive the anointing upon my life?

[*Jesus*] *went up out of the water ... and he saw the Spirit of God descending like a dove and lighting on him. And a voice from heaven said, "This is my Son, whom I love; with him I am well pleased"* (vs 16-17). The Father blessed Jesus and the Holy Spirit anointed Jesus. He continually sought the anointing of the Holy Spirit upon His work and ministry while He was on earth.

Prayer

My Father, I come before You in gratitude for the example set by Jesus. Jesus, You are my Lord and Saviour, help me to have the same mind that was in You. Fill me with Your Holy Spirit, I pray, so that I can walk in the anointing to fulfil Your purposes and plans for me. Amen.

14 November

Anointed to fight Goliath

Read Matthew 4:1-11

Then Jesus was led by the Spirit into the wilderness to be tempted by the devil. After fasting for forty days and forty nights, he was hungry. The tempter came to him.
- Matthew 4:1-3a

Jesus went through His wilderness experience. He faced His Goliath. David had to fight Goliath before he could become king. You and I need to fight our Goliath's as well. This can be a stumbling block that prevents us from walking in our anointing. We come to the scene of battle where we come face to face with our Goliath, and we run away; instead of depending upon God and His Spirit to undertake for us.

My life is not at the mercy of the enemy – it is controlled by God.

The time in the wilderness is not important; it is what we do with it that counts. God led Jesus into the wilderness to face Satan. Jesus had to go through this to teach us some important lessons. God was the One who put it in David's heart to fight Goliath. It was God who made him believe he could overcome the giant. Our lives are not at the mercy of the enemy – they are controlled by God.

Prayer

Father God, I do not need to fear my Goliath. I do not need to fear the time in the Wilderness. Your Spirit will not lead me anywhere that He cannot keep and sustain me. Thank You, Lord, that like Jesus, and like David I can have implicit faith in You and Your love for me. Amen.

15 November

Anointed to destroy strongholds

Read 2 Corinthians 10

The weapons we fight with are not the weapons of the world. On the contrary, they have divine power to demolish strongholds. We demolish arguments and every pretension that sets itself up against the knowledge of God, and we take captive every thought to make it obedient to Christ. - 2 Corinthians 10:4-5

Aldo walks in the Spirit. The Spirit shows him all manner of things. People have spoken negatively over him and caused him great hurt. Resentment sprang up in him and the root of resentment is rebellion. None of this was from God. The enemy used these feelings and emotions to gain a foothold in his life. The enemy used this to wage a war against Aldo. Like Jesus he has been through his wilderness experience. Aldo has had to learn how to fight the enemy. This is a daily lesson that is a part of our lives now.

God says I must bless those who curse me. He has told me to speak blessing upon people.

This is the dimension God has called us to walk in. God has told us to bless those who curse us. He has told us to speak blessing upon people. I have learnt that I have to be obedient to what God tells me to do irrespective of what people think or say.

Prayer

Father I come before You with a humble spirit. I know that there is a dimension of living that is far removed from the 'normal'. As Your child You call me to live and walk in the supernatural. It is in this dimension that Your Spirit operates. Father, lift me into this dimension, I pray. Amen.

Anointed to minister

Read Luke 4:1-21

"The Spirit of the Lord is on me, because he has anointed me to proclaim good news to the poor. He has sent me to proclaim freedom for the prisoners and recovery of sight for the blind, to set the oppressed free, to proclaim the year of the Lord's favour."
- Luke 4:18-19

This is a description of walking in the anointing. God uses us to proclaim Good News to the poor, freedom to prisoners, recovery of sight for the blind and to set free the oppressed. God wants to use you to do these things! It is so thrilling; this is living life to the full. This is fulfilling your purpose. God did not create us for mediocrity; He created us to fulfil a divine destiny.

I must be about my Father's business, building His Kingdom.

Living in this dimension is not about building your own kingdom; no to the contrary it is about building God's Kingdom. This is not about us – this is about God. The anointing is not to be used for our own selfish ends. We will only be effective if we are walking in humility before God. Sadly too many Christians try to build their own kingdoms. This will not stand the test of time. God will not share His glory.

Prayer

My Father, You have given me the wonderful privilege of being Your child. You have anointed me for ministry. I am to spread the Good News, proclaim freedom, help the blind to see, and set the oppressed free. Not in my own power, but in the power of Your Spirit. Amen.

17 November

An anointed life

Read Matthew 4:1-17

From that time on Jesus began to preach, "Repent, for the kingdom of heaven has come near." - Matthew 4:17

There is a pattern that we can trace as we look at an anointed life. Someone is called of God. They lay down their lives, yielding to the purposes of God. There is a wilderness experience where their commitment is tested. Then their ministry begins. This is exactly the pattern that Jesus' life followed.

It is no different with us. God will manifest His power through us in order to destroy the work of the enemy in our life. Jesus gained the victory over Satan. We have to claim our victory in Jesus' Name. God wants His Kingdom to become increasingly stronger in our lives. It is so sad when the works of the enemy are more evident in a child of God's life than what the Kingdom of God is. Jesus lived His life only doing what the Father told Him to do. How much more should we live like this?

I have to be obedient to His voice and no one else's. There is no other way to live if I want to walk in the anointing.

Prayer

Father, I realise that there is a price to be paid to walk in the anointing. I realise that I cannot please people and You at the same time. If I want to walk in Your power I have to be totally yielded to You. I have to be prepared to go through the wilderness experience. Help me to discern Your will and walk in obedience to what You reveal to me. Amen.

Paul anointed for ministry

Read Acts 9:1-19

Then Ananias went to the house and entered it. Placing his hands on Saul, he said, "Brother Saul, the Lord – Jesus, who appeared to you on the road as you were coming here – has sent me so that you may see again and be filled with the Holy Spirit." Immediately, something like scales fell from Saul's eyes, and he could see again. He got up and was baptised, and after taking some food, he regained his strength.
- Acts 9:17-19

It was Paul's life's mission to annihilate the followers of the Way. After encountering Jesus on the road to Damascus he was blinded for three days. Did you notice this sentence when you were reading? *"I will show him how much he must suffer for my name"* (v 16). God had a purpose for Saul's life. God was going to use him mightily, but Saul would also suffer much for the Kingdom of God.

I must not allow anything to stand in the way of me fulfilling my purpose.

God told Ananias to lay hands upon Saul, and anoint him for ministry. We are told that scales fell from his eyes, and he was a changed man. The zealous persecutor of the Christians became the zealous preacher of the Gospel of Jesus Christ. If anyone ever needed the anointing it was Paul. His was a hard road. Yet he counted it all as nothing for the surpassing greatness of following Jesus. Paul did not allow anything to stand in the way of his fulfilling his purpose.

Prayer

My Father, thank You for the wonderful testimony of the Apostle Paul. His life is an inspiration to me. Thank You for his witness and his single minded devotion to You. Lord, I pray that You will help me to have the same commitment to You – help me to put aside everything that would hold me back so that I can focus wholeheartedly upon You. Amen.

Anointed power

Read Acts 19:1-13

God did extraordinary miracles through Paul, so that even handkerchiefs and aprons that had touched him were taken to those who were ill, and their illnesses were cured and the evil spirits left them. - Acts 19:11-12

In Acts 19 we see evidence of the anointing that was upon Paul's life. He preached the Gospel in Ephesus. Paul stayed with them for three months teaching in the synagogue. Paul taught in the power of the Holy Spirit. Sadly we see that some of the religious people rebelled against the Way. So Paul left the temple and went and preached in another venue.

Some people tried to imitate Paul. They tried to drive out evil spirits. *One day the evil spirit answered them, "Jesus I know, and Paul I know about, but who are you?" Then the man who had the evil spirit jumped on them and overpowered them all. He gave them such a beating that they ran out of the house naked and bleeding* (vs 15-16). God will not share His glory. There is no short cut to the anointing and the power, my friend. It cannot be bought, it cannot be copied.

> *Anything I do for God of lasting value is done through the power of the Holy Spirit at work within me.*

Prayer

Father, again thank You for Your instruction. Thank You for showing me in Your Word the importance of walking in the power of Your Spirit. You give Your anointing to Your children. You empower me to do Your work. Help me to seek the Giver not the gift, I pray. Amen.

No Holy Spirit, No anointing

Read 1 Corinthians 2

My message and my preaching were not with wise and persuasive words, but with a demonstration of the Spirit's power, so that your faith might not rest on human wisdom, but on God's power. - 1 Corinthians 2:4-5

Paul had an excellent education. He was learned in all aspects of the Law. Intellectually there were few people who were his equal. Yet Paul only operated in the power of the Holy Spirit. He knew that he had to become less and Jesus had to become more. Paul understood that nothing he said could change people. It was only the power of the Holy Spirit at work in people's lives that could bring about change. It is not our cleverness or our abilities that count.

I was speaking at a meeting recently when the Holy Spirit interrupted me and told me that He wanted to work among the people. At first I was concerned about what people would say if I didn't finish my message. Then I realised that it was important for me to obey God and not worry about people. God moved in a mighty way that day.

This is the key to walking in the anointing; walk in obedience to the Holy Spirit.

Prayer

My Father, thank You that You are the All-Powerful God. Help me to be available and open to being used by You. Give me the courage to do the things You are telling me to do, even if they go against popular opinion. Help me only to be a God-pleaser – not a people-pleaser. Amen.

Anointing Oil

Read Exodus 30:22-33

Then the Lord said to Moses, "Take the following fine spices: 500 shekels of liquid myrrh, half as much (that is, 250 shekels) of fragrant cinnamon, 250 shekels of fragrant cane, 500 shekels of cassia – all according to the sanctuary shekel – and a hin of olive oil. Make these into a sacred anointing oil, a fragrant blend, the work of a perfumer. It will be the sacred anointing oil." - Exodus 30:22-25

God gave Moses a recipe for the anointing oil he was to use to anoint the tent of meeting and all its contents. There were five ingredients that he had to use. Five is the number for grace. Grace means favour. God longs to anoint us with His Spirit. He wants to favour His children with His ability and strength.

The fire of the Holy Spirit is not for my destruction but for my purification.

These ingredients are not only for the anointing oil, but also ingredients we should have in our lives, within our spirits. The first one is myrrh – it is purifying in its application and very costly. Myrrh is bitter to the taste. It is used as a balm to soothe hurt and sore parts of the body. It brings relief when applied in this way. So the Holy Spirit is given as a gift of healing to the Body of Christ. He cannot be bought because He is priceless.

Prayer

My Father, thank You for Your precious Holy Spirit. Thank You that You give me Your Holy Spirit not for my destruction but for my purification. I pray that the fragrance of Your Spirit will flow from my life. Amen.

Myrrh for healing

Read 2 Timothy 2:14-26

Those who cleanse themselves from the latter will be instruments for special purposes, made holy, useful to the Master and prepared to do any good work. - 2 Timothy 2:21

Myrrh is bitter to the taste. When you apply it to the hurting parts of your soul though, the myrrh begins to have a soothing, calming, healing effect upon your pain. Many people are walking around with soul wounds that go deep and often seem to be incurable. There is no such thing as an incurable hurt, when brought to the Great Physician. After you have been through the healing process the fragrance and oil that will come from you, no money can buy; nothing and no one can take it away from you.

We have to go through the purification process. The Holy Spirit is the purifier, but He is also our Comforter. The pain can be physical, it can be spiritual or it can be emotional. This is where the Comforter comes in. He will apply the balm of the Myrrh, bringing healing and restoration in our lives.

Once I have been through the purifying process I will be a vessel set apart to be used by God.

Prayer

Father, I come before You in submission. I lay my hurt and wounded soul before Your throne of grace. Lord, I know that I can only get through this with the help of Your Holy Spirit. I pray that You will touch my pain so that Your healing power can flow through me. I don't shy away from the bitterness but know that through it You will be glorified and I will be useful to You. Amen.

23 November

Cinnamon - aroma of obedience

Read 1 Samuel 15:1-23

But Samuel replied: "Does the Lord delight in burnt offerings and sacrifices as much as in obeying the voice of the Lord? To obey is better than sacrifice, and to heed is better than the fat of rams. For rebellion is like the sin of divination, and arrogance like the evil of idolatry. Because you have rejected the word of the Lord, he has rejected you as king." - 1 Samuel 15:22-23

Cinnamon, the second ingredient, comes from the bark of the cinnamon tree and has a wonderful aroma. The Bible speaks about the aroma of sacrifice. God is not pleased with our sacrifice unless it is accompanied by obedience. God says, 'Obedience is better than sacrifice.' It costs to obey God. Sometimes we have to be prepared to give up things that are important to us. Maybe you have to give up a friendship that means a lot to you, but you know it is not right in God's eyes. God asks, 'Will you obey Me, will you turn your back on this friendship?'

The cost of obedience is dear but the aroma emitted before God's throne is worth it.

When the bark is removed from the cinnamon tree; there is a tearing as the bark is removed from the trunk of the tree. As this happens the aroma is released. This signifies the pain we can experience which leads to the aroma of obedience being released in our lives.

Prayer

My Father, I bow before You in obedience. Help me to surrender my will to Your will. Help me to be prepared to let go of the things that are preventing me from bearing fruit. I want to live a life that is pleasing to You. I want to give off the sweet aroma of obedience. Amen.

24 November

A broken reed

Read Isaiah 66:1-11

"Has not my hand made all these things, and so they came into being?" declares the Lord. "These are the ones I look on with favour: those who are humble and contrite in spirit, and who tremble at my word." - Isaiah 66:2

The third ingredient is the cane. This plant grows very tall but when it is crushed and broken it gives off an incredibly sweet fragrance. The more it is broken up the greater the fragrance that comes from it. This is what God wants to teach us in our spirits. Cane speaks of brokenness. *"Has not my hand made all these things, and so they came into being?" declares the Lord. "These are the ones I look on with favour: those who are humble and contrite in spirit, and who tremble at my word."*

When we live out of our abundance it is so easy for self and the flesh to creep in. If I am feeling strong and I am in control then I do not need to depend upon the Lord. However, when I am in that place of brokenness; when I have nothing left to give – that is when He can use me.

When I am in that place of brokenness; when I have nothing left to give – that is when He can use me.

Prayer

My Father, Your Spirit works within me. As I come to You in my brokenness, You cause the broken reeds of my life to give off an aroma – a sweet perfume, that attracts people to You. Father, I submit to You – use me, I pray. Amen.

Jesus anointed to suffer

Read Mark 14:1-11

"Leave her alone," said Jesus. "Why are you bothering her? She has done a beautiful thing to me. She did what she could. She poured perfume on my body beforehand to prepare for my burial. Truly I tell you, wherever the gospel is preached throughout the world, what she has done will also be told, in memory of her." - Mark 14:6,8-9

Jesus was anointed by a woman (the Gospel of John tells us it was Mary). She broke open a precious jar of perfume and poured it over Jesus' head. The aroma spread throughout the house. The disciples (and particularly Judas) were upset over the 'waste' of money. Jesus said Mary was anointing Him for His burial. Mary was anointing Jesus for the suffering that lay ahead of Him on Calvary.

I come to Him as an empty vessel and I allow His sweet perfume to flow through me, attracting people to Christ.

Mary didn't realise the importance of what she did. She was simply expressing her love and gratitude to Jesus for all He had done for her. It is the aroma of Jesus' suffering on Calvary that has drawn men and women to God down through the ages. He hung on the Cross, broken and battered, so that we could have Salvation. He had to suffer so that we can have Eternal Life. Without suffering there is no life. God uses the broken reed to bless others.

Prayer

Lord God, I come to You a broken reed. Help me, I pray, to see the bigger picture. I submit my brokenness to You and I ask You to use me. Make me a sweet smelling perfume sharing the love of Jesus with everyone I meet. Amen.

26 November

The anointed are ridiculed

Read John 12:1-11

But one of his disciples, Judas Iscariot, who was later to betray him, objected, "Why wasn't this perfume sold and the money given to the poor? It was worth a year's wages." He did not say this because he cared about the poor but because he was a thief; as keeper of the money bag, he used to help himself to what was put into it.
- John 12:4-6

Judas became mad at Mary. All she wanted to do was express her gratitude, and it was misunderstood. Instead of it being a meaningful moment between her and her Saviour, it became an embarrassment. In order for the fragrance to be poured out, the flask had to be broken. It is the same with our lives. Something that often blocks this brokenness is pride. If you are proud then you cannot have a deep anointing upon your life.

You do not need to fear when man reviles you because God says to you. 'Yes, you have lost your reputation, you have been broken, and people do not approve of you. I am your approval. My anointing over your life is My approval, and I regard you with pleasure. I respect you, I love you and I bestow My favour upon you. Your sweet smelling fragrance is pleasing in My sight.'

God bestows His favour upon me. My sweet smelling fragrance is pleasing in His sight.

Prayer

Father, thank You for Your stamp of approval upon my life. Thank You for Your words of encouragement. I do not care about what people say about me. My eyes are focused upon You. My only desire is to please You and to serve You. Make me a blessing, I pray. Amen.

27 November

Humility, bending, and bowing

Read 1 Peter 5:1-11

Humble yourselves, therefore, under God's mighty hand, that he may lift you up in due time. Cast all your anxiety on him because he cares for you. - 1 Peter 5:6-7

Cassia means to bend, bow and stoop. I don't know if you are aware of it but pride is a demon spirit that tries to destroy the very life of God's people. Peter also says, *'All of you, clothe yourselves with humility toward one another, because, "God opposes the proud but shows favour to the humble"'* (v 5). The name of the demon spirit of pride is Leviathan; his influence is with spiritual pride and the blocking of deliverance.

Submission is the path to humility, and humility is the path to promotion. When we walk in humility we can know that there is a double portion of God's anointing poured out upon us. Cassia speaks of humility that is the exact opposite of pride. As we allow God to work in our lives; bending, bowing and stooping us. He will take our lives and use us as a sweet smelling incense to draw people to Himself.

Cassia speaks of humility which is the exact opposite of pride.

Prayer

Lord God, I come before You in deep humility. Father, forgive me for all the times that I have allowed pride to creep into my life. I renounce it today, in Jesus Name. I ask You to fill me with humility. I want my life to represent cassia so that I can be bendable and humble. Amen.

28 November

Olive oil: Spiritual trial

Read Matthew 22:1-14

"For many are invited, but few are chosen." - Matthew 22:14

The last ingredient in the anointing oil is olive oil. The Olive tree can withstand long periods of drought. It is a tough tree. The fruit has to be pressed under a considerable weight to remove the oil. The spiritual meaning of the olive oil is 'trial'. We see that so many Christians, including Jesus, went through a period of trial. There is a price to be paid to carry the pure anointing. It does not come free. The Lord showed me that Salvation is free, but the anointing costs you your life.

God sets His stamp of approval on our lives, by bestowing the anointing upon us.

Holy Spirit is my best friend. He has taught me that all the ingredients of the anointing oil are characteristics that He uses to bring us into total dependence upon God. They cause us to live in obedience to Him. When we live like this then we can go into the world, and spread the sweet aroma of Christ to everyone we meet.

Prayer

Father, my life feels like it is being squeezed from all sides. I am at the end of my own abilities. I choose in this time of trial to look to You. You are my Living Water. Father, keep me faithful through the trial, I pray. Help me to emerge from the wilderness victorious in Jesus. Place Your anointing upon me, I pray. Amen.

29 November

Dying to self

Read 1 John 2:18-17

As for you, the anointing you received from him remains in you, and you do not need anyone to teach you. But as his anointing teaches you about all things and as that anointing is real, not counterfeit – just as it has taught you, remain in him.
- 1 John 2:27

When one walks in the anointing of God, there is no place for self. It is all about God. It is His aroma that we give off. His strength and His energy work through us making the anointing evident. There is a high price to pay for walking in the anointing – dying to self. This is a day by day process, not a once off experience. The anointing needs to be nurtured and renewed.

The level of the anointing upon my life and in my life has everything to do with the relationship I have with Holy Spirit. It all flows from fellowship with Him. Each day I have to follow His leading and obey His voice. As I follow Him step by step I live a life that is borne upon His wings. My burden is light when I walk with Him, even when I am going through difficult times.

My burden is light when I walk with Him, even when I am going through difficult times.

Prayer

Father, thank You that my birth-right is to be filled with Your Spirit. Your anointing is mine as Your child. Help me to handle my inheritance with care. Help me to nurture and walk in Your Spirit. I pray that the anointing will become more and more evident in my life. Amen.

Anointed to bring life

Read Ezekiel 47:1-12

...so where the river flows everything will live. - Ezekiel 47:9c

The stronger my relationship with the Holy Spirit, the more the fruit of the Spirit will be evident in my life. The more the fruit of the Spirit is evident, the more like Christ I will become. As I live like this my life is open for the anointing of God to become ever stronger within me and upon me. *As the man went eastward with a measuring line in his hand, he measured off a thousand cubits and then led me through water that was ankle-deep. He measured off another thousand cubits and led me through water that was knee-deep. He measured off another thousand and led me through water that was up to the waist. He measured off another thousand, but now it was a river that I could not cross, because the water had risen and was deep enough to swim in – a river that no one could cross* (Ezekiel 47:3-5).

> *So the more I die to self, the more I step out of the way, the greater the anointing can flow.*

According to these verses we have just read I believe there are levels and degrees of anointing. Some walk ankle deep, others walk in up to their knees, still others at waist height, and then there are those who swim in the river of anointing. The degree to which we live in the anointing is dependent upon our relationship with the Almighty God. Those that swim are carrying high levels of El Shaddai power.

Prayer

My Father God, I long to walk in the fullness of Your anointing. Lord, I praise You and I commit myself to You anew. Lord, keep me faithful and keep me strong. Amen.

Christus se bruid sien
ons sal deur bid,
vas sy stem gehoor
saam. Sy woord
en Gees wat ons lei.
sien hoe hy ons
voorberei om sy bruid
te wees. Jy en ek
wat ons lewe neerlê
vir Christus sal sy
bruid wees dankie!
Sy bruid is baie
baie vry van
die wêreld. Sy sien
hy sal haar nooit
begewe of verlaat nie.
Wysheid sê sy is
baie lief vir haar
bruidegom en sy soul
is rooi alles oorgegee
aan Jesus Christus.
dankie so dankie
vir ouers wat vir
my na rustige waters
waar rus is gelei het
met hulle gebede
geloof in Christus.

Letter 12:

Bride of Christ

I see that the Bride of Christ will obey His voice through fasting and prayer. He leads us through His voice and by His Spirit. I see how He prepares us to be His Bride. The ones that lay down their life for Christ will be His Bride. His Bride is completely free from the world. She knows that He will never leave her nor forsake her. Wisdom says that the Bride truly loves her Bridegroom, and that her soul is red [covered by the blood of the Lamb] and completely surrendered to Jesus Christ. I am so thankful for my parents who led me to peaceful streams where I can rest, through their prayers and their faith in Christ.

Intimacy with God

Prayer for December

My Father God, I praise You and worship You for Your faithfulness to me during this year. Thank You that I have been able to walk with You. Thank You for what You have done for me. You have seen me through many situations – some that have been joyful, others that have brought sorrow and even unhappiness – yet through everything You have been with me. As I enter this last month of the year I look forward to spending time with You in Your Word. Your call to intimacy with You is one that I long to yield to. I want to know the joy of having moved from the Outer Court – where I have come with joyful praise – into the Holy Place where Your Spirit has filled me. Then the wonder of walking into the Holy of Holies where You are waiting for me so that we can have sweet communion, and I can sit in Your presence. Thank You for Your great love for me.

I love You, my Lord, and bless Your Holy Name.

Amen.

Living my highest life

Read Luke 8:40-48

But Jesus said, "Someone touched me; I know that power has gone out from me." Then the woman, seeing that she could not go unnoticed, came trembling and fell at his feet. In the presence of all the people, she told why she had touched him and how she had been instantly healed. Then he said to her, "Daughter, your faith has healed you. Go in peace." - Luke 8:46-48

We have to choose where we are going to live: In the Outer Court, the Holy Place, or in the Holy of Holies – the throne room of the Father. The call God has placed upon our lives is to live in His fullness. This is our purpose. God's plan for you and me is to lead us into a deeper spiritual walk and to teach us Kingdom principles.

Many things can keep us from living our highest life: sin, bad habits, a heart that refuses to forgive, disobedience, prayerlessness, bitterness or a lack of spiritual discipline. These are all barriers that keep us from true intimacy with Christ. The woman with the issue of blood did not allow the obstacle of the crowd to keep her from reaching out and touching Jesus' robe. She persevered until she connected with Him. We must have a determination to experience intimacy with Jesus Christ.

> *I must not allow anything to detract or keep me from intimacy with Jesus Christ.*

Prayer

Father, as I begin the last month of this year I come before You to worship You. I say thank You for Your hand upon my life. Thank You that I have such a clear purpose for my life – to walk with You each day. Nothing else matters, nothing else is important. Amen.

The narrow gate leads to life

Read Matthew 7:1-14

Enter through the narrow gate. For wide is the gate and broad is the road that leads to destruction, and many enter through it. But small is the gate and narrow the road that leads to life, and only a few find it. - Matthew 7:13-14

A shift is coming in the Spirit realm. I believe we will all start to experience what Jesus was talking about in Matthew chapter seven. We will experience the rain descending, the floods and the winds blowing, lashing our houses. When this happens will we find out if our houses are built upon the Rock or upon the sand? As we enter the final hour it will become more evident where people are living. Some will be in the Outer Court, others in the Holy Place and then there will be those who are in the Holy of Holies.

In the Holy of Holies comes the full understanding of the revelation of the Father, the Three in One.

People who live in the Outer Court are only interested in their own pleasures. They have accepted Jesus, but there is no spiritual discipline. There isn't a longing for God in the Outer Court. Everything is about them. They have not yet come to the place of intimacy with God.

Prayer

Father, I realise that the time has come for me to become serious about my choices. I do not waant to live in a house that is built upon the sand. I come to You asking You to forgive my complacency. Fill me with Your Spirit. I want to live in the Holy of Holies. Amen.

Jesus is the Life

Read John 14:1-15

Jesus answered, "I am the way and the truth and the life. No one comes to the Father except through me." - John 14:6

Jesus is the Way, the Truth, and the Life. In the Holy of Holies we begin to live the abundant life. The Outer Court is all about the body and the desires of the flesh. In the Holy Place we feed and please our souls, but in the Holy of Holies, we live and move in the Spirit.

In the Outer Court there are glorious stars. In the Holy Place there is the glory of the moon. However, in the Holy of Holies, is the Sun, the greater light. We live in the King's domain, in His living Kingdom. We realise that we cannot fight our giants on our own. We enter His rest and trust God to help us. When we move into the Holy of Holies, we are operating in the realm of an open heaven. This is a dimension that can only be attained in the Spirit.

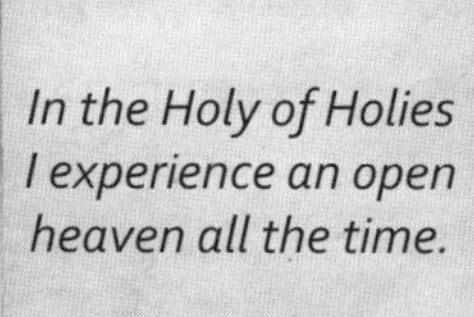

In the Holy of Holies I experience an open heaven all the time.

Prayer

Father, I am no longer satisfied living in the Outer Court, or in the Holy Place. There is only one place I want to be and that is in the Holy of Holies. I long for Your presence and Your blessing upon my life. Amen.

Moses in the Outer Court

Read Exodus 3:10-22

God said to Moses, "I AM WHO I AM. This is what you are to say to the Israelites: 'I AM has sent me to you.'" - Exodus 3:14

One day he encountered a burning bush. Moses was curious when he saw the bush burning, and approached it from the flesh (the Outer Court). God spoke to him, and told him to remove his shoes, because he was standing on holy ground. His shoes were a symbol of removing the contaminated things in his life.

Moses heard God's voice telling him what he had to do. Moses reacted in the flesh (Outer Court). He said; no. Moses hadn't yet learnt that it was not about his abilities but about the ability of the great I AM. He made excuses about why he couldn't do what God asked him to do. Are you making excuses? Is there something God is calling you to do? Maybe God has been speaking to you, but because you are living in the Outer Court your spiritual ears are closed. You cannot have intimacy without obedience.

I will never know true intimacy with God if I am not prepared to hear and obey Him.

Prayer

Dear Father, thank You that I can learn from Moses' life. Help me to listen with my spiritual ears and not in the flesh when You speak to me. I want to have intimacy with You, help me to be obedient. Amen.

5 December

Moses in the Holy Place

Read Exodus 4:18-31

The Lord said to Moses, "When you return to Egypt, see that you perform before Pharaoh all the wonders I have given you the power to do." - Exodus 4:21

Even after God identified Himself and said to Moses: *"Take off your sandals, for the place where you are standing is holy ground"* (Exodus 3:5). Moses did not get it. It took quite a while longer before Moses accepted the mission God had for him. Once Moses took on his destiny he moved forward into the Spirit realm (into the Holy Place). The power of the Holy Spirit was upon Moses, empowering him and giving him what he needed to fulfil God's commands.

The Children of Israel tested the patience of God and Moses on many occasions. It is incredible to see how Moses was able to handle them. Moses had evolved from someone who lacked confidence and was insecure to being a leader that we still can learn lessons from today. How did this transformation take place in Moses' life? He had an encounter with the living God. He chose to obey God and begin to move into his destiny.

I need to trust God each day to help me to do what He calls me to do.

Prayer

My Father, I realise that I cannot move forward with You and remain in the Outer Court. I thank You, Lord, that You don't call me to do anything that Your Spirit cannot help me to do. Amen.

Moses in the Holy of Holies

Read 2 Corinthians 3:7-18

Now the Lord is the Spirit, and where the Spirit of the Lord is, there is freedom. And we all, who with unveiled faces contemplate the Lord's glory, are being transformed into his image with ever-increasing glory, which comes from the Lord, who is the Spirit.
- 2 Corinthians 3:17-18

Moses took the next step and moved from the Holy Place into the Holy of Holies. Moses asked God, *'Let me know Your ways that I may know You ...'* (Exodus 33:13b NASB). This had become the main desire of Moses' life – to know God. We read God's response to Moses *"I will also do this thing of which you have spoken; for you have found favour in My sight, and I have known you by name"* (Exodus 33:17 NASB).

Moses understood what it means to worship in the Holy of Holies before the throne of God.

But whenever Moses went in before the Lord to speak with Him, he would take off the veil until he came out; and whenever he came out and spoke to the sons of Israel what he had been commanded, the sons of Israel would see the face of Moses, that the skin on Moses' face shone. So Moses would replace the veil over his face until he went in to speak with Him (Exodus 34:34-35 NASB).

Prayer

My Father, I long to experience You in a way that my face will glow as a result of the encounter we have. I long to have You say to me *I have known you by name.* Amen.

7 December

Lessons from the Life of Moses

Read Hebrews 11:23-29

By faith he left Egypt, not fearing the king's anger; he persevered because he saw him who is invisible. - Hebrews 11:27

We can learn some lessons from Moses' life. Moses would not be your first choice if you were recruiting a dynamic person to lead a large crowd of people on an epic journey. Moses was comfortable in the Outer Courts. He was not looking for the grand project. God had other plans. Often God has to interrupt our lives to get our attention.

Moses began to learn what it means to walk in the Spirit. God moulded Moses to fulfil his destiny. The closer Moses got to God the less Moses became and the greater God became. It is the same for us. All we have to do is rest in Him. When Moses moved into the Holy of Holies we see a man who was totally sold out to God. He reached a level of intimacy with God where God listened to Moses, and did what he asked Him to do.

God will lead, guide, teach and nurture me as He grows me for His purposes.

Prayer

My Father God, so much of my life is about me. I know that You are speaking to me through Your Spirit. It is time for me to become serious about what You are saying to me. I know that You will give me everything I need in order to fulfil Your purposes. I surrender to You. Amen.

Transparency

Read Romans 12

Do not conform any longer to the pattern of this world, but be transformed by the renewing of your mind. Then you will be able to test and approve what God's will is – his good, pleasing and perfect will. - Romans 12:2

The Lord said to me; 'If you don't make time to be in My presence you cannot expect to become radiant the way I am.' Aldo calls it transparency. Our transparency is determined by the degree to which we have laid down our lives; on how much of our bitterness we've worked through. It is measured by the lack of selfishness and self-centredness in our lives.

If I spend time with God I will begin to reflect His glory.

We live entrenched in our comfort zone inhabiting a world of hurt, darkness and unbelief. We can remain trapped in the Outer Court for years in this cycle. We become like the people we spend our time with – so it stands to reason that the more time we spend with God, the more we'll become like Him. We saw this in Moses' life. When he had been with God his face literally glowed. It is the same with us. His power will be evident in our lives.

Prayer

Lord, it is only in Your presence that I find everything I need. Father, I give You all the things that are holding me back from experiencing You. As I stand before You shine Your Light upon me. I want to reflect Your glory to the people I come into contact with. Amen.

9 December

Mixed seeds

Read Matthew 13:24-30, 36-43

The Son of Man will send out his angels, and they will weed out of his kingdom everything that causes sin and all who do evil. They will throw them into the blazing furnace, where there will be weeping and gnashing of teeth. Then the righteous will shine like the sun in the kingdom of their Father. He who has ears, let him hear.
- Matthew 13:41-43

The Lord has been speaking to me about 'mixed seeds'. The Church is full of people who are living with mixed seed. The Lord told me that because I was living in His Promised Land there was no place for mixed seed in my life. Generally people do not want to hear this word preached. It does not make them feel secure in their comfort zones. God tells us in Matthew 7:22-23 that the day is coming when He will say to some of the people who come before Him; '*I never knew you. Away from me ...*' These must surely be the hardest words that anyone could ever hear.

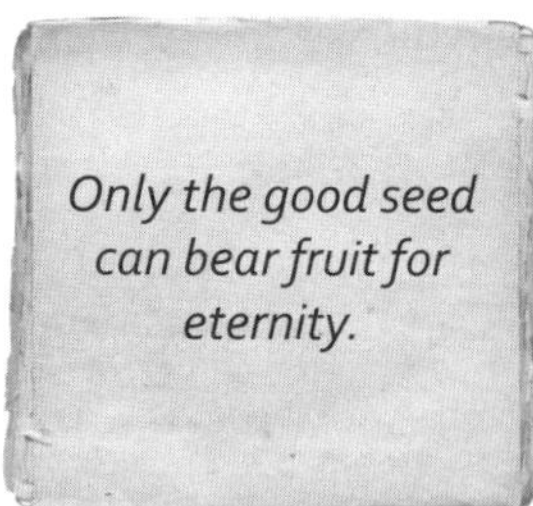

Only the good seed can bear fruit for eternity.

The truth is that God is not interested in what we do for Him. What we do for Him should be a by-product of our relationship with Him. The mixed seed must be burnt out of our lives. We have to have a single-minded focus; intimacy with God.

Prayer

My Father God, I lay myself on the altar – I pray that You will burn away the mixed seed in my life. I want to have a single minded focus as I walk with You. Lord, make my life count for eternity. Amen.

Stones that weigh us down

Read Romans 12:9-21

Love must be sincere. Hate what is evil; cling to what is good. If it is possible, as far as it depends on you, live at peace with everyone. - Romans 12:9,18

So many of us are weighed down by the stones we carry around inside of us. Our stones of anger, greed and hatred, to mention a few, keep us from entering the Holy of Holies. We are kept in the Outer Court where the flesh rules. Our prayers sound like this: 'Lord, please give me more...' The 'more' that we ask for are things that will benefit us. Our prayers are not about furthering God's Kingdom – it is all about me, me and me.

In the Holy of Holies it is totally different. It is all about God. He is the focus; He is the centre of my worship, my thoughts and my life. It is the Holy of Holies where we can worship Him as He deserves to be worshipped. It is there that we give Him the honour that is due His Name. It is there that I praise Him; Holy, holy is the Lord God Almighty.

The more I praise His Holy Name, the more His Name is upon my lips.

Prayer

My Father God, forgive me that so often my prayers are all about Me. Lord, give me a fresh infilling of Your Spirit so that I can have a change of heart and mind. I worship You; I give You praise. You are the Almighty God – Holy, holy, holy is Your Name. Amen.

The Love of God

Read John 3:1-21

For God so loved the world that he gave his one and only Son, that whoever believes in him shall not perish but have eternal life. - John 3:16

When I look at the cross I see LOVE. God's love for me drove Jesus to Calvary. God's love is not selective – He loves everyone – even my enemies. Therefore I have no right to judge you. If God loves you then I cannot speak evil against you. I cannot curse you if I know that Jesus died for you. At the cross I die to self. When I experience His love I have no option but to love in return. He will fight for me. I do not need to fight on my own behalf.

Holiness in my life is my main goal. I am willing to shed anything and everything that tries to hold me back from this goal. I stop striving and am at rest as His peace fills my soul and my spirit. All this is possible because of the love of God. It is possible because of the Cross of Calvary.

I stop striving and am at rest as His peace fills my soul and my spirit.

Prayer

Father, thank You for the Cross of Calvary. Thank You for Jesus' sacrifice. Thank You for Your great love for me and for every human being. Help me to live in the fullness of all that is mine as a result of Calvary. Fill me with Your peace, I pray, so that I can rest in You. Amen.

Choosing against the flesh

Read Psalm 100

Know that the Lord Himself is God; It is He who has made us, and not we ourselves; We are His people and the sheep of His pasture. For the Lord is good; His loving kindness is everlasting, and His faithfulness to all generations. - Psalm 100:3, 5 (New American Standard Bible)

We come to God with joyfulness and gladness. How can we be anything other than joyful when we recognise Him for who He is? I come into the Outer Court to worship and praise God – I make His Name Great – The purpose of the Outer Court is to help us focus upon Him. It is in the Outer Court that we deal with the flesh. We repent of our sin. It is here we choose to die to self.

God reminds us of His love and faithfulness. *For the Lord is good; His loving kindness is everlasting, and His faithfulness to all generations* (v 5 NASB). The phrase loving kindness – is a covenant word. It is because of God's faithfulness that I can choose to die to self. I do not need to worry about my life or my needs because my Covenant Keeping God is taking care of me. It is in dying to self that I gain life.

I cannot move out of the Outer Court until I have chosen to die to self and deny the flesh.

Prayer

My Father, I come before You with praise and thanksgiving. I come into Your presence joyfully and with gladness. I lift my eyes away from my circumstances and I look to You. You are my Covenant Keeping God. I place myself on the altar at the foot of the cross – I surrender to You. Amen.

13 December

I can do all things through Christ

Read Philippians 4

I can do everything through him who gives me strength. - Philippians 4:13

It is when we choose to die to self in the Outer Court that our spiritual eyes are opened. God will not ask you to do anything that He cannot give you the ability to do. The Living Bible puts it beautifully when it says, *I can do anything God asks me to through Christ who strengthens me.* Paul who penned these words understood exactly what it meant to die to self. Paul learnt that it was all about God and nothing of himself. It is no different for us. It is all of Him and nothing of us.

Dying to self is a daily process. Each new day I have to choose to move on from the Outer Court by laying down my life. We can do this because it is Christ who strengthens us. We want to be in His presence where we can communicate with Him face to face.

My focus is on God; I want to live before the throne of God in the Holy of Holies.

Prayer

My Father God, thank You for the assurance that You will never ask me to do anything that You will not give me the ability to be able to accomplish. I can lay my life before You because I know I can trust You. I can rest in Your love and faithfulness to me. Amen.

The path to intimacy

Read John 13:18-38

One of them, the disciple whom Jesus loved, was reclining next to him. - John 13:23

Jesus had twelve disciples who followed Him. Peter, John and James went further; they became Jesus' friends. He chose to take them with Him to pray in the Garden of Gethsemane (Matthew 26). They were willing to take that extra step. John went even deeper. A special bond existed between Jesus and John.

At the last supper Jesus told the disciples that one of them would betray Him. They looked around trying to figure out who it would be. *One of them, the disciple whom Jesus loved, was reclining next to him* (v 23). John had the liberty to ask. *Leaning back against Jesus, he asked him, "Lord, who is it?"* (v 25). Jesus told him. They were all sitting there but only John heard and understood. Jesus invites us to take the extra step. He invites us to be prepared to move from the Outer Court, through the Holy Place into the Holy of Holies – into the very presence of God.

He invites me to recline in His presence and to have fellowship with Him.

Prayer

My Father, You invite me to have a special relationship with You. The door to Your throne room is open – I need to walk through the door. It is only in the Holy of Holies that I can be in Your presence. Help me to be prepared to pay the price for this kind of intimacy with You. Amen.

15 December

Crucified with Christ

Read Galatians 2:16-21

I have been crucified with Christ and I no longer live, but Christ lives in me. The life I live in the body, I live by faith in the Son of God, who loved me and gave himself for me. - Galatians 2:20

Not many people are prepared to pay the price for true intimacy with God. Even the disciples who walked with Jesus; only one pushed through into true intimacy while Jesus was with them. It is tragic that so few experience this intimacy, when it is the very thing that Jesus died to give us. There are not many who are prepared to enter through the narrow gate – most choose the broad road.

Being crucified with Christ is a daily experience. Each day I have to lay my life upon the altar of sacrifice. This is the only way that leads to life. We do not find life on the broad road; that is the route to destruction. It is on the narrow road that I have fellowship with Jesus. Paul says in Galatians 5:25: *If we live by the Spirit, let us also walk by the Spirit* (NASB).

In the Spirit I find the faith, wisdom, knowledge, truth and understanding to live the crucified life.

Prayer

Father, help me to pay the price. I want to walk in intimacy with You. Fill me with Your Spirit so that I can walk the narrow way. Give me grace to lay my life on the altar of sacrifice. I can only live this life through faith in You – I cannot do it in my own strength. Amen.

God's heart for us

Read John 17:1-12

Now this is eternal life: that they may know you, the only true God, and Jesus Christ, whom you have sent. - John 17:3

We find it so difficult to simply rest in God. We want a ten point plan to follow. Living in intimacy with God is not like that. We no longer have control of our lives. Jesus died so that we can know God. The more we know God the easier it will be to rest in Him. Our birth right is to walk in intimacy with God.

In His prayer Jesus also prayed that we, His children, will be one in Him. *"My prayer is not for them alone. I pray also for those who will believe in me through their message, that all of them may be one, Father, just as you are in me and I am in you. May they also be in us so that the world may believe that you have sent me. I have given them the glory that you gave me, that they may be one as we are one."* - John 17:20-22

Knowing God and walking in intimacy with Him is my birth right in Jesus.

Prayer

My Father, I long to know You in the way that Jesus spoke of in His High Priestly prayer. I realise that my experience of You is lacking in so many ways. Help me to turn from the things that prevent me from having this relationship with You. Amen.

17 December

One in the Spirit

Read John 16:5-15

But when he, the Spirit of truth, comes, he will guide you into all truth. - John 16:13a

It is in the Holy Place that the Holy Spirit works in our lives. He teaches us what it means to live and walk in the Spirit realm. The more we get to know Him the more we want of God. The greater our desire will be to move into the Holy of Holies where we can worship before the throne of God.

In Jesus' High Priestly prayer He prays that His children will be one as He is one with the Father. His heart is that we demonstrate His love by the way we treat each other in His family. When we live in intimacy with Him then there will be no place in our hearts for hatred and strife. We will find it easy to forgive; we will bless when cursed; and we will not allow bitterness to take a hold in our lives. He calls us to be one with Him.

God's heart is love and if I am one with Him, then my heart will also be overflowing with love.

Prayer

Father, You have called me to choose the narrow way. You invite me to intimacy with You. Your heart is that I should show the world Your love through the way I love my brothers and sisters in Christ. The way for me to do this is through being one in the Spirit with You. Fill me with Your Spirit, I pray. Amen.

The altar of sacrifice

Read Romans 12

Therefore, I urge you, brothers, in view of God's mercy, to offer your bodies as living sacrifices, holy and pleasing to God – this is your spiritual act of worship.
- Romans 12:1

We will never move from the Outer Court unless we lay our lives upon the altar of sacrifice. We saw this in the life of Abraham. God called him to offer up his only son – the son of promise. This was a mirror picture of the sacrifice of Jesus on the cross to save the world. The difference is that there was no lamb in the thicket, because Jesus was the sacrificial Lamb, who would take away our sins.

It was the moment of truth for Abraham. It was his passage through – into the Holy of Holies. The same is true for us. You cannot by-pass the sacrifice. Oneness with God, intimacy with Him, is what He is calling us to. I want to encourage you if you find yourself in the line of fire today. Be sure that if God is at work in You then You can trust Him. The end result will be intimacy with Him.

I rejoice in the fire as He works in me. The end result will be intimacy with Him.

Prayer

Father, as I bow in Your presence I submit to Your work in my life. I surrender to You. Have Your way with me. I trust You for the results and rejoice in the privilege of being Your child whom You love. Lord, I want more of You, I want to walk in intimacy with You. Amen.

19 December

Revelation of the deep things of God

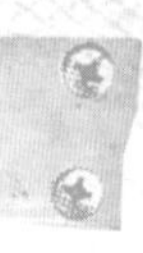

Read John 16:1-15

"I have much more to say to you, more than you can now bear. But when he, the Spirit of truth, comes, he will guide you into all truth. He will not speak on his own; he will speak only what he hears, and he will tell you what is yet to come. He will bring glory to me by taking from what is mine and making it known to you. All that belongs to the Father is mine. That is why I said the Spirit will take from what is mine and make it known to you." - John 16:12-15

Through this scripture Yeshua said that He has many things to teach us. The things that the Spirit teaches us can only be learnt as we move from the Outer Court into the Holy Place where He dwells. Once we have come to the place of sacrifice and we move into the Holy Place, God's Spirit is ready and waiting to take us to the next level in our road toward intimacy with God.

God's presence is the greatest gift that I can experience as His child.

It is Holy Spirit who takes us into the greater and deeper things of God, into intimacy with Him. It is through the Spirit working in us that we become an instrument of God's anointing. It is the Spirit that ushers us into the very presence of God where we can enter His throne room. This is our reward for persevering and not giving up. This is the end result of choosing the narrow way.

Prayer

Father, thank You for Your Spirit who teaches me the deep things about You. He instructs me leading me into all truth. I am so grateful that the end result of my journey is intimacy with You. Amen.

Spiritual discernment

Read 1 Corinthians 2:6-16

We have not received the spirit of the world but the Spirit who is from God, that we may understand what God has freely given us. - 1 Corinthians 2:12

H*owever, as it is written: "No eye has seen, no ear has heard, no mind has conceived what God has prepared for those who love him"* (1 Corinthians. 2:9). There are truths that God has for us that are beyond our human capacity to understand. God reveals these truths through Holy Spirit to those who wait upon Him. He reveals them to those who are totally dependent on Him. Holy Spirit searches the deep things of God's heart and reveals them to His children.

When my eyes are fixed on Him, and not the world, I discover the depths of who God is.

All of God is available to us, but we have to seek His heart for every situation and need in our lives. Sacrificing our lives on the altar means that we are no longer in control of our lives. When we live with Him in the Holy of Holies – in that place of rest and dependency on God, it is there that we can know the deep things of God.

Prayer

Father, I long to know the depths of You. I long to see the things You want to reveal to me. I long to hear the truths Your Spirit wants to share with me. My Father what a privilege to be Your child. I thank You for Your love for me. Amen.

21 December

Hunger and thirst for righteousness

Read Matthew 5:1-12

"Blessed are those who hunger and thirst for righteousness, for they will be filled."
- Matthew 5:6

When someone is not filled with Holy Spirit, they will never understand the deep things of God's heart. Aldo wrote in one of his letters: 'Your soul cannot hear Gods voice – it is spirit to Spirit.' We need to ask God to shine His light into the deep and hidden places that are the cause of all the trouble in our lives.

Often because we want for nothing in the physical realm our spirits are dulled to our spiritual malnutrition. We do not realise that we are dying as a result of our lack of spiritual nourishment. Hungering after God means we constantly want more and more of Him, we seek Him and wait upon Him for new strength. It is a longing and a desire for intimacy with Him. People don't move higher into the dimension of the Spirit, because they are not hungry (or should I say broken) enough to desperately seek Him.

Only when I reach the stage of desperation the Spirit of God can feed me and nourish me with the meat of the Word.

Prayer

Father, thank You that You give me my daily bread. I realise that so often I am not nearly as concerned about my spiritual diet as I am about my physical diet. Fill me with a hunger for righteousness and a thirst for the Living Water. Amen.

The mind of Christ

Read 1 Corinthians 2:12-16

"For who has known the mind of the Lord that he may instruct him?" But we have the mind of Christ. - 1 Corinthians 2:16

There is a battle for the control of our minds. The enemy is constantly firing his darts of fear and lies at our minds. He knows that if his darts find a chink in our armour he is able to break through our defences and gain a foothold. When our minds are filled with the things of God, and we are listening intently to His voice we will develop strong minds.

God longs to communicate with us. He waits for us in the Holy of Holies. It is in the throne room that we can feel safe and secure. In the throne room we can have our minds fortified and strengthened. Once you walk in an intimate relationship with God so many of the struggles, fears and concerns of your life will be put into perspective. Peace is a Person, not a state of mind or circumstance. Choose the mind of Christ.

When I have the mind of Christ regarding my life I will walk in peace and contentment.

Prayer

Father, thank You for Your provision for me. Thank You that I can choose the mind of Christ. That as my mind is focussed upon You, I can be strong both mentally and spiritually. It is in Your presence that I receive the strength that I need to overcome the attacks of the enemy. Amen.

An enlightened heart

Read Ephesians 1:18-23

I pray also that the eyes of your heart may be enlightened in order that you may know the hope to which he has called you, the riches of his glorious inheritance in the saints, and his incomparably great power for us who believe. - Ephesians 1:18-19b

An enlightened heart trusts God rather than the noise of the stormy situation you are in. The enemy might try and convince you otherwise, but you will know that God is in control of your situation. If you have an enlightened heart you will not waste precious time talking about people or situations in a negative way. You have far more important things to do. Negative thoughts and words fill the earth with negative vibrations.

An enlightened heart worships God for who He is, walking a path of intimacy with Him. Continually pray that the Lord will enlighten the eyes of your understanding, so that you can start delving into the deeper things of God. An enlightened heart will not be satisfied in the Outer Court or even the Holy Place. It is only in the Holy of Holies, in the throne room of God, where we can experience intimacy with God and where we can hear Him speak to us.

> *An enlightened heart speaks and thinks positively; sending out good vibrations of life.*

Prayer

My Father, I pray that You will open the eyes of my understanding. I ask that You will give me an enlightened heart so that I can live in the fullness of all that You have for me to enjoy. Amen.

God is faithful

Read Psalm 89:1-8

I will sing of the Lord's great love forever; with my mouth I will make your faithfulness known through all generations. - Psalm 89:1

In January 2012 we went on holiday to America for 12 days. One morning Aldo woke Tinus up at 3 am asking him repeatedly where he would be able to find a ring the next day. Aldo insisted, 'Wisdom keeps telling me today is the day.' The next morning our hostess handed me a box of rings and said, 'Retah, at 3 am this morning the Lord impressed it on my heart to give these rings to Aldo.'

Aldo took one look at the rings and said 'thank You, Abba', over and over again. Then he went to Chans, bent down on one knee and proposed to her. We watched in awe as this scene unfolded before us. Only later did I hear the whole story of how Holy Spirit had been preparing Tinus from 3 am that morning for the big occasion. It was a testimony to a God who gives life, and who is faithful to all His promises.

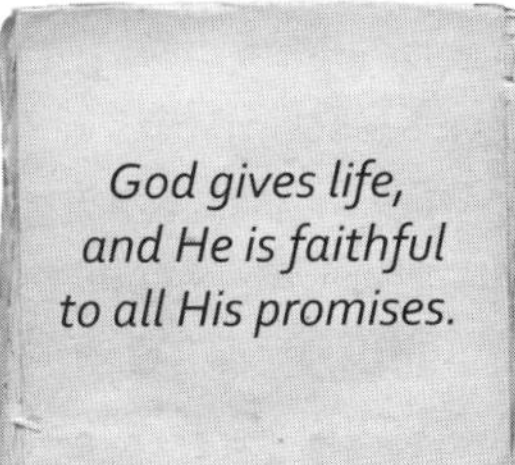

God gives life, and He is faithful to all His promises.

Prayer

Father, thank You that You are a life-giving God. You speak life into dry bones. You are faithful to every promise You make to me. Thank You that I can rejoice in Your goodness, love and favour. Amen.

25 December

God keeps His promises

Read Psalm 145:1-13

Your kingdom is an everlasting kingdom, and your dominion endures through all generations. The Lord is faithful to all his promises and loving toward all he has made. - Psalm 145:13

So, on 7 January, 2012 Aldo and Chans were engaged! The Lord is preparing them for the future He has planned for them. Their engagement was a Godly thing. I think back on the many nights I spoke life over Aldo's situation. How I told him of his beautiful bride, and how she would be filled with the Holy Spirit, and have God's glory upon her. *"Commit your way to the Lord, trust also in Him, and He shall bring it to pass"* (Psalm 37:5 King James Version).

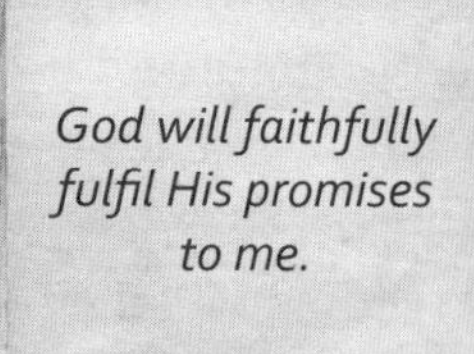

God will faithfully fulfil His promises to me.

Give God the glory in your life! Are you placing your trust in Him as you face a New Year? You do not need to be fearful when you have a loving God who holds your days in His hands. *For no matter how many promises God has made, they are "Yes" in Christ. And so through him the "Amen" is spoken by us to the glory of God* (2 Corinthians 1:20).

Prayer

My faithful God, I stand in awe of Your goodness and love. You have confirmed in Your Word that every promise is yes in Christ. Help me, Lord, to trust You in every situation and circumstance of my life. I know that as I live in intimacy with You I will become closer to You each day of my life. Amen.

Faith comes by hearing

Read Romans 10:8-21

Consequently, faith comes from hearing the message, and the message is heard through the word of Christ. - Romans 10:17

I stood with a farmer in the Lichtenburg area looking at the mealie-fields a while back. He said: 'Nothing can water my mealies like the rain that comes from heaven.' I smiled at his comment and thought, 'this is exactly how it works in our faith walk.' Bible study group, attending church and prayer meetings are all important, but nothing can compare to your 'knee-time' with Abba Father in your inner room.

The farmer continued: 'The change in the mealies can clearly be seen after a good rainfall. Nothing compares to the goodness of heavenly rain.' When we spend time with God in our inner room, in the Holy of Holies, we meet Him spirit to Spirit. It is in the throne room that He breaks open the living Word in our hearts. In the Holy of Holies we receive first hand revelation of His character, we learn to trust Him, and He deposits faith into your hearts.

In the Holy of Holies God deposits faith into my heart.

Prayer

Father, I thank You for this lesson that I can learn from the story of the mealies. I realise how much I need the rain of Your Spirit in my life. I need Your life giving revelation. Help me to be open to Your Spirit ministering in my life. Amen.

27 December

The gift of faith

Read Matthew 21:18-22

Jesus replied, "Truly I tell you, if you have faith and do not doubt, not only can you do what was done to the fig tree, but also you can say to this mountain, 'Go, throw yourself into the sea,' and it will be done. If you believe, you will receive whatever you ask for in prayer." - Matthew 21:21-22

The gift of faith is distinguished from other forms of faith by the fact that it is the supernatural manifestation of the Holy Spirit working through a believer. It is the 'God kind' of faith – it is a gift from God. It is rooted in faith in God, and not faith in man or man's abilities. It is an aspect of God's own eternal nature. Through the gift of faith, the Holy Spirit imparts a portion of God's faith supernaturally into a believer. This is faith on a divine level. It is elevated above mere human faith, in the same way as heaven is above the earth.

Intimacy with God will open the floodgates for me to receive the gift of faith from God.

This promise from Jesus is as true today as it was when He spoke it. Jesus did not put a restriction on who may ask in prayer, by faith in the Living God. Our power comes from spending time with God in the Holy of Holies, in the throne room of God.

Prayer

Father, I thank You for the wonderful, super natural gift of faith. I pray that You will give me this faith. Lord, as I spend time in Your presence I ask that You will fill me with Your Spirit so that I can manifest Your power in my life. Amen.

Keep your eyes on Jesus

Read Luke 8:22-25

"Where is your faith?" he asked his disciples. In fear and amazement they asked one another, "Who is this? He commands even the winds and the water, and they obey him." - Luke 8:25

Jesus asks you the same question as you approach the end of this year: 'Where is your faith?' Jesus is our example when it comes to operating in faith. We must look to the Father and trust in His goodness, and His love for us. He is the Almighty God, the Creator of heaven and earth for whom nothing is impossible. Jesus opened His heart to the Father and received 'God-like' faith. We need this supernatural gift of faith to deal with the day-to-day storms we face.

Don't look around at other people; instead focus on Jesus, and the path He has laid out for you. God has called you to walk in intimacy with Him. He has opened the way so that you can enter the Holy of Holies. You do not need to remain in the Outer Court. It is your choice as to whether you will live with Him in the Holy of Holies. Keep your eyes on Jesus.

I am walking my own unique road of faith with God. I must keep my eyes on Jesus.

Prayer

My Father, You have invited me to live a life in Your presence. I want to walk in supernatural faith. I realise that I cannot operate in this domain in my own strength – it is only as I keep my eyes focussed upon You, and walk in Your Spirit. Amen.

Our need for intimacy with God

Read 2 Corinthians 1:1-11

Praise be to the God and Father of our Lord Jesus Christ, the Father of compassion and the God of all comfort, who comforts us in all our troubles, so that we can comfort those in any trouble with the comfort we ourselves receive from God. For just as we share abundantly in the sufferings of Christ, so also our comfort abounds through Christ. - 2 Corinthians 1:3-5

God has created us with a desire and need for intimacy with Him in our hearts. Nothing else on earth can fill the God-shaped hole in our hearts. People have tried. I have tried, in fact to tell you the truth, in the past I tried everything possible to fill the hole in my heart – but nothing could. It was only when I cried out to the Living God with a shattered heart, kneeling beside a car-wreck on a highway, that He filled the void in my heart with Himself. What should have been the most devastating day of my life became the best day of my life.

As I approach the beginning of a New Year I hear and respond to God's call for intimacy.

For more than eight years now we have walked this road of healing and restoration as a family. I have learnt lessons on our journey that the world doesn't want to hear. The world is always looking for the easy way out. COMPROMISE is the trap that Satan uses to ensnare so many of Yahweh's children. Hear and respond to God's call for intimacy today.

Prayer

Father, it is almost the end of the year. As I reflect back upon all You have done for me – I want to thank You that You are inviting me to a closer walk of intimacy with You. I am so excited about all the things You want to share with me and teach me. Thank You, Lord. Amen.

No room for compromise

Read 2 Corinthians 5:14-21

For Christ's love compels us, because we are convinced that one died for all, and therefore all died. And he died for all, that those who live should no longer live for themselves but for him who died for them and was raised again. - 2 Corinthians 5:14-15

As we have spent this month learning about intimacy with God I hope and pray that the Holy Spirit has broken this message open to you as only He can. Not by human arguments, but by the power and conviction of the Spirit. I pray that as you have spent time in God's Word your desire to live in intimacy with Him has grown, and that you have realised this is the only way to true and lasting happiness.

It is only in God's presence that I will find wholeness. Compromise will no longer be an option for me.

In popular Christian culture, we have looked for short-cuts to survive without Yahweh's direct presence. We have started walking down paths we carved out for ourselves, and we have followed our own ways. The call to move from the Outer Court where we live in flesh is a call to put a stop to compromise. When we move into the Holy Place we begin to walk in the Spirit and the things of God become more important to us than our own plans and ideas. Then as we step into the Holy of Holies our whole lives become consumed with God and His presence in our lives.

Prayer

Father, You have been calling me to a life of intimacy with You. Today You have added to that call the instruction not to compromise. I want to obey You – I want to honour You in the way that I live. Amen.

31 December

Sanctification leads to intimacy

Read Ephesians 1:18-23

I pray that the eyes of your heart may be enlightened in order that you may know the hope to which he has called you, the riches of his glorious inheritance in his holy people, and his incomparably great power for us who believe. - Ephesians 1:18-19

I believe that God is calling us to 'sanctification'. The result of intimacy with Him is that we will be one with Him; completely yielded to Him; and reflecting His holiness. Our lives will not be marred by compromise with the world. We will showcase His love and His character to the world. We will be His hands and feet here on earth. People will see Him reflected on our faces, without us having to say one word.

The things of the world will fade away. All our voids will be filled with His love and His peace as we yield to Him. Our Father carries our best interests in His heart, and He wants us to fulfil the purpose that He created us for, and to enjoy the good things He blesses us with. He knows that His plan for our lives will only work out if we are fully yielded to Him. We are to reflect His holiness.

I choose the road of sanctification that leads to holiness and intimacy with God!

Prayer

My Father, I choose to lay down my own plans and I yield to Your plans and purposes for my life. As I walk into the New Year I choose the road of sanctification. I want to dwell in the Holy of Holies with You, rejoicing in Your presence. I commit my life to You again and pray that You will use me to the honour and glory of Your Name. Amen.